Nativism and Modernity

SUNY series

EXPLORATIONS

in

POSTCOLONIAL STUDIES

Emmanuel C. Eze and Arif Dirlik, editors

A complete listing of books in this series
can be found at the end of this volume.

Nativism and Modernity

Cultural Contestations in China and Taiwan under Global Capitalism

MING-YAN LAI

State University of New York Press

Published by
STATE UNIVERSITY OF NEW YORK PRESS, ALBANY

For information, contact State University of New York Press, Albany, NY
www.sunypress.edu

Production, Laurie Searl
Marketing, Michael Campochiaro

Library of Congress Cataloging-in-Publication Data

Lai, Ming-yan, 1961–
Nativism and modernity : cultural contestations in China and Taiwan under global capitalism / Ming-yan Lai.
p. cm. — (SUNY series, explorations in postcolonial studies)
Includes bibliographical references and index.
ISBN 978-0-7914-7285-9 (hardcover : alk. paper)
ISBN 978-0-7914-7286-6 (pbk. : alk. paper)
1. Nationalism—China. 2. Nationalism—Taiwan. 3. Nativism. 4. Modernism (Literature)
I. Title. II. Title: Cultural contestations in China and Taiwan under global capitalism.

JC311.L14 2008
320.540951—dc22

2007010151

10 9 8 7 6 5 4 3 2 1

Contents

Acknowledgments

This book has traveled with me through so many personal and intellectual developments that it is impossible to adequately acknowledge all to whom thanks and gratitude are due. Research for various parts of the book has been supported by the Wisconsin Alumni Research Foundation, the John D. and Catherine T. MacArthur Foundation, the China Times Cultural Foundation, the Pacific Cultural Foundation, and the Purdue Research Foundation. I am grateful to those who made possible my receiving such generous support. Unlike research funding, intellectual debts are much more difficult to trace and credit, considering their interstitial, transforming, and transformative power. My sincere thanks go to the teachers, friends, colleagues, and students in the University of Wisconsin-Madison, Purdue University, University of California, Santa Barbara, and the Chinese University of Hong Kong who have enriched my life and understanding in innumerable ways. I want especially to thank Arif Dirlik, Leo Lee, David Wang, Geri Friedman, Paddy Fumerton, Dick Hebdige, and Shu-mei Shih for sparing time and energy from their hectic schedules to read all or parts of the manuscript, and offering wonderful and insightful comments, not all of which I managed to incorporate into a necessarily limited study. For boundless support and everyday sustenance, without which none of my intellectual work is possible, I thank my family, particularly my mother, Cham Yuk Sing, whose help relieves me of the guilt of occasional absent-minded parenting; Raymond Wong, whose love and computer skills have seen me through various scrapes in our years together; and Hanwey Wong, who brings enormous joy into our lives and inspires me to keep faith in an alternative future.

INTRODUCTION

Interrogating (through) the Native

What and why does the native matter in a world where capitalism has apparently extended its reach into all corners and globalization has become a household term even in former margins of the capitalist empire like the People's Republic of China? This question haunts us as our supposedly global world witnesses an intensification of "fundamentalist" revival and separatist movements laying claim to native cultural identity disrupt the putative force of cultural homogenization under global capitalism. For all our celebration of global culture, transnationalism and cosmopolitan sensibilities, imaginations and evocations of the native keep turning up with renewed rigor. Yet our dominant discursive paradigms seem indisposed to address the question or engage the paradox of an insistence on native claims in a world of shifting and perforated borders. The privileging of travel, diaspora, and hybridity in current cultural theories tends to sidestep nativism. It circumscribes the native within the historical legacy of imperialist cultural mapping, which denies equality and coevality to non-Western cultures by relegating them to the primitive and the exotic. Though not without critical potential, this common way of framing the native in terms of (post)coloniality and the impossibility of leaving Western imperialism and its epistemic violence behind fixes the concept in hegemonic knowledge production.[1] It thus categorically denies the very possibility of a nativist alternative that motivates the discursive (re)turn to the native, seeing evocations of the native by the (ex)colonized as ultimately little different from Western imperialist constructions of the native. So delimited, contemporary references to the native can only be cast in the light of nostalgic conservatism that maintains Western dominance and hegemony in a binary opposition.

Are all nativist claims to alternative grounding merely a derivative of Western imperialist discourse establishing and confirming the power and identity of the West? Is self-Orientalism necessarily the fate of nativist claims by the "natives" themselves? What happens when the "natives" self-consciously engage in nativist discourses? What oppositional strategies and possibilities can such nativist discourses offer? Without denying the continued importance of the legacy of imperialism and colonialism, this book explores these questions by shifting the frame of reference and examining specific discursive constructions of the native in concrete contemporary contexts of global capitalism and its imaginary. If the historical legacy of imperialism and its disruptive effects on cultural origins, authenticity, identity, and subjectivity are very much with us today, their specific effects are mediated by and situated in different sociohistorical conditions of global capitalism in the wake of national independence and geopolitical realignments in the international division of labor. The critical frame of imperialism alone will not enable us to understand how the native serves as an alluring figure of rootedness, deep tradition, and communal identity under these different sociohistorical conditions, what desires it articulates, and what intervention it seeks to effect.

In his influential book on travel and translation in the late twentieth century, James Clifford perceptively argues that the homonymous roots and routes are not opposites but coupled concepts, one implicating the other. Recognizing the intertwining nature of routes/roots means that one has to "focus on hybrid, cosmopolitan experiences as much as on rooted, native ones . . . in specific cases of historical tension and relationship."[2] Though Clifford's rhetorical and substantive emphasis on travel runs counter to the explicit concern with native assertions in this book, his critical intervention into ethnography's propensity to localize natives and essentialize cultural roots suggests a dynamic understanding of the native that is apropos here. Underlying my interrogation of the place and politics of the native in contemporary cultural contestation is precisely an understanding of roots and natives as discursive constructions responding to concrete local-national-global power dynamics in specific historical encounters involving physical and/or symbolic travel. "What does it take to define and defend a homeland? What are the political stakes in claiming (or sometimes being relegated to) a 'home'?" These questions that Clifford considers necessary for probing and comparing distinct routes/roots are among issues I try to address in this exploration of nativist discourses in contemporary engagement with global capitalism as well.

Given the hegemonic understanding of and ideological investments in "home," it is perhaps not surprising that gender is invariably central to various efforts to define and claim a "homeland" and "native place," even if the specificities of the discursive constructions differ. By virtue of such difference in commonality, the particular ways in which gender figures in the construction and consolidation of the native place and its symbolic meanings are illuminating of the cultural politics of specific nativist discourses, including their oppositional possibilities and limits. Following this lead, my study will trace how gender ideologies intersect with ethnic, class, national, and other concerns to shape the particular imaginations and constructions of native alternatives under global capitalism, and explore what oppositional possibilities are thus opened up and what limits and limitations ensue.

As global capitalism seeks to totalize the world into a nexus of common yet differentiated markets of labor, production, and consumption, pitting one social location against another while drawing all into its compass, the native is arguably an overdetermined ideological site for working out and contesting the meaning of capitalist development or modernity—the inclusive sign under which capitalism and its social effects are often referenced—for those (once) relegated to the margins of history by the historical development of capitalism. Defined negatively in relation to the West's self-image of and as modernity, the native in its incarnation of exotic otherness, primitive backwardness, infantile innocence, and/or noble savagery captures various dimensions of opposition and difference in time-space and social constructions that the (ex)colonized must confront in their engagement with global capitalism. By the same token, it also marks a space of (re)construction and re-vision where local historical and cultural specificities can be mapped and interpreted to offer a different ground of imagining the meaning of capitalist development and modernity. Nativism in this light is a deliberate mobilization of specific local differences to intervene in the construction of modernity.

Importantly, as a form of assertion of local culture and identity, nativism is distinct from the localism that has claimed much critical attention under global capitalism as the counterpart of globalism. Though localism has sometimes be taken as resistance to both the abstract modern formations of the nation-state and the equally abstract, deterritorialized globalism of transnational capital, the mutual implication of the global and the local, concisely captured in the term glocalism, has also been noted.[3] Rather than homogenizing the world into interchangeable markets of standard commodities and identical consumers, as in the modernist conception, global capitalism thrives on weaving local cultural differences into commodity expansion, product differentiation, marketing strategies, and consumer cultivation, as well as inducing localities to distinguish themselves in the competition to attract transnational capital. The global, then, takes concrete forms only in the local while the local is actively shaped by global forces. With this mutual implication, localism is more often than not an appropriation and manipulation of local cultural identity to accommodate rather than resist global capitalism.

Inasmuch as nativism foregrounds the native rather than the local, it suggests a different relation to global capitalism in its affirmation of local specificities. With its nascent grounding in a particular place—the native place—and its implied opposition to the foreign, the notion of the native explicitly evokes two forms of politics that do not necessarily figure in the local-global pair of signification—namely, a place-based politics and a mutually exclusive structure of opposition. If place is a necessary location for glocal operations, its importance is often eclipsed in the hegemonic privileging of transnational forces in the workings of global capitalism, rhetorical affirmations of localism notwithstanding. Nativism, in contrast, highlights the centrality of a place of origin and attachment in its articulation of local particularities against the abstraction of global forces of modernity and capitalism. As such, nativism is a form of place-based politics that mobilizes a native-inflected local to resist global capitalism and its propensity and capacity to commodify cultural differences and reduce concrete places with established communities and ways of life into commodity and labor markets of various exchange values. And yet, by virtue of its constitutive opposition to the foreign, the native in nativism is not solely defined by local particularities grounded in a concrete place. As the polar opposite of the foreign, the native is also determined in negation by hegemonic understandings of what constitutes the outside and foreign, including global and translocal elements that shape boundaries and threaten established identity, community, and everyday life. That is, of the many local beliefs, customs, and practices, what comes to define the native depends on perceived differences from received notions of the outside and the foreign. Furthermore, insofar as the nation-state marks an almost naturalized form of cultural and political boundaries in modernity, the native is inextricably linked to the national, even though the two are conceptually distinct and possibly conflicting. Thus, contingent on a variable interface of opposition, the native is concretized in a global-national-local dynamic that does not automatically privilege any one of these terms of demarcation. It is ultimately grounded in a place, the native place, but what distinguishes the native place is determined by an oppositional structure against the foreign that not only selectively accentuates particular local features as distinctive, but also potentially translates place-based local specificities into deterritorialized, supraplace beliefs and practices against imported modernity under global capitalism.

Precisely because of its emphasis on local specificities, nativism's cultural politics and oppositional possibilities cannot be ascertained without a close analysis of concrete constructions of the native against particular historical contexts of global-national-local interactions. In other words, there is no generic nativism with definite political parameters beyond an implied oppositional structure. The political stakes in claiming a root or native place have to be explored contingently, case by case, in terms of historical and discursive particularities in engaging hegemonic concepts and praxis such as those of modernity and global capitalism. Accordingly, this book seeks to explore the oppositional possibilities and limits of nativist intervention into the discursive construction of modernity outside the imperial center of Euro-America through a detailed analysis of two nativist discourses emerging from different sociohistorical contexts of "Chinese" articulation of modernity under global capitalism, namely the *xiangtu* nativism of Taiwan in the 1970s and *xungen* nativism of the People's Republic of China (PRC) in the 1980s.

As leading literary discourses of their times, *xiangtu* and *xungen* nativisms were immensely important in their respective sociohistorical contexts. Their significance goes well beyond literary issues, for they are conscious cultural statements on the contemporary historical conjuncture and deliberate intervention into the course of national development. Interestingly, while their literary contribution is recognized separately in a wealth of critical and scholarly discussion, there has not been any comparative study of the two bodies of work, even in literary terms. This arguably reflects the intensity of their local focus and distinct emphasis on particular concerns of the time. Their acute engagement with the contemporaneous national context easily makes the two nativisms look parochial and dated, hence not amenable to comparative analysis. In offering the first comparative study of the two nativisms while situating their local focus in a common negotiation with questions of alternative modernity under global capitalism, this book not only contributes to a better understanding of nativist cultural politics, but also brings new perspectives to the analysis of the two literary nativisms and individual works therein.

Flourishing separately over a period of major restructuring in global capitalism in the politically divided yet traditionally and historically linked spaces of Taiwan and mainland China, *xiangtu* and *xungen* nativism offer a rich ground for comparative analysis and critique of nativist cultural politics. Beyond the obvious comparative interest of two different "Chinese" contexts, they encode significant differences in local-national-global dynamics, particularly vis-à-vis the development of global capitalism. In terms of national development, both emerged at a historical conjuncture when their respective states had embarked on a course of increased articulation with global capitalism for economic development, but the values of such capitalist modernity had not (yet) been normativized into the national belief system and become hegemonic in the everyday experiences of the people, leaving room for contestation. In a brief window of about a decade, the two similarly partook in a social struggle to determine the vision and meaning of modernity within their specific national contexts against the universal domination and claims of global capitalism. Arguably, only in such moments of national ideological instability can nativism thrive, given its constitutive commitment to alternatives, however doomed, remote, or imaginary.

In terms of the transnational development of global capitalism, however, *xiangtu* and *xungen* nativisms came into place in very different historical conjunctures. From *xiangtu* nativism in the 1970s to *xungen* nativism in the 1980s, the possibility of a socialist alternative has essentially fizzled out and global capitalism has gained much ground with the advancement of flexible accumulation through the operation of multinational corporations and offshore production in what was once known as the "third world." East Asia played a particularly noticeable role in this transition, as active integration into global capitalist production brought phenomenal economic growth and celebratory attention to the region. Led by Japan's escalating economic power, the region's "miracle" has not only transformed Taiwan into a lauded success in economic development through strategic participation in the international division of labor and capitalist market system, but also fostered the articulation of a new geo-imaginary of global capitalist development in the figure of the Pacific Rim, which projects boundless growth and dynamism on the linked horizons of capitalist economies along the East and West coasts of the Pacific. Culturally, the economic feat also renewed transnational interests and local confidence in the significance of East Asian traditions in modernity, as testified in numerous conferences on East Asian cultures and modernization/economic development. Fueling this revival of cultural confidence, the trans-Pacific formulation of an East Asian model of development that putatively blends traditional values and practices harmoniously into the capitalist mode of production reached a zenith in the mid-1980s, just as *xungen* nativism made its mark on the mainland Chinese cultural scene.

Situated in different moments of this epochal transformation in the relation and meaning of the East Asian region to capitalist development, *xiangtu* and *xungen* nativisms encode different parameters of local-national-global dynamics. In addition to the country's engagement with global capitalism, these local-national-global dynamics were simultaneously determined by the different positioning of their respective states in the international political order, as well as the historical particularities and local struggles within their respective social formations. These include, most notably, the crisis of "national" identity Taiwan faced in being displaced by the PRC as the internationally recognized legitimate Chinese state, and the traumatic socialist legacy the PRC had to confront in its efforts to forge a different path to modernity.

As detailed in chapter two, when *xiangtu* nativism was radicalized into a pointed cultural political discourse intervening in Taiwan's construction of modernity in the 1970s, Taiwan as a nation-state faced simultaneously global and local challenges. Globally, Taiwan had to reposition itself in the international political order as the capitalist powers led by the United States shifted toward recognition of the communist regime's political representation of the Chinese nation. Exposing the state's vulnerability and dependency, this national delegitimation at the global level created openings for local challenges to the authoritarian state's construction of the nation, especially since the state-orchestrated articulation into global capitalist production had yet to deliver the capital accumulation that would make the island-state a celebrated economic success in a decade's time. Rather than economic gains, more immediately noticeable was a neocolonization of the country with foreign capital controlling and exploiting local labor that was drawn predominantly from rural Taiwan, especially the population of young rural Taiwanese women, many of whom were compelled or seduced to leave home for exploitative and oppressive jobs in foreign-owned factories or even work in the burgeoning sex trade catering to foreigners in the cities. Taiwan's loss of national recognition globally sharpened this sense of neocolonization experienced at the local level. The class, ethnic, and gender lineup in this experience of neocolonial development, in turn, determined the specificities of the local challenges to the state and its construction of modernity in the name of the native place, as elaborated below.

A different global-national-local dynamics underlay the emergence of *xungen* nativism in China in the 1980s. With significant contribution from East Asian countries, global capitalism was by then well on its way to conquer the world. Emerging from decades of Maoist opposition to capitalist development into this era of global capitalism, China experienced a devastating awakening to the country's material and technological backwardness, even as the exceptional success of the East Asian articulation with global capitalism fed into a postmodern affirmation of difference to boost confidence in East Asian cultural traditions and their values in modernity. As a national response, the postsocialist state's effort to catch up with the capitalist powers through importation of capital, science, and technology under the Four Modernization program and "open-door" policies mobilized renewed cultural nationalism for legitimation while creating regional tensions that put pressure on national identification in promoting the enrichment of urban areas over rural hinterlands. Given the Maoist legacy of ideological investment in the rural areas, this marginalization but continued exploitation of the rural hinterlands in the name of national modernization made the rural hinterlands a resonant site of local contestation of the postsocialist state's construction of modernity in a discursive search for native alternatives.

In view of such underlying contextual differences, a comparative analysis of *xiangtu* and *xungen* nativisms promises to illuminate the way nativist discourse operates in and through a dynamic local-national-global nexus to articulate alternatives under global capitalism. In particular, whether/how the two nativisms generate different cultural political interventions will be instructive about the possibilities and limits of nativism in proffering alternative constructions of modernity under global capitalism.

Tracing the critical intervention of nativist discourses in two different yet related sociohistorical locations of "Chinese" modernity also facilitates an exploration of differences in the construction and representation of the native beyond "national traditions" to show its intricate and multifarious mappings onto such common social classifications as class, ethnicity, and gender. As elaborated in chapter one, nativism is commonly conflated with nationalism and its valorization of a primordial folk and timeless tradition in current critical discussions, a trend that arguably parallels the tendency to circumscribe nativism within the historical legacy of imperialism and its opposition. Yet, even if there has been a close historical association between nativism and nationalism, the conceptual grounds of the native and the nation are distinct. Being an implicitly relational term with a claim on the local and congenial in opposition to the foreign, the native has no intrinsic link to national demarcations. Historically, furthermore, as Prasenjit Duara notes with reference to representations of the native place in China during the first half of the twentieth century, national appropriation of the native/local, though undeniable, was but one of many ways in which the native/local figured in the cultural politics of modernity.[4] Embodying cultural authenticity bombarded by Western values in a field of competing forces of imperialism, capitalism, nationalism, regionalism, and revolutionary ideologies such as socialism and anarchism, the native/local constituted an intense locus of contestation, the complex politics of which was enacted in the production and reception of particular texts and practices across a wide discursive spectrum ranging from academic disciplines such as anthropology, folklore studies and geography to local history writing, native place literature, and visual representations. A critical appraisal of the political possibilities of nativist discourses thus requires an analytical framework that enables an interrogation of the relation between the native and the nation, one that encompasses without privileging national tradition and identification in a full range of potentially contradictory issues and concerns that can be articulated through the figure of the native. Such a framework underlies the comparative analysis of *xiangtu* and *xungen* nativism undertaken in this study.

Between Taiwan and the PRC, the thorny question of national identification and representation has always loomed large, giving a wide opening for interrogating the place of the nation in nativist oppositional politics. The ambiguity of Taiwan's national identity, especially after the U.S.-led international recognition of the PRC as the legitimate Chinese regime in the 1970s, renders particularly intricate a relation that is never straightforward. The irreducible disjuncture between the native and the nation surfaces clearly in *xiangtu* nativism, which is literally torn between a tradition-informed Chinese nationalism and a class-inflected identification of the native with the marginalized in the local realities of Taiwan. The native place (*xiangtu*) in *xiangtu* nativism, in other words, is mapped on a dual grid of hierarchical opposition in terms of nation and class. In its representation of the everyday lives of manual laborers, *xiangtu* literature such as the stories by Wang Zhenhe, Wang Tuo, and Huang Chunming discussed later in the book constructs a native alternative to Western-originated and oriented modernity that is simultaneously class conscious. The inclusion of class concerns into the configuration and representation of the native expands and complicates *xiangtu* nativism's critique of modernity along the line of nationalist protest against Western domination and neocolonial exploitation. It brings capitalist exploitation "home" within the national space through a keen focus on the experiences and realities of manual labor, thus fracturing the sanguine affirmation of nationalist opposition to Western modernity. This opens up diverse possibilities of configuring native critiques and alternatives in a variable matrix of social justice, equality, and national independence, which are differently enacted in the literary and critical writings that constitute the core of *xiangtu* nativism. As chapter two will show, Wang Zhenhe's famed story "Xiaolin lai Taibei" makes use of an almost paradigmatic mapping of class and national opposition to highlight the exploitative and oppressive structure of Western modernity and proffer an alternative that privileges manual labor primarily as the uncorrupted custodian of the Confucian moral order necessary for founding a native modernity. In contrast, Wang Tuo's "Jinshuishen" valorizes not so much manual labor as the sacrificing spirit of a native "sacred mother" in a fishing community to critique an imported, greed-driven modernity that breeds a general ethos of exploitative, egotistic materialism, leading to an erosion of communal solidarity and neglect of the common good. If both ultimately ground the native in a patriarchal moral tradition linked to the exploited, Huang Chunming's "Pinguo de ziwei" eschews a readily available native alternative to lay bare the necessity of engaging multiple lines of intersecting national, class, ethnic, and gender oppression and exploitation to establish a contingent ground of critical dialogues and collective struggles for a congenial, just future for all.

Inasmuch as class figures centrally in *xiangtu* nativism, *xungen* nativism offers an interesting comparison, for class was precisely what the postsocialist regime sought to downplay in its effort to forge a new era of "modernization" and economic development through the introduction of market competition and importation of Western capital and technology. The excesses of the Maoist emphasis on class struggles during the socialist era and the traumatic memories they brought also made it impossible for class to assume a critical interrogatory role in postsocialist China as it did in Taiwan's *xiangtu* nativism. Yet, the Communist Party-state's dependence on nationalism to legitimate its modernization program made necessary a differentiation of the native from the nation for a nativist alternative to be articulated. *Xungen* nativism locates such a native ground through re(dis)covering "roots" in regional ethnic cultural traditions in remote hinterlands, a strategy that is itself partly a return to the legacy of *xiangtu* writings in the 1930s.[5] Like Taiwan's *xiangtu* nativism, however, *xungen* nativism does not totally jettison nationalist concerns in its mapping of an alternative modernity. Instead, subtle negotiations between national identity and regional ethnic cultural traditions crisscross the configuration and representation of roots in various *xungen* texts, effecting different oppositional possibilities and limits in the process. For instance, while Han Shaogong's *xungen* manifesto affirms the refreshing vitality of marginalized ethnicized cultural traditions in remote areas and the value of (re)turning to these traditions for native alternatives to the staleness of a Confucianism-dominated national tradition and the regimentation of modern industrial lives, his *xungen* fiction employs a literary style of regional color only to articulate a nationalist concern with the self-destructiveness of a tradition-bound, inward-looking community, thus indirectly supporting the postsocialist state's "open-door" policies of national development. Similarly, Li Hangyu's elegiac celebration of a regional culture of spontaneous daring and lively abandon in his *xungen* stories expresses not only his professed desire for a vital native alternative to a nationally enforced cultural identification of shallow mediocrity, but also a reluctant confirmation of the inevitability of the postsocialist state's national construction of a bureaucratic capitalist modernity redeploying the pragmatic principles of the Confucianism-based orthodox cultural tradition.

Thus featuring a common tension and negotiation with national and nationalist concerns irrespective of their different focus on class and regional ethnic culture to identify the native, *xiangtu* and *xungen* nativisms together suggest that nativism's oppositional edge may very well lie in positing and locating other natives than the state's dominant construction of national identity and tradition. That is, more than an opposition to the foreign in terms of Western importation, the native being sought or constructed in the two nativisms encodes an implicit challenge to the dominant national order and the visions and traditions it enforces, marking the space of marginality in this order and the state's construction of modernity it underwrites. On such a ground of marginality, alternatives are imagined and advanced. Thus the two nativisms inscribe a different global-national-local dynamics than that prevalent in globalization discourse, which relegates the nation to a historical legacy that is becoming obsolete if not already so, and privileges a trope of decentered web over the center-margins power structure that the two nativisms maintain in their critiques. In recognizing the importance of the nation while challenging its marginalization of other natives, *xiangtu* and *xungen* nativisms offer a thought-provoking alternative to the positioning and representation of the nation vis-à-vis the local and the global in either state nationalism or globalization discourse.

Besides affording critical reflections on the native-nation relation and the variable mappings of the native on the marginalized in terms of class or regional ethnic culture, a comparative study of *xiangtu* and *xungen* nativisms illuminates, above all, the gender politics of nativist opposition. If their common focus on the differently invested marginalized suggests variable oppositional possibilities beyond nationalism and conservative nostalgia, their different inscriptions of the native alternative ironically fall back on a common, familiar gender bias. Whether it is *xiangtu* nativism's patriarchal tradition vested in the manual labor family or *xungen* nativism's masculine subjectivity lodged in regional ethnic cultures, the native alternative in both rests on a gender hierarchy that feminizes the problems of the state's dominant construction of modernity and excludes or relegates women to a subordinate position in the native order. In this light, the fact that all the major figures associated with *xiangtu* and *xungen* nativism are male assumes particular significance. Informed by masculine concerns and anxiety about the feminizing effects of a capitalist modernity based on market competition and commodity exchange, both nativisms displace the political economic issues of exploitation and internal colonialism onto gendered problems of native tradition, national identity, and individual subjectivity to effect an ideological resolution in a cultural re(dis)covery of a masculine tradition. Thus the oppositional possibilities of a class critique based on the experiences of manual labor or an interrogation of hegemonic conceptions from the perspective of marginalized ethnic cultures are circumscribed and undermined by the conservatism of a masculinist, patriarchal gender politics. By the same token, gender emerges as a key figure for unpacking and assessing the oppositional possibilities and limits of the two nativisms, as later chapters will demonstrate in detail.

In sum, the comparative analysis of *xiangtu* and *xungen* nativism undertaken in this book brings out the variable importance of such common social classification as class, ethnicity, and gender besides the nation in shaping the cultural politics and oppositional contours of nativist intervention in the discourse of modernity. Herein lies a significant guidepost of the study. Through opening up the conceptual frame of nativism with emphasis on different engagement with particular power structures of social differentiation in the configuration of the native, I endeavor to lay bare the variability and contingency of nativism's cultural intervention and oppositional effectiveness. The same stroke highlights the critical importance of attending closely to the textual and contextual specificities of particular nativist discourses in exploring their politics. Precisely because nativism accentuates particular differences in its construction of the native as an oppositional site, its critical evaluation must be based on a corresponding focus on specificities and particularities. Thus the study charts a course that allows the nativist texts under examination to bring forth the relevant categories of analysis—be it class, ethnicity, or gender—and follows their meandering and at times contradictory reach for a native alternative.

Accordingly, though this book seeks to go beyond the literary framework in which *xiangtu* and *xungen* texts have been studied to address interdisciplinary issues of global capitalism, modernity, and oppositional discourse, it continues to employ strategies of close reading and textual analysis that are the strength of literary criticism. Besides the literary writings that constitute the core of the two nativist discourses, other texts of significance such as official documents of the state ideological apparatuses, policy papers, or critical commentaries in newspapers and journals are similarly read when appropriate. This is not to deny differences between literary and social texts, but to bring out the discursive and rhetorical elements of nonliterary writings that are no less central to their meaning constitution than the substance and subject matter. In thus putting strategies of literary criticism to work for a cultural studies addressing interdisciplinary concerns, this book not only follows the spirit of nativist intervention in making the local meaningful in and against the global, but also sheds light on significant discursive tactics and textual practices performing and intervening into ideological functions that would otherwise remain obscure and enigmatic.[6]

Reflecting the nativist focus on local particularities, detailed analysis and discussion of the two nativist discourses are given in separate lengthy chapters that offer an integrated textual and contextual exploration of the internal dynamics of nativist intervention into the discursive construction of modernity within the social formation of the respective "nation-states." Each of these chapters first locates the nativist discourse in the specific "national" struggle to construct a congenial modernity while crafting a place for the nation-state in a world dominated by global capitalism. The chapters then examine various local perspectives on and understanding of the social and cultural contexts of the struggle, and trace the commonality and differences in the articulation of the native as the site of alternatives in key texts shaping the discourse. Specifically, the chapters investigate the terms and discursive strategies that local intellectuals employ to make sense of and represent the experiences and visions of their societies' integration into the international order of global capitalism. In the close textual analyses that follow, the chapters perform three related tasks: (1) they draw out the contestatory nature of the nativist constructions and the various meanings attached to or associated with the native; (2) they relate the different glosses on the term to social and ideological differences; and (3) they interrogate the underlying assumptions and ideological implications of the specific textual constructions of the native into a site of resistance and/or opposition to dominant constructions of modernity.

Framing these chapters of close reading of the national/local scene of *xiangtu* and *xungen* nativism are general discussions that put the two discourses in a global and comparative context. Chapter one situates the two nativisms in a global relational context of capitalist development and (post)modernity that features especially the advancement of the geopolitical imaginary of the Pacific Rim to include East Asia in a new discourse of postmodern global capitalism. With reference to this historical and discursive context, the chapter discusses how nativism proffers alternatives and what theoretical framework enables a critical assessment of its oppositional possibilities. Chapter four offers a comparative analysis of the gender politics of *xiangtu* and *xungen* nativism, which makes clear that the limits of these two nativist discourses lie not so much in the conservative nostalgia for primordial communities and the security of timeless identities with which nativism is often charged, but rather in an ideological representation and resolution of the issues and problems of a derivative modernity that is simultaneously culturalist and masculinist. Thus the alter/natives proffered inscribe a gender and class exclusion that must be opened up to engender genuine alternatives. Upon such alternatives the impetus of this study ultimately rests.

The last chapter extends the book's concern with nativism as a local articulation of alternatives under global capitalism into a discussion of developments in place-based politics and global-national-local dynamics in China and Taiwan as global capitalism's grip on the two countries tightens. In drawing out the continued significance of the issues the two nativisms grapple with, albeit in somewhat different forms, the discussion also brings out the distinctiveness of nativism as an oppositional discourse grounded in a cultural affirmation of the significance of place.

CHAPTER ONE

Of Alter/Natives, Margins, and Post/Modernity at the Rim

This stretch of the Gechuanjiang harbored at least a hundred-plus fishermen. Just their Xiaozai Village alone had over seventy households. Most moored all year long on the west bank, going downstream to fish every morning and evening, selling the catch to the villagers in Xixi nearby. During the day, they mended fishing nets and fixed roll-hooks. That life was real comfortable—plenty of fish in the water, wine in the flask, and a young wife with big breasts and big buttocks on the boat bedding; even her loud curses felt sweet to him. That's called life!

—Li Hangyu, "The Last Fisherman"

Spring finally returns to Badouzi. Like a mother who is full of life, spring enables infinite vitality and vivacity to reappear on the earth, nurturing innumerable tiny lives to leap, jump and cheer under the sun, in the wind. People busy themselves in a joyful, brisk rhythm on the beach, preparing to welcome the coming fishing season.

—Wang Tuo, "Jinshuishen"

My father's life of ever-chewable richness, from Xiaoxingan Range to Daxingan Range, left much that impassions me, warms me, yet also deeply torments me. I started my life tracing his footsteps to walk out of that splendidly solemn and mighty forest. Looking back from afar at that forest as I come near to completing half of my journey, it is still very close but I have also walked far enough away.

—Zheng Wanlong, *The Totem of Life*

The warmth and bonds of childhood, the landscapes, livelihood, and familiar faces of a rustic hometown, the nurturance and earthiness of roots—these common impressions and images of the native enthrall with their apparent simplicity and authenticity. The organic representations project a sense of native identity that is natural, abiding, and self-referential. Standard definitions of the term in English dictionaries reflect and reinforce such an identity: native, as a noun, signifies "a person born in a specified place or associated with a place by birth" (The Concise Oxford Dictionary); as an adjective, its litany of meaning centers on a radical assertion of "in"—"instinct, inborn, inherent, innate, connate, built in, intrinsic, instinctive, intuitive, natural, natural-born, congenital, hereditary, inherited, in the blood, in the family, inbred, ingrained" (The Oxford American Thesaurus of Current English). On the surface, then, the self-referentiality of a native identity seems unremarkable and incontrovertible. Yet, beneath its reference to an apparently self-evident and determinable origin, the significatory significance of the idea of native ultimately lies in the recognition of difference and predicates an implicit opposition: without something "foreign" to pit against, native identification makes no sense. That is, regardless of the visceral intimacy and emotional immediacy with which a particular embodiment of the native may be experienced, the discursive and social practice of demarcating and maintaining a native realm itself is a deliberative act of differentiation and an exercise of power in social relations. Thus an invocation of the native is neither natural nor innocent, however common or commonplace. It is always already an engagement with others, a struggle of naming and meaning over boundaries that mark off literal, symbolic, and cultural territories, as the refrain of "in" in the list of synonyms for the adjectival use of native above makes evident. Precisely because of this constitutive engagement, while distinctions like native-versus-foreign, inborn-versus-grafted, and indigenous-versus-imported are as old as human history, their specific contours and substantive meanings may vary significantly in history, depending partly on the global, national, and local power structures in which they are embedded and partly on the visions of alternatives they embody.

Yet, such engagement with others, mobilization of difference, and imagination of alternatives in the configuration of particular native identities are often overlooked in critical analysis, which predominately associates native identification with conservative nostalgia. Ironically, this is especially the case with current scholarships informed by poststructuralist questioning of origins. What results is a tendency to short-shift historical and contextual specificities and differences in constructions of the native, reducing nativism to a generic form of conservative identity politics akin to collective navel-gazing. Against such a priori dismissal of possibilities of progressive cultural politics in nativism, I argue here the importance of contextualizing nativist discourses not only in their sociohistorical particularities but also in relation to cultural contestations and social struggles of the time. With reference to *xiangtu* nativism in Taiwan in the 1970s and *xungen* nativism in the PRC in the 1980s, I explore contemporary nativist discourses in terms of critical intervention in the construction and debate of modernity, which has become an urgent universal concern ever since the West colonized and made the world in its image. Specifically, I examine how their different representations of the native articulate a discourse of identity in/and modernity that interrogates dominant conceptions received from the West, and whether/how nativism constitutes an oppositional discourse that proffers alternative visions of modernity.

For better or worse, modernity has been the sign under which Euro-America constructs, maintains, and legitimizes its global dominance in the past few centuries, radically altering social structures, cultural imaginations, and geopolitical positioning for all coming into its pathway. China was no exception. Displaced from its long-standing self-anointed position of the "Central Kingdom" by this Euro-American discursive construct, China found itself caught in a "storm of progress," to borrow Walter Benjamin's evocative phrase. With modernity bearing down on them in the form of Western cannons, gunboats, traders, and missionaries, Chinese intellectuals, sharing the fate of countless all over the dominated world, had to confront the dilemma of incorporating or resisting a system of knowledge and a way of seeing that presume to subjugate them and conquer the world. If hybridity emerged as the predominant figure of countermodernity in Latin America and has lately become the privileged sign of inclusive decenteredness in postmodernity and globalization, the Chinese struck a different tone. Arguably because of pride and confidence nurtured by the long history of Chinese dominance in East Asia, Chinese intellectuals kept turning to the native for utopian projections and discursive articulation of alternatives, even in the face of great display of Western power.[1] Indeed, nativism, or the deliberate advancement of a discursive movement advocating a (re)turn to the native, has shadowed Westernization throughout modern Chinese history, emerging in times of intense efforts to "modernize" through importation of Western knowledge, culture, technology, and industry. Within the literary field, nativism has seen different elaborations throughout the twentieth century since Lu Xun made it a vital part of modern Chinese literature in the 1920s. From the critical realism of Lu Xun's "homecoming" stories to the romantic nostalgia of Shen Congwen's *xiangxi* stories, the conservative localism of Zhou Zuoren's "Beijing School" (*jingpai*), and the "national resistance" literature against Japanese occupation in Manchuria, nativism has spanned a wide cultural political spectrum to renegotiate the place of local cultural identification and affiliation in a world of foreign incursion and Western domination. The two nativist discourses discussed in this book are but recent manifestations of a persistent dialectic in Chinese modernity under specific historical conditions.

The entanglement of nativism with Westernization efforts underscores the relational nature of nativist constructs. In contrast to hybridity's destabilization of polar opposites, nativism foregrounds a binary structure of opposition. As such, it raises some fundamental issues of resistance and contestation in the (post)colonial world: In the aftermath of imperialism and colonization, (how) is it possible to claim a realm of knowledge and value outside and independent of the value-coding system and epistemological dominance that is (Western) modernity? If not, what constitutes a viable ground for native (oppositional) claims, and how does it relate to hegemonic modernity? How and to what extent can alternative visions of modernity be articulated in the name of a separate "native" tradition? (How) does the politics of native identification limit oppositional possibilities and articulation of alternatives? These questions have particular resonance in the period under discussion, when postmodernity erupted in the discursive horizon of Euro-America, subjecting the grand narratives of universal modernity to intense interrogation and deconstruction, while East Asia became a celebrated "model" of modernization for its putative success in integrating capitalist development and participation in the new international division of industrial labor with a selective continuation of traditional culture and assertion of "national" difference. In this historical conjuncture of a multinational turn in capitalist practices and a revaluation of identity and difference in discourses of (post)modernity in the West, the nativist discourses of *xiangtu wenxue* and *xungen wenxue* emerged to articulate alternatives that depart from, if not directly contest, dominant constructions of modernity proffered by the Euro-American center and their respective developmentalist state, Taiwan and the PRC. The specific oppositional articulations of these two nativist discourses and their efficacy in proffering alternatives will be discussed in later chapters with particular reference to their national and local contexts. Here, I will first situate the discourses in a global, relational context and explore its historical specificity in terms of the development of what Bruce Cumings calls "Rimspeak" to include East Asia in a new discourse of postmodern global capitalism. I will then explore the oppositional possibilities that nativism may encode in such a historical and discursive context, as well as the theoretical contours of a critical framework for assessing these oppositional possibilities.

MODERNITY IN THE MARGINS, NATIVISM, AND EAST ASIAN PARTICULARITIES

> In its relational dimensions, modernity is a diffusionist project, assigned to interpellate others from a center. . . . Modernity [i]s an *identity discourse*, Europe's (or the white world's) identity discourse as it assumed global dominance.
>
> —Mary Louise Pratt

> What gets called modernity in China is neither a purely localized matter nor a mere instantiation of a universal discourse. It exists instead . . . as a repeatedly deferred enactment marked by discrepant desires that continually replace one another in an effort to achieve material and moral parity with the West. These deferrals reflect cross-cultural translations that Chinese elites and government leaders undertake as "China" continues to represent, for universalizing projects—and theories—of modernity, the formative "outside."
>
> —Lisa Rofel

> The project of modernity is itself rendered so contradictory and unresolved through the insertion of the "time-lag" in which colonial and postcolonial moments emerge as sign and history, that I am skeptical of those transitions to postmodernity in Western academic writings which theorize the experience of this "new historicity" through the appropriation of a "Third World" metaphor.
>
> —Homi Bhabha

With the postcolonial coming to voice of the marginalized in modernity, the Eurocentrism of hegemonic modernity discourse is increasingly unmasked. Ironically, the recognition of modernity and its later variant of postmodernity as an undeniably Western construction and temporal-spatial delineation of the world serves to underscore its very real effects on discursive significations of and in the rest of the world. As Mary Louise Pratt argues in her illuminative survey, modernity is fundamentally an ideological configuration of power relations placing white Euro-America at the center, with diffusion and interpellation of others as its most central features.[2] This means not only that the center-margins structure is inherent to modernity, but also that modernity is by definition different in the margins,[3] entailing what Homi Bhabha calls a time-lag of cultural difference that is productive of the very understandings of modernity.[4] Whether characterized as discrepant, dissonant, deferred, belated, pseudo, or contra, modernity in the margins serves to establish and affirm the normativity of the center and its "identity discourse" of modernity.[5]

Unfortuitously, then, identity looms large as a central issue of modernity in the margins. As prescribed others against which modernity constitutes the center, non-Euro-American societies experience a perpetual identity crisis in their encounter and engagement with modernity. "Progress," that privileged state in the center's identity discourse, is translated there into an imperative of "catching up" or reproducing what has already been achieved elsewhere that destabilizes all available grounds of identity formation. This imperative further reinforces the condition of "imposed receptivity" characteristic of modernity in the margins, under which the supposedly backward margin finds itself compelled to reckon with developments in the center, however incongruous and outlandish they may seem. Thus fragmentation, decenteredness, and coexistence of incommensurate realities become part and parcel of modernity in the margins. Any discursive attempt to make sense of modernity in the margins, then, necessarily involves some forms of double consciousness, as Paul Gilroy's groundbreaking discussion of "the black Atlantic" as a counterculture of modernity makes clear.

Insofar as nativism engages the question of modernity in the margins, it, too, partakes in double consciousness, despite its claims to the contrary in referencing the native. By virtue of its situation in the margins, it cannot but be, at best, a creative engagement with imposed receptivity, undertaking what Gayatri Spivak calls the catachrestic project of "seizing the apparatus of value-coding."[6] In this sense, nativism after the epistemic violence of Western imperialism in the name of modernity is already a hybrid discourse, embodying within its discursive structure, in opposition, differentiation, and/or complementarity, assumptions, values, and ways of seeing developed from the experiences and perspectives of the Euro-American center and disseminated through modernity. Still, nativism's open contestation of the dominant Western discourse of modernity marks a conscious departure from contemporary affirmation of hybridity, especially the saccharine strand that celebrates seamless mixing and fusion. Its assertion of an alternative ground of identification rather than an outright embrace of hybridity makes it a distinctive form of oppositional discourse that demands serious consideration of its own terms and the critical possibilities it encodes.

Situating nativism thus in the context of modernity in the margins highlights its critical intervention and historical contingency while drawing attention to its relational nature and contextual specificity. In this light, the advancement of nativism in response to the imposed receptivity of modernity is a contingent praxis that cannot be understood without reference to the particular historical relations of the specific margin to the Euro-American center. In the cases of Taiwan and China, the privileging of the native rather than hybridity as a ground for alternative discourses of modernity is arguably overdetermined by the unique success of East Asia in countering Euro-American domination in the name of modernity.

In her discussion of alternative modernities in China, Lisa Rofel argues that China occupies a distinctive position of otherness to modernity at the center by being "the constitutive 'outside' of western civilization . . . shap[ing] modernity by representing to Europe everything modernity is not."[7] A key component and signifier of this constitutive outside is of course the long, supposedly monolithic heritage of "Confucian culture," against which Max Weber, in one of the most influential studies of the role of culture in capitalist development, opposes the Protestant or Puritan ethic he considers key to the emergence of capitalism.[8] Yet, important as this constitution of the cultural outside has been, not least in reinforcing the tendency among Chinese intellectuals to focus the struggle for modernity on culture and the iconoclastic mode this often takes, the specificities of East Asia's historical resistance to capitalist domination and its changing practices are arguably just as significant, if not more, in shaping the emergence of nativist discourses of alternative modernity in Taiwan and China.

In the world of capitalist domination, East Asia stood out in its capacity to resist full-scale colonization by Euro-America. China of course was long preyed upon by various imperialist powers, but it managed to maintain a formally independent state to the end, a fact often considered a major factor in Chinese intellectuals' propensity to project onto traditional culture their desires and frustrations in modernity.[9] More important, insofar as colonization occurred in East Asia, the key colonizer was one of its own—Japan—rather than any of the European powers. Indeed, what made East Asia stand out in the history of Euro-American domination is Japan's exceptionality in becoming the first non-Western modern imperialist power while mobilizing a nativist ideology of opposing Western aggression. It was, above all, Japan's legendary ability to withstand direct domination by the Western powers and quickly learn their tricks and trades to rise itself as a modern power rivaling Euro-American dominance (even if in a limited geopolitical area) that generated the particular dynamics and conflicts shaping the experiences of modernity in East Asia in the twentieth century. In colonizing Taiwan, Korea, and Manchuria, as well as occupying various parts of Southeast Asia, Japan's efforts to become a competing center of modernity through the establishment of the "Greater Asian Co-prosperity Sphere" complicated the center-margins structure of Euro-American modernity. It made a fragmented China ironically an "ally" of European struggles against fascist aberrations of modernity, boosting Chinese nationalist aspirations and self-understanding of their nation's position in the world despite its plight of semicolonial subjugation. At the same time, Japan's apparent ability to forge its own path to modernity opened up the possibility of an "East Asian" alternative that inspired Chinese intellectuals and state officials even as it threatened their nation's very survival. Temporarily suspended and displaced by Japan's defeat in World War II and the prospect of a socialist alternative with the Communist victory in China, this possibility of an "East Asian" model of capitalist modernity was to become immensely significant again in the 1970s and 1980s, when socialism began to wane in China and the Japanese economy had grown so strong that it seemed poised to displace Euro-America from the center of capitalist modernity.

If modernity was once identified with and centered on Euro-America, that center no longer seemed able to hold by the late 1970s. Even as Euro-America faced severe economic crises with the oil shocks of the 1970s, Japan, which had been benefiting from U.S. strategic and economic deployment in East Asia as part of the Cold War to recover quickly from its war wreckages and become a formidable engine of the world economy, continued to boast significant growth and provide an unimpeded economic drive for the Pacific region. At the same time, the development of a new mode of flexible capital accumulation and deterritorialized production, of which the subcontracting system commonly adopted by Japanese corporations constituted a distinctive and pioneering trend in East Asia, led to a loosening of the ties between capitalist development and Euro-America.[10] With the rise of multinational companies and the parceling out of the industrial production process to different countries, notably the export processing zones established in newly industrializing countries such as Taiwan, it became questionable whether Euro-America continued to be *the* center of capitalist development and locus of progress, even though the multinational companies still maintained their bases there.

There is of course no direct connection or translation between economic power and cultural dominance, and the relative decline in economic supremacy of the United States in the 1970s does not automatically mean a corresponding loss in ideological domination and cultural legitimacy of Western modernity. But the relative decline, particularly the perception of a decline, opened up a discursive space for rethinking the presumed link between capitalist development and Western culture long accepted in Euro-American circles and their satellites in the margins. Specifically, the general ascendance in economic power of East Asia led by Japan generated interest in what came to be formulated as an "East Asian development model" and, concomitantly, a reevaluation of the compatibility and role of traditional culture, particularly Confucian culture, in modernity. The rise in Japan in the 1970s of a nativist discourse, the *Nihonjinron*, highlighting a set of distinctive national cultural characteristics, a Japaneseness, that remains intact even in modernity also fueled such speculative efforts.[11] Out of this discursive opening emerged different attempts to reposition East Asia and renarrativize cultural identity in capitalist modernity by various interested parties across the Pacific, including the media, policy and public opinion makers, and academics in the West, as well as the ideological apparatuses of the East Asian states and local intellectuals. In particular, the possibility of an East Asian modernity inflected with indigenous values and its challenge to dominant universalist conceptions of modernity became subjects of intense intellectual and policy debates in the United States no less than in East Asia. In the United States, it precipitated a discursive reconstitution of global capitalist relations around the new imaginary of the Pacific Rim to harness the emerging sources of economic vitality, as well as speculative projections of a culture-based, economics-driven East Asian challenge to Western supremacy. On the Asian side of the Pacific, the postulation by Western trained and/or based academics of an East Asian development model harmoniously integrating cultural traditions into capitalist development triggered and reinforced officially sponsored revival of (interests in) national cultural heritages, even as locally based scholars and intellectuals questioned whether and how traditional cultures could indeed remain vital and alive in (capitalist) modernity. With such renewed attention to East Asian cultural traditions and competing articulations of their relationship to modernity, what constitutes native culture and who/what represents the native easily became key sites for contesting modernity and conceiving alternatives in the East Asian societies.

Besides the contested terrain between East Asia and global capitalist development, the global context of this discursive opening also includes a concomitant rethinking of modernity in the name of postmodernity in the Euro-American center. Just as East Asian economic ascendance fostered nativist articulation of alternatives locally, the perceived decline in U.S. economic might and corresponding shift of capitalist momentum toward Asia fed into a general questioning and reexamination of modernity in the center that heralded the emergence of postmodernity. Whether new developments in the capitalist world of the late twentieth century constitute a significantly different historical formation meriting the designation of postmodernity and what exactly defines postmodernity have of course been controversial issues that remain unresolved as the discursive dominance of the postmodern came to pass with the recent ascendance of globalization discourses. Be that as it may, cognates of the postmodern were key terms for interrogating modernity and contemporary conditions in the last two decades of the twentieth century, especially in Euro-America, with theoretical intervention and elaboration by scholars of various persuasions. As such, postmodernity constitutes a critical part of the global context for *xiangtu* and *xungen* nativisms, even if (or precisely because) it is highly debatable.

As the reference to postmodernity rather than postmodernism suggests, what concerns us here is not so much the specific cultural, aesthetic, and literary trend that has become, in the words of Fredric Jameson, "the cultural logic of late capitalism."[12] Despite some innovative attempts to locate signs of such postmodernism earlier in Taiwan and China, it is generally accepted that postmodernism did not become significant in Taiwan and China, if at all, until the late 1980s and 1990s, respectively.[13] For the period under discussion, in contrast, postmodernity signifying the socioeconomic transformation and historical experience of the global extension of capitalist development through the institution of flexible accumulation, the formation of multinational corporations, and the advancement of technologies (especially information and computer technologies, which greatly facilitated production coordination, financial transactions, capital movements, and media transmissions across the globe) was quite relevant to Taiwan and China, particularly as a controversial marker of the changing global condition that had become dominant in the Euro-American center.[14] Inasmuch as the global extension of capitalist practices corresponds in part to the Japanese-led ascendance in economic power of East Asia, postmodernity encodes a particular way of understanding local and regional developments in East Asia in relation to Euro-America. Conversely speaking, postmodernity's affirmation of local differences constitutes, in part, a response to the decentering threat that East Asia, particularly Japan, posed to Euro-America's identity discourse of modernity.[15] With the media hype of such publications as *Japan as Number One*, the prospect of multiple centers including an Asian component, if not necessarily Japan assuming *the* center, called into question the established center-margins structure of modernity, rendering it difficult to confirm Euro-America as self-identical with modernity.[16] On this historical ground of a compelled recognition of different modernities in the margins or outside Euro-America, postmodernity resignifies the world from the experience and perspective of the Euro-American center. While registering significant changes in Euro-America's self-imagery and understanding of their relation to modernity and the margins, which facilitate nativist articulations of alternative modernities in the margins, postmodernity underscores the continued global dominance of Euro-American discursive constitution of the world. As a dominant global term, it has critical purchase beyond Euro-America in discussions of "newly industrializing" areas like Taiwan and China, especially for highlighting the mediated connection between local developments and global capitalist practices.

And yet, by virtue of its Euro-American centrism, the global designator of postmodernity alone is not sufficient to define the historical and discursive context in which *xiangtu* and *xungen* nativism emerged to articulate alternatives. What postmodernity signifies in the center corresponds to something quite different in the "newly industrializing" East Asian countries, which, by and large, stayed in the margins of economic decisions and discursive constructions of global capitalism even as they were incorporated into the global capitalist assembly line as outlying satellite factories.[17] The economic practices taken to characterize multinational capitalism in postmodernity, such as offshore production in export processing zones, are precisely what enabled capitalist development to "take off" in Taiwan and China, resulting in conditions that approximate (earlier) modernity at the center, namely industrialization, urbanization, and the rise of an urban bourgeoisie together with an escalation in social inequality. Also, quite contrary to the decentered order and delegitimation of grand narratives highlighted in postmodernity, these developments took place under the strong authoritarian control of a "modern" nation-state in the name of modernization and national development. The importance of a strong state in orchestrating and overseeing economic development is indeed highlighted as a key feature of the "East Asian development model." Thus, countering the global claims of postmodernity, modernity (or modernization) has remained the primary operative concept and hegemonic vision locally, both for the state and oppositional forces within the national space.

Of course, as suggested in the idea of modernity in the margins, modernity is constitutionally different in Taiwan and China from the Euro-American center. Indeed, modernity in the margins is arguably always already postmodern in the sense (per Ernesto Laclau) that the values of (Western) modernity cannot maintain any absolutist hold there, and that it entails an acute sense of the loss of mastery, a recognition of ineradicable differences, and the necessity to take others, especially powerful Euro-America, into consideration. Put differently, the supposedly postmodern experience and condition of fragmentation, decenteredness, and what Arif Dirlik and Xudong Zhang call "spatial fracturing and temporal desynchronization" are very much a part of modernity in the margins.[18] Postmodernity as a global term, then, conceals significant differences and disjuncture between the contemporaneous experiences and understanding of global capitalism in the Euro-American metropolitan centers and the margins.

Between the designators of modernity in the margins and postmodernity, at issue is not so much a problem of periodization as the problematic that governs what and how alternatives and oppositions to the status quo can be articulated. If the designator of postmodernity captures the changed power dynamics between the Euro-American capitalist establishment and East Asia that enabled the confident articulation of alternative modernities, it also obscures the chain of power relations in effect on national and local grounds. Under the sign of postmodernity, with its inscription of a decentered order, there is no discursive space for the center-margin opposition that structures nativist conceptions of the power relation between the West and East Asian nation-states like China and Taiwan, as well as the related hierarchy between urban centers and rural hinterlands. Without such an oppositional structure, nativist alternatives simply cannot be articulated.

To fully cover the global and local designation of the historical and discursive context for the advancement of *xiangtu* and *xungen* nativism as critical intervention and alternative articulation, then, a simultaneous reference to postmodernity and modernity is needed. For this purpose, I adopt the heuristic term post/modernity. As a sign specifying the historical and cultural conditions under which nativism seeks to rewrite modernity under global capitalism, post/modernity draws attention to coeval yet different discursive identification of the conditions in the Euro-American center and in the margins. Marking both the disjuncture and connected simultaneity between global postmodernity and local modernity, the term highlights tensions between local perspectives and dominant global signification from the Euro-American center. It registers the need to simultaneously attend to different locations and perspectives along the center-periphery spectrum and across the global-local divides in accounting for contemporaneous experiences and aspirations in the margins. Post/modernity, in short, situates Euro-America and East Asia in the same temporality of global capitalism and highlights the structural relation between practices in the center and developments in the margins while drawing attention to the tensions and incommensurabilities between global and local standpoints in making sense of this contemporaneity. Historically, it corresponds to the chronotope of the last quarter of the twentieth century, before globalization captured the imagination of the capitalist world, displacing postmodernity with the vision of a singular global network of simultaneous if differentiated markets. Discursively, it marks a dynamic opening up of modernity to multiple alternative formulations in response to the global extension of capitalism and shift of economic power toward East Asia.

THE PACIFIC RIM PROJECTION OR GLOBAL CAPITALISM'S NARRATIVE OF POST/MODERNITY

> Pacific Rim Discourse presumes a kind of metonymic equivalence. Its world is an interpenetrating complex of interrelationships with no center: neither the center of a hegemonic power nor the imagined fulcrum of a "balance of power." . . . The Rim was a perfect image for a centeredness with no central power.
>
> —Christopher Connery

> The language of the Asia-Pacific myth, with its invocation of "Third-Wave" civilizations and its focus upon the "basic commonalities" of economic prosperity, rhetorically reconciles the tensely coexisting multiple rival capitalisms and usefully blurs potential battle lines among them. Its votaries on both sides of the Pacific Rim become imaginative shareholders in a common utopianized marketplace.
>
> —Alexander Woodside

In the discursive opening of post/modernity, a new geo-imaginary, the Pacific Rim, emerged prominently to give shape to a cognitive (re)mapping of the world according to capitalist imperatives and desires. As such, the Pacific Rim discourse constitutes a particular postmodern articulation of the global discursive context for understanding the social and cultural intervention enacted in the *xiangtu* and *xungen* nativist texts.

Given East Asia's significance in the global shift of capitalist power and the ensuing disidentification of modernity and Euro-America, it is hardly surprising that capitalism's postmodern narrativization of its global future should take the form of reimagining East Asia and the region's relation to capitalist development. Even as cultural critics in Euro-America tried to make sense of contemporary changes in terms of the postmodern, American futurologists, policy makers, and social scientists projected their hopes, visions, and predictions of global capitalist development onto a construct of the Pacific Rim. In rendering a "growth"-oriented and technology-driven account of the shift in capitalist power underlying post/modernity, Pacific Rim discourse may be characterized as global capitalism's preferred narrative of post/modernity, offering a capital-centered representation of the fluid advancement of global capitalism into a decentered rim. Against this imaginary of a free flow around a hollow center, *xiangtu* and *xungen* nativism's emphasis on the abiding hold of the native place as a locus of marginality in modernity encodes a telling alternative.

Contrary to its image of circularity without origins or ends, the Pacific Rim, as most commentators concur with Arif Dirlik, is fundamentally a Euro-American invention serving primarily Western capitalist interests. It is so in the dual sense that the Pacific region itself has been historically constituted by Euro-American forces of capitalism and colonialism, and that the concept was informed and advanced by Euro-American interests and visions.[19] Tracing the concept's rise in prominence, Alexander Woodside notes that though the idea of a Pacific Ocean free trade zone was first proposed by Japanese politicians and economists in the 1960s, it became significant only with U.S. espousal in the latter half of the 1970s, when the economic achievements and potential of East Asia became apparent, especially after China's adoption of "open-door" policies to attract foreign capital and technology. As a "mobilization myth" of U.S. liberal economists and futurologists, the Pacific Rim discourse features an "international capitalist utopianism" that projects a vision of boundless economic growth based on technological advancement, free trade, and global market integration. Presumably drawing on the historical experience of phenomenal economic development in East Asia, its capitalist utopianism finds expression in two ubiquitous motifs in accounts of the East Asian success story—miracle and dynamism.[20] With these two motifs, the East Asian historical experiences are economized and universalized into an exemplary realization of the promises and prospects of global development, "progress," and limitless growth under the capitalist machine, which are open and available to all who are willing to plug into the machine and play by its rules. The World Bank's 1983 report on the "East Asian miracle" mints such a narrativization in attributing economic success in East Asia to "a market-friendly strategy with limited state intervention and a high degree of openness to trade and capital movements."[21] Following this classic liberal economics narrative of development, the Pacific Rim discourse presents a capitalist dynamism that is "all on the up-and-up, a whoosh of progress transforming the region,"[22] with no sign at all of contradictions between Euro-America and the Asia Pacific or rivalry within the Pacific region that later took on cultural accoutrements and escalated into the open in the form of "Japan bashing." In this light, the Pacific Rim may be seen as a new imaginary and conceptual construct to manage the shift of capitalist power out of the established Euro-American center with the multinationalization of industrial production and capital accumulation, articulating a common economistic concern of prosperity, progress, and development to cover (over) different interests of capitalist elites across national boundaries and cultural traditions.

The particular cultural politics of this management is accentuated in the trope of the rim, which is decidedly American in conception and usage, but masked in scientific aura. Whereas the metaphorically, if not geopolitically, neutral term "Asia Pacific" was and is generally used on the Asian side, the Pacific Rim has been the preferred reference with most currency in the United States. In substituting the rim for Asia, the American term conveniently elides cultural and historical constitution of the region beside and beyond the Pacific, as well as the contradictions between Euro-American and Asian constructions of the region. The term Pacific Rim's geological origin lends a scientific aura that underlines the discourse's proclivity for technology and economic rationality to the exclusion of cultural signification.[23] Metaphorically, the rim also evokes a sense of frontier that echoes the earlier American frontierism of "going west" toward the Pacific to discover wealth and create a man of oneself.[24] It renews and enlivens the dream of an infinite capacity of expansion into the future and progressive transformation of the world seen as space rather than historically, socially, and culturally constituted places. The brave new world of the Pacific Rim, as a rim, connects and unites capitalist pioneers into a dynamic nexus of growth and advancement with no fixed centers, outsides, or hierarchical divides. Always on the edge of development, it circumscribes and encompasses all into the capitalist dream, rendering antiquated and obsolete the other Euro-American image of the Pacific as a timeless paradise, an "escape" from the protean power of capitalism.

This myth of the rim is of course an ideal American imagery of the Pacific region, subject to challenges and alternative formulations from those with eyes more trained to the concrete data and politics of trans-Pacific exchanges. As Arif Dirlik stresses, the Pacific region is rife with contradictions that the Pacific Rim discourse is intended to suppress, not least the "failure" of Euro-American capitalism to contain the "success" of East Asian economic development within its cultural narratives.[25] In a self-consciously benchmarking overview of the Pacific Rim, Peter Gourevitch notes a vigorous debate over the role of culture, specifically Confucianism broadly conceived as the East Asian cultural tradition, in bringing about the East Asian miracles.[26] Participating and having a stake in the debate were not only American futurologists and social scientists specializing in East Asian societies, but also diasporic intellectuals and the East Asian states and local scholars. Just as the Pacific Rim discourse elides the significance of culture in its economistic representation of the capitalist "success" of East Asia, cultural traditions figure centrally in competing narratives of the "East Asian economic miracle" advanced by those identifying with the Asian side. In broad strokes, if the Pacific Rim myth promotes a form of universal class-based narrative that locates and celebrates the wellspring of East Asian miraculous growth in the unfettered operation of capitalist forces through free trade and open markets, counternarratives highlighting particular cultural factors in the East Asian success were advanced from the Asian side, often with reference to "native" perspectives, to suggest a culturally inflected capitalism beyond monolithic Euro-American domination.

Common to these counternarratives is a deterritorialized transnational Confucian culture that presumably challenges the supremacy of Western (Protestant) culture in cultivating the right ethic for advancing capitalist development in post/modernity. In a popular, influential version of these narratives, Herman Kahn identifies the "neo-Confucian cultures" of Taiwan and South Korea as a key factor in the two countries' rapid development and summarizes the kernel of the "Confucian ethic" into two related sets of characteristics: "the creation of dedicated, motivated, responsible, and educated individuals and the enhanced sense of commitment, organizational identity, and loyalty to various institutions."[27] Following Kahn, Roderick MacFarquhar proposed "the Post-Confucian Challenge" while Peter Berger put forward the "East Asian Development Model" to highlight the cultural dimension in East Asia's exceptional success in capitalist development.[28] With few variations, what came to distinguish East Asian culture in these accounts is a Confucian tradition of orientation toward the collective rather than Western culture's emphasis on the individual. That this rather reductive formulation of a common ground among the diverse cultural traditions of East Asia is motivated by a deliberate contrast with Western culture, especially the Protestant ethic Max Weber identified at the origins of capitalism, is particularly evident in Hung-chao Tai's summary formulation of "the Oriental alternative":

> The cultural setting [of Japan, South Korea, Taiwan, Hong Kong, and Singapore] has created what may be called an Oriental or affective model of economic development, which emphasizes human emotional bonds, group orientation, and harmony. It stands as an alternative to the more established Western model of development. The latter may be called a rational model, which stresses efficiency, individualism, and dynamism.[29]

In openly proposing an "Oriental" alternative, this diasporic scholar was obviously capitalizing on the newfound economic power of East Asia to challenge Euro-American hegemony (though the use of "Oriental" ironically betrays his continued subjection to the very hegemony he sought to challenge).[30] Such a challenge went in tandem with the Pacific Rim discourse in the 1980s, when the East Asian states entered the fray and took an active part in asserting their national/cultural identity even as they sought to consolidate their economic ascendance through further integration into the global capitalist system. The revival and promotion of interests in Confucianism lay at the heart of these state efforts. Starting in the 1980s, state-sponsored conferences on Confucianism and/or East Asian culture, especially the relationship between Confucianism and economic development/modernization, were regularly held in Taiwan, Hong Kong, Singapore, and even the People's Republic of China, generating copious discussions in conference volumes, scholarly journals, and cultural magazines.[31] While many, especially "local" scholars living and working in the East Asian countries, expressed skepticism toward arguments about a particularly congenial connection between Confucian culture and modernization, or a common (neo)Confucian culture in East Asia, these proceedings and discussions nonetheless normativized the centrality of Confucianism to East Asian cultural identities and legitimated the efforts to make a Confucian-based cultural tradition relevant to modernity in East Asia.

Inasmuch as these discussions assert cultural differences between the Asian and Euro-American sides of the Pacific and affirm the importance of cultural factors in economic development, they suggest efforts at an alternative account of the historical shift in capitalist power that the Pacific Rim discourse seeks to manage and contain. Yet, in articulating (neo)Confucian or East Asian culture to capitalist development, they also uphold and underscore the value of capitalist development and its centrality to modernity in East Asia. As such, they are arguably more a variant than a counterhegemonic alternative to the Pacific Rim discourse. Like the Pacific Rim discourse, they subscribe to a developmentalism that affirms capitalism as the motor for universal economic progress while registering the advance of multinational capitalism beyond singular Euro-American dominance and the attendant disarticulation of capitalism from Western cultural traditions. In this sense, they are an Oriental articulation of the Pacific Rim, even as or precisely as they seek to counter the cultural barrenness and fill in the empty form of the geological Rim with substantial representation of the Asian contents of the Pacific. Together with the Euro-American version of the Pacific Rim discourse, they constitute the hegemonic discursive context against which *xiangtu* and *xungen* nativisms posed significant alternatives.

Marginality, Oppositionality, and Nativism at the Rim

If the Pacific Rim discourse, in its tacit affirmation of the possibility of other cultural articulation with capitalist modernity, encodes an alternative conception to the Euro-American identity discourse of modernity, *xiangtu* and *xungen* nativisms can be seen as yet a different articulation of alternative modernities arising from the same historical context of post/modernity. While the two nativisms are not necessarily deliberate contestation of the Pacific Rim discourse, especially *xiangtu* nativism whose key texts predate the heyday of the Pacific Rim discourse, they advance alternative constructions that give different meanings and significance to the key concerns, motifs, and images of the Pacific Rim in both the American and Oriental versions. Foremost is their focus on the native as marginality, which interrupts and interrogates the developmentalism driving Taiwan and China's state construction of modernity that also finds expression in the Pacific Rim discourse's language of growth and progress. As later discussions will detail, in both *xiangtu* and *xungen* nativisms, this focus broadens the concerns of modernity beyond issues of capitalist economic development. It also enables *xungen* nativism to explore local cultures that contest the hegemonic representation of Confucianism as *the* native/national/East Asian culture.

Briefly, *xiangtu* nativism's figuration of the native in terms of exploited labor mapped variably onto hierarchical oppositions between the nation and the West, and between the urban and the rural inserts questions of social justice and the value of a traditional moral order into the consideration of the meaning and ends of modernity, challenging the Pacific Rim discourse's presumption of economic development as the indisputable yardstick and goal of modernity. Whereas *xiangtu* nativism tends to reaffirm Confucianism in its representation of the traditional moral order, the deliberate mapping of the native onto a "primitive" hinterland characterized by a marginalized ethnicized regional culture in *xungen* nativism explicitly challenges Confucian values and their hegemonic claim to representation of the native/national/ East Asian culture. In sum, in foregrounding marginality, the two nativisms highlight the persistent structuring effects of center-margins power dynamics in post/modernity and resignify the figure of the rim, thus articulating alternative visions of modernity in the margins that recenter social inequity and underscore issues of class, gender, ethnic and/or regional disparity in mapping the past, present, and future. Rather than a frontier of capitalist growth and expansion, the native place located in the margins is a rim of neglected values and traditions that stand against the ruthless exploitation and instrumental mentality of capitalist modernity.

To explore the two nativist discourses as such an intervention into the narrativization of post/modernity, however, requires an interruption and displacement of the entrenched conception of nativism as a conservative identity politics keyed to nostalgic nationalism. Situated against the domination and hegemony of capitalism and Western culture in modernity, nativist claims outside Euro-America tend to be critically mapped on a superimposition of oppositions between the rural and the urban, and between the nation and the West. The dominant conception of these terms along a universalist trajectory of modernization further translates the spatial imaginary into a temporal frame of the past versus the future, tradition versus progress. Thus, the invocation of nativeness to anchor one's being and orient one's action in the contemporary world easily becomes harnessed to nostalgia and aligned to cultural and political conservatism.

Such a spatiotemporal positioning is evident in established critical readings of nativism in modern Chinese culture. A telling example is David Wang's summary characterization of the *xiangtu* line of modern Chinese literature from its inception in May Fourth writings in the 1920s to its reincarnation in the *xungen* movement of the 1980s in mainland China. Contrasting *xiangtu* writings with urban literature, Wang notes that the former highlights "such themes as the clash between traditional, rural values and modern, urban civilization; the confrontation between intellectual-revolutionaries and peasant-conservatives; [and] nostalgic evocations of the past or of childhood."[32] In its unassuming association of nativism with a nostalgic orientation toward the rural and traditional past, this characterization reveals entrenched spatiotemporal assumptions about nativism as a modern discourse. Indeed, the nostalgic nature of nativism and its articulation of rural-urban and traditional-modern oppositions are so taken for granted that it becomes a platform for critical advancement in discussion of modern Chinese culture. Wang's insightful development of the term "imaginary nostalgia" to discuss certain nativist work is made on this very ground. While the term productively underscores the nuances and complexity of the nostalgic orientation in nativism by suggesting that the past to which nativism turns is not strictly representational, but incorporates imaginary elements motivated by present desires and concerns and steeped in intertextuality, it simultaneously affirms nostalgia as the structure of feeling and signification in nativism. Even as it opens up imaginative readings of nativist texts, it locks nativism within the spatiotemporality of nostalgia. Imaginary or otherwise, a nostalgic turn to a traditional past marks Wang's delineation of the nativist impulse in *xiangtu* literature.

Nativism's tie to conservative nostalgia is even more pronounced in Rey Chow's categorization of Chinese cultural resistance to colonialism.[33] To highlight the radical alternative offered by postcolonial cultural productions in Hong Kong, Chow situates nativism against postmodern celebration of hybridity as the two common but problematic poles framing contemporary cultural practices. Her critique of nativism centers on what she calls the "totalizing nativist vision of the Chinese folk," which is entwined in "a nostalgia for ever-receding origins" that shores up "the practice of centrism."[34] Nativism, in other words, engages in a nostalgic mobilization of the idea of a monolithic folk in support of the dominant culture. This characterization is noteworthy on two related fronts, each bringing up issues that are central to our critical assessment of the oppositional possibilities of nativism. First, there is an implicit identification of nativism with nationalism and the native with the folk/nation, which is also discernible in Chow's book, *Primitive Passions*, where, with the term "primitive" standing in for native, she criticizes "Chinese intellectuals' tendency to see everything in terms of the primitive that is China—to the exclusion of other issues, other peoples, and other struggles elsewhere."[35] As a correlative to this native-nation identification, Chow further links nativism to centrism and the "suppression of the fundamental impurity of native origins."[36] On account of this suppression of difference, nativism is deemed antithetical to postmodernism and its signatory celebration of "hybridity," "diversity," and "pluralism," of which Chow is no less critical for being contemporary culture's readily proffered panacea for the malaise of monolithic cultural domination in modernity. In positing such an opposition, Chow explicitly grounds nativism in a modern cultural paradigm of nationalism, linear temporality, and monolithic identity. With this grounding, nativism's critique of modernity is inextricably tied to nostalgia for an (imaginarily) wholesome past and its political possibilities as an alternative articulation of modernity can only be retrogressive and conservative. Chow's critical schema thus exposes the consequential link of nativism to nationalism and the modern paradigm that underlies nativism's common critical reception as a nostalgic response to the challenges of a Western-dominated modernity.

Significantly, the association of nativism with a conservative politics opposing hybridity and diversity is not limited to debates on modernity. It also figures centrally in discussions of postmodernity, notably David Harvey's widely influential study on the condition of postmodernity.[37] As a form of place-based identity politics, nativism is, in Harvey's critical framework, a fundamentally "reactionary" response to the (post)modern experiences of time-space compression intensified under the regime of flexible accumulation in late twentieth-century capitalism. At its root lies the desire and quest for "secure moorings in a shifting world," where experiences of fragmentation, insecurity, and ephemerality are pervasive under global capitalism's exploitation of spatial differences and uneven development to maximize profits through increasing financial and production mobility. This desire fosters an aestheticization of politics that displaces class solidarity with place-based identities and traditions, hindering the emergence of global political opposition and reinforcing the very condition of fragmentation that enables mobile capitalism and flexible accumulation to thrive.

Despite its unrelenting negative assessment, by virtue of situating place-based politics in the postmodern development of capitalism, Harvey's analysis suggests the possibility of reading nativism as a cultural response to postmodernity that is coeval with the ascendance of postmodernism in Euro-America. Inasmuch as nativism is often associated with conservative third world resistance and postmodernism with first world cultural currents, this accordance of coevality productively avoids the pitfall of temporalizing cultural differences into backwardness that plagues such universalizing theoretical undertakings. Yet, Harvey's global analysis from the perspective of capitalist development still perpetuates a reductive universalism that makes no distinction among place-based identity politics by different social groups in different locations within the global capitalist system. Particularly significant is its elision of differences in oppositional possibilities between nativist identity politics in the Euro-American center and the margins. If, as argued earlier, modernity in the margins always entails negotiations with powerful others that dislocate and decenter identity, the possible meanings of affirming a place-based identity—a native position—in the margins will be quite different from those in the center, however destabilized and shifting the center may have become.

It is precisely an emphasis on this crucial difference that allows critics such as Trinh Minh-ha to affirm nativism as a productive oppositional strategy for the colonized amid prevalent negative assessment of its politics. Trinh's appreciation of nativism hinges on a distinction between two invocations of "native" that highlights the term's variable valence depending on its location of enunciation, and thus the critical importance of attending to contextual differences in references to the native.[38] Evoking the world of difference between its use against others and for oneself, she suggests that in contrast to being othered as natives, which relegates one to the margins of history according to the dominant, colonizing culture, native self-identification strives to recenter a marginalized culture and tradition as the ground in which to root oneself and on which to project and build an independent future. From this perspective, nativism in the margins is fundamentally a project of reclaiming a denigrated identity in an act of postcolonial self-affirmation. In place of a native origin that is primordially fixed on a centrist idea of the folk/nation, the focus here is the oppositional impulse behind nativist constructions in a struggle against marginality. In other words, from a supposedly conservative orientation toward the past and primordial origins, critical attention is shifted to exploring what contemporary interests, desires, and concerns are expressed and contested in discursive efforts to reclaim and reconnect with some forms of the native and cultural traditions that have been marginalized.

Stuart Hall's affirmation of the return to roots as the ground on which margins came into representation in recent decades corroborates such a positive reading of nativism's oppositional possibilities in post/modernity. As Hall points out, while a return to the local is often a response to the global postmodern, it has a special significance and history for those in the margins.[39] Historically, the related moves of returning to some kind of roots, rediscovering hidden histories, and locating another place of enunciation were crucial for the coming to voice of the margins. Inasmuch as the center covers over, with universal claims, the particular traditions, histories, and contexts in which its representations and discourses are situated, those in the margins must rediscover their place of "origins," their past, and their "roots" to reclaim their voices and develop their own discourses and representation. A nativist return to roots is, in this light, a key discursive strategy in the struggle against marginality.

With such a shift from nostalgia to marginality as the theoretical fulcrum and interpretative lens, nativism is no longer inextricably tied to an ideological consolidation of the nation and the attendant suppression of differences in native origins, which account for much of its negative reception as reactionary identity politics. Instead, it is keyed to power relations, which can cover a multitude of social differentiations including class, gender, and race/ethnicity. From this critical perspective, there is nothing inherently regressive or conservative in nativist discourses. Nor does a nativist call for return to the homeland necessarily inscribe an exclusionary identity. Hall's emphasis on the mediatory role of narration and desire in the discursive return to a homeland and the recovery of a marginalized identity makes this clear.

Indeed, in drawing attention to nativism's negotiation of the very power structure of consolidating a center through the marginalization of others, the critical focus on nativism's underlying oppositional impulse opens up the possibility of identifying therein multiple lines of opposition to oppression and marginalization beyond a general nationalist resistance to Western domination. That is, insofar as nativism is understood primarily in terms of an attempt to reaffirm the devalued and marginalized in specific relations of power under a Western-dominated post/modernity, the native that is reaffirmed can be variously inflected with multiple social differentiations such as gender, class, race, ethnicity, region, religion, and/or generation besides nationality, depending on the particular power relations against which it situates itself in concretizing and substantiating marginality. By the same token, nativism needs not be seen as necessarily antithetical to postmodern attention to diversity and differences, even if in addressing specific power relations, it tends to stay largely within the either-or binarism of modernity.

It may be countered, with certain credence, that inasmuch as this notion of the native is deeply entwined in the history of colonialism and Western domination, its postcolonial maneuver in the name and hands of the marginalized would still amount to little more than derivatives of Western colonial discourses. In this vein, the danger of nativism making real the imaginary identities of the native to which Western colonial power has subjected the peoples under its domination has frequently been sounded. Or, as Ben Xu argues in his discussion of nativist cultural theory in China during the 1990s, the spirit of opposition to the West and imperialism ends up generating only a negative construction of the native, an identity of "past hurt, pain, or injury" that leaves the native forever under the shadow of the West.[40] Given the staying power of the rhetoric of alterity and the seductive simplicity of polarized identities, this danger of nativism reconfirming the power of colonialism and Western hegemony needs to be heeded and taken seriously. Yet it is just as important not to let the potential danger dispose us toward a facile dismissal of nativism and blind us to the oppositional possibilities of specific nativist constructions. The very double-edgedness of the term "native" in our recent history of colonialism and imperialism means that its mobilization in the (re)construction of identity and (re)claiming of traditions for a congenial future requires close examination and critical vigilance.

It is perhaps worth noting that to focus on the oppositional impulse behind nativist constructions and to acknowledge the possibility of nativism interrupting the binary oppositions of modernity to engage polymorphous differences certainly does not entail overlooking the exclusionary or centrist tendencies of many nativist practices. Nor is it to deny that nativism often appeals to some "natural," "innate" qualities as the native foundation. Rather, it is to consciously maintain a productive distinction between the native and the nation, to keep open the multivalence of the native, and to create a critical wedge between nativism and the modern paradigm of universal teleology and monolithic identity so that the oppositional potentialities of specific nativist critiques can be explored rather than shortchanged to a standard mode of nostalgic nationalism.

In view of the common conflation of nativism with nationalism, a critical framework that foregrounds the conceptual distance between the ideas of native and nation is especially important for understanding the specificity of nativism as an oppositional discourse in and of post/modernity. Arguably because of the prima facie importance of the nation-state in Western experiences of modernity, the ideological valorization of the nation-state into the proper, at times even natural, unit of collectivity in modern Western discourses, and most significantly, nationalism's consequent centrality in anticolonial struggles for independence, nativism is easily associated with, indeed often taken to imply, nationalism of some kind. Yet, as Kwame Anthony Appiah reminds us, there is an irreducible chasm between nativism and nationalism, for not only are they "different creatures," but they "fit together uneasily."[41] However closely related they might have been in the historical struggles for national independence, nativism and nationalism are set apart conceptually by their distinctive core notions. Insofar as the term "native" evokes natural belonging to a particular place and the culture and tradition "rooted" in that place, it has no necessary connection to the nation as a collective unit. The native place, in other words, can be a village, town, region at the subnational level, or an entire continent at the supranational level. Indeed, considering the "imagined" nature of the nation and the technology involved in such imagination, as Benedict Anderson's influential study points out, any linking of the native to the nation is a laborious process not to be taken for granted. If nationalism and its imaginary and symbolic constitution of a common folk as the natural subject of a nation-state are quintessentially parts of modernity, the transmutability of nativism's cultural reference to local traditions and practices suggests the possibility of different articulations of time, space, and sociality. In fact, nativism's invocation of the local place may in some instances be a subversive contestation of the authoritarian nationalism of the modern nation-state, as detailed analyses of Taiwan's *xiangtu* nativism and China's *xungen* nativism in the following chapters will show.

Nativism, Place-based Identity, and Difference

Given nationalism's embeddedness in hegemonic discourses of modernity, to maintain a critical distance between nativism and nationalism also means attending to nativism's possible interruption, suspension, or refusal of the universalism, linear temporalization of space, and what Horkheimer and Adorno called "abstract identity" of modernity.[42] This entails taking seriously nativism's literal emphasis on and rhetorical construction of place and locality as a discursive site for interrogating the meaning of modernity and imagining alternatives in the margins rather than translating it temporally into a nostalgia for origins and the past. In this critical light, nativism can be seen as a deliberate turn to the local and the particular embedded in specific places, with an insistence on the situatedness of human experiences and visions of modernity.[43] Against the global claim and globalizing force of capitalism in post/modernity, specifically, such a turn to the place-based local encodes an affirmative recentering of the marginalized, enabling a reinscription of past territorialization of social relations to engage the politics of identification and representation in a world in which previously underdeveloped places are relentlessly incorporated and transformed into replaceable units of production and manufactured markets of consumption under capitalist post/modernity.

The oppositional potential of *xiangtu* and *xungen* nativism's alternative configuration of/at the Pacific Rim arguably lies precisely in this focus on local rendition and inflection of historically grounded places, especially as/in the margins. As global capitalism's narrative of post/modernity, the Pacific Rim discourse inscribes an interchangeability of places as spaces of capitalist development and a universal teleology of technological and economic progress that accords little significance to local representation and figuration of the diverse localities in the Pacific region. Even with the Oriental insertion of a (neo)Confucian component to the Pacific Rim, the specificity claimed is still a transnational East Asian cultural difference that is deterritorialized and devoid of local signification of its social meaning in different places. In calling attention to local constitution of meanings and construction of identities rooted in concrete places, *xiangtu* and *xungen* nativism establish alternative grounds for imagining and narrating post/modernity that challenge the teleology of capitalist development and its hegemonic worlding of modernity.

To understand how such a focus on local signification of the native place can go beyond nostalgic conservatism to effectively negotiate the meaning of modernity, we need a conception of place that is open to dynamic interaction rather than fixed in geological space. Here, Doreen Massey's elucidation of the irreducibly social constitution of places is useful:

> Places . . . are not so much bounded areas as open and porous networks of social relations . . . their 'identities' are constructed through the specificity of their interaction with other places rather than by counterposition to them . . . [and] those identities will be multiple (since the various social groups in a place will be differently located in relation to the overall complexity of social relations and since their reading of those relations and what they make of them will also be distinct). And this in turn implies that what is to be the dominant image of any place will be a matter of contestation and will change over time.[44]

This conception of place as open, contested, and constituted through interaction—including differences and conflict—brings out the variability, multiplicity, and heterogeneity that are potentially inscribed in the place-based identity and cultural construction of nativism. With such a conception, place-based identity is definitely not confined to a monolithic, fixed cultural category. Rather, it is embedded in a nexus of social relations and processes that make up the contested terrain of the variable local in post/modernity, inextricably tied to relations and processes that actualize, reconfigure, disrupt, and reconnect familiar social categories such as class, ethnicity, and gender. In other words, the place that grounds native identity in nativist discourse, variously conceptualized as the "homeland," the "native village," or "roots," is to be seen not so much as a fixed location as a particular situatedness specified by a nexus of social relations and processes that, however, do not remain uncontested and unchanged. As textual analyses of *xiangtu* and *xungen* writings in the following chapters will show, though "*xiangtu*" or "*gen*" generally references a particular geographical location, such as the fishing village of Badouzi in Wang Tuo's *xiangtu* fiction or the Heilongjiang border area in Zheng Wanlong's *xungen* works, this specific place is constituted not so much by its geographical location as by the social relations and moral order that give it its distinctive feature—the patriarchal order of selfless maternal sacrifice in Wang Tuo's fishing village or the moral economy of an autonomous yet caring masculine subject in Zheng Wanlong's border zone. In its capacity to engage relations of power and domination pertaining variously to gender, ethnicity, class, and other social categories of producing and managing identities in post/modernity, this socially defined place enables nativist writers to enact different interruption and interrogation of dominant constructions of modernity in their particular mappings of the native.

In view of such variability in nativism's place-based identity politics, a wholesale dismissal or celebration of nativism as a strategy of resistance and opposition is clearly untenable. The oppositional possibilities encoded in specific instances of nativist construction depend on what and how power relations are engaged in the discursive process. Only through a careful excavation of the ground—the native place as a discursive construct of social relations within particular situatedness—on which each nativist text configures its figures of modernity can we explore tension between its challenge to and continued reliance on dominant modalities of modernity, and determine its politics of identity and difference in inscribing alternatives.

Particularly, inasmuch as nativism mobilizes identity politics and local differences to challenge universalist notions of/in modernity, a critical assessment of its oppositionality calls for a close examination of how it grounds and deploys difference. Just as differences can be mobilized to destabilize entrenched categories and wrest open a space for new articulations of modernity and identity under certain conditions, existing boundaries and hierarchies can be consolidated in the name and interest of preserving differences against the relentless, homogenizing force of modernity, like the (neo)Confucian articulation of Pacific Rim discourse. Relatedly, differences and otherness may be appropriated to consolidate the social and discursive power of various national elites as well. Though situated in the margins vis-à-vis Euro-American construction of modernity as well as their respective states' project of modernization, *xiangtu* and *xungen* nativisms are not immune to the pernicious danger of appropriating otherness and marginality, given the multiple axes of power crisscrossing their locations of discursive production. As noted earlier, much of the oppositional vitality of these nativisms lies in their flexible construction and signification of place that allows the encoding of different power relations covering the range of sociality from gender, ethnicity, and class to age and generation. This, in effect, compounds the possibilities of appropriating marginality and otherness and consolidating existing power structures in the guise of maintaining differences against cultural homogenization through Westernization. In particular, the class, gender, and ethnic makeup of the intellectuals mobilizing the nativist discourses suggests a propensity for male intellectual appropriation of the voices and marginalized positions of female subalterns to shore up the moral authority of their discursive opposition and articulation of alternatives, as detailed analyses in the following chapters will corroborate.

Mindful of the potential treachery of nativism's identity politics of multiple differences, my examination of specific instances of *xiangtu* and *xungen* discourses will interrogate how they delineate and situate themselves in the global-national-local nexus of post/modernity, whether/how they mark their locations of articulation, and how their politics of difference are articulated and play out in this nexus. Specifically, the interrogation would include questions along the following lines: What are the acknowledged and unacknowledged global, national, and local contexts of the discourse? How are the global, national, and local conceived and mapped in the discourse? Where is the native place located in this mapping? Against what is the assertion of native identity and local differences directed? In particular, is the native counterposed to the homogenizing forces of global capitalism with its valorization and universalization of the market penetrating into and commodifying every aspect of life? Or is the native pitted against the hegemony and domination of Western culture, expressing a primary concern with modernization as Westernization that leaves the social and political-economic impacts of capitalist transformation and their relation to everyday life and cultural experiences unexamined and uncritiqued? How is the native positioned and local differences aligned vis-à-vis the perceived domination? What social categories are the differences mapped onto? Is the native identified with the nation? If so, how is the nation conceived, and how does it relate to the state? In addition, (how) is the native mapped onto social relations of class, ethnicity, and/or gender? Are differences allowed within the mapping of the native? (How) is the mapping of the native complicitous with the status quo or replicating existing power hierarchies? Finally, what subject positions are mobilized to speak for and assert local differences? (How) is otherness or marginality deployed structurally in these positions? Together, these questions probe the politics of difference in a particular nativist discourse along the global-national-local nexus, enabling a dynamic assessment of the oppositional potentials and limits of the discourse's engagement with post/modernity. It is my contention that only such a dynamic assessment can illuminate nativism's variable purchase and significance as alternative articulation of modernity under global capitalism, and thereby deliver us from the pitfall of a blanket dismissal of nativism for reputed conservative nostalgia, overlooking the richness of its persistent contemporary appeal.

CHAPTER TWO

Beneath the Claims of Native Soil

Class, Nation, Gender, and *Xiangtu* Nativism in Taiwan

Xiangtu Nativism and Post/Modernity

There is perhaps no better illustration of nativism's significance in the oppositional politics of post/modernity than the case of Taiwan, which stands as an exceptional success in riding the postmodern wave of multinational capitalism to ascend the global economic order. Before the island-state settled into its celebratory status as a "little dragon" or "tiger" skillfully weaving together Chinese traditional culture and capitalist development, an intense questioning of the meaning and course of modernity took place in the form of a revival of nativist discourse. In the 1970s, when Taiwan was actively adapting to and cooperating with capitalism's exploratory global shift to offshore production by instituting export processing zones on its territory, "nativist literature" (*xiangtu wenxue*) emerged as the country's preeminent form of literary expression and quasipolitical dissent, gaining wide popularity and critical notice. Nativist literature's conscious social criticism and its advocates' provocative political positions drew public attention and posed significant challenges to the state's vision and construction of modernity. From sharp depictions of the exploitative working conditions of laborers in foreign-operated factories and the dislocation and oppression suffered by migrant workers from rural villages to parodic and satiric representations of the corruption and decadence of urban life dominated by the consumption of imported goods and Western lifestyles, as well as the degradation of native intellectuals caught in the ruthless operations of global capitalism and forced into guiding sex tours and pimping hometown girls for Japanese businessmen, nativist literature vividly exposed the underbelly of the post/modern beast of capitalist development in Taiwan. To counter these implicit and explicit challenges, state-sponsored writers and critics launched a concerted attack on nativist literature and some of its advocates and writers, culminating in a ferocious debate in 1977–1978. Ostensibly about literature, the debate actually centered around the meaning of the term "native" (*xiangtu*) and its relation to Taiwan's post/modernity. In the course of the debate, critical questions about what modernity means for Taiwan and how it relates to national independence, cultural identity, and social (class) injustice were raised and heatedly pursued. An advancement of nativist discourse in literature thus brought forth what is arguably the most public and engaged cultural contestation over post/modernity in the history of Taiwan.

As argued in the last chapter, if recourse to the native is a common form of resistance against Western domination and exploitation, what is invested in specific conceptions of the native may not be common at all. While nationalism is often involved, specific mappings of the native and its relation to the nation vary significantly according to particular needs and concerns in different sociohistorical and cultural contexts. In the case of Taiwan's *xiangtu* nativism of the 1970s, issues of class were central, creating a tension with nationalist sentiments that have often been taken to be synonymous with nativism. Though class was not explicitly deployed as a discursive category or oppositional strategy in the nativist struggle to redefine (and perhaps redirect) Taiwan's modernity, class consciousness clearly informed most of the writings, and the class content and implications of nativist fiction were major causes of contention during the nativist literature debate. This strong class inflection of the native brings out the importance of looking beyond the apparent nationalist reference of nativist discourses to examine their textual and rhetorical specificities, as well as the particular sociohistorical conditions that elicit those specificities.

With the demise of socialism as a viable progressive alternative and the ascendance of postmodern play and attention to multicultural diversity, gender, and ethnic identities, class concerns have fallen into the wayside of contemporary cultural criticism. Indeed, not only has class ceased to be the central oppositional category, but its invocation and role in progressive cultural politics have become a point of contention between postmodern cultural critiques and established Marxist lines of radical opposition. Whereas Marxist critics fault postmodernists for neglecting and jettisoning class in their analysis of and intervention into oppression and marginalization, postmodern cultural critiques lay bare the culpability of conventional class politics in the reductive and oppressive logic of binary oppositions and polarizations in the regime of modernity. From a global perspective of oppositional strategies, then, the centrality of class concerns in Taiwan's nativist discourse of the 1970s clearly aligns it with an earlier moment of oppositional politics structured under the sign of modernity. From a local standpoint, however, *xiangtu* literature's cultural politics is complicated by the intricate interweaving of nation, class, ethnicity, and gender in the discursive constitution and cultural representation of modernity, even if the association of nativist opposition with modern rather than postmodern cultural politics is by and large on the mark.

The investment of class concerns in Taiwan's nativist discourse of the 1970s is arguably traceable to the island's development strategy and political climate since the Nationalist takeover in 1945. Because class was institutionalized into the Chinese Communists' building of a modern nation on the mainland, any direct reference to class in public discourses was too politically charged to be tolerated by the Nationalist government. In fact, the suppression of discussions of class through censorship and other disciplinary mechanisms under the institution of martial law necessitated the expression of class concerns in other idioms.[1] That they eventually found expression in terms of the native is understandable given the particular nature and trajectory of Taiwan's economic development under Nationalist rule, which was in turn deeply entwined in global politics and capitalist economy.

Since becoming the seat of the Nationalist government after Communist victory in the Chinese mainland, Taiwan has been heavily dependent on the United States for its political and economic survival. American aid, which resumed in 1950 as part of the Cold War anti-Communist strategy after the outbreak of the Korean War, was indispensable to the Nationalist government's maintenance (or, more precisely, enforcement) of economic and political "stability" on the island for more than a decade. The extent to which Taiwan's development was directed by U.S. interests can be surmised from the unabashedly self-congratulatory assessment N. H. Jacoby made on behalf of the U.S. Agency for International Development (AID) when the Taiwan program was terminated in the mid-1960s:

> Given a clear mutual objective, a relatively high level of aid was provided. This "saturated" Taiwan's absorptive capacities, produced manifest evidence of progress, and gave the U.S. Mission strong influence upon Chinese policies. . . . AID followed an activist policy in using its influence upon the Chinese government to inaugurate a favorable climate for private investment and enterprise. It rejected the fallacious view that aid should have "no strings." . . . [I]t underwrote the stable political framework for economic progress provided by an authoritarian government, and let political reforms come later. . . . AID administered assistance to the Republic of China through semi-autonomous Chinese institutions outside of the government budget. It jointly controlled with them U.S. dollar projects, NT dollar projects, and imports.[2]

This retrospective celebration of U.S. power in determining Taiwan's policy and course of action reveals not only a high degree of U.S. control over Taiwan's economic development throughout the aid period, but also the extension of such control and its underlying mentality of legitimate U.S. domination beyond the mechanism of direct aid. Even after the official termination of aid in 1965, Taiwan's heavy dependence on U.S. capital investment, technology, and trade continued unabated, though in a different form. Under U.S. prompting and in response to the global restructuring of capitalism with the introduction of flexible production, Taiwan adopted an export-oriented industrial development policy in the 1960s and set up its first export processing zone in Gaoxiong (Kao-hsiung) in 1966. This policy catapulted Taiwan into the forefront of global capitalism, turning the island essentially into a supplier of cheap labor for offshore production by foreign multinational companies, which retained control of capital flow, technology, and markets while increasing their profit margins with overseas manufacturing operations. If this development of multinational corporations and offshore production signifies a shift away from Eurocentric capitalism that marks the rise of postmodernity in the West, it was experienced by many in Taiwan at the time as modernity, especially a form of neocolonial modernity that left their country dependent on foreign capitalist powers. To the locals, such arrangements not only kept Taiwan's economy under the thumbs of U.S. capital interests, but also enabled Japanese companies to return and rapidly regain their share of economic dominance over the former colony. The result was that the United States and Japan together effectively controlled Taiwan's industrial development and foreign trade by the early 1970s.[3]

The domination of American and Japanese capital in Taiwan created a situation in which capital-labor contradictions easily corresponded to a foreign-Chinese opposition.[4] This made possible a displacement and superimposition of class consciousness onto a desire for national autonomy and independence, which remained legitimate and socially sanctioned under the repressive Nationalist regime. The displacement allowed a critical reading of Taiwan's modernity in terms of neocolonialism, with the "nation" as a whole being exploited and oppressed by Japan and the United States.[5] Such a view, which informed most of the writings in the magazine *Xiachao* (China Tide), began to take shape in Taiwan's intellectual circles in the early 1970s.[6] Its persuasiveness and relevance were particularly enhanced by a series of incidents that starkly exposed Taiwan's subordinate position in the international order and its dependency on the United States for political survival as a nation-state.

The exposure first came with the so-called Diaoyutai incident, when the United States decided to turn over the contested Diaoyutai islands to Japan rather than Taiwan.[7] This brought public attention to Taiwan's weakness and dependence on U.S. patronage as the internationally recognized Chinese nation-state. Chinese intellectuals and students in Taiwan and overseas immediately considered the reversion an act of joint U.S.-Japanese aggression against their nation, and quickly turned Diaoyutai into a rallying point for their Chinese nationalist sentiments.[8] Strikingly, amid the popular fervor, the Nationalist government made no stronger protest than a formal declaration of sovereignty over the islands. The paltry response bespoke a reluctant acquiescence that drove home to Taiwan's intellectuals the dependent nature of their "nation-state," and deepened their awareness and resentment of U.S. and Japanese domination over the Chinese nation and the Nationalist government's complicity in the perpetuation of such domination. This gave rise to a sense of national crisis, which continued to aggravate as the following years saw further erosion of international support for the Nationalist's claim to the representation of the Chinese nation. In 1971, Taiwan was forced to leave the United Nations after the United States withdrew support for its representation of China. The following year, the United States further signaled its de facto recognition of the Beijing regime with Nixon's presidential visit, while Japan went so far as to officially sever diplomatic ties with the Nationalist government in Taiwan.

The early 1970s thus found Taiwan struggling with a deepening national crisis that brought into the open the unequal relationships underlying its post-World War II economic development and political survival. To local intellectuals, the crisis made urgent the articulation of alternative bases for imagining and building the nation and modernity, alternatives that could effectively resist both foreign domination and the state's complicit construction of modernity and the nation. It was such a quest for alternatives that led to a reconsideration and consolidation of the native as a strategic locus of critique and opposition.[9] Arising from a recognition of the dependent and neocolonial nature of postwar Taiwan, and a keen awareness of the state's failure to represent and act in the interests of the nation, this discursive (re)turn to the native incorporated an understanding of Taiwan's condition as a form of "internal colonialism," where the state and its elites colluded with international capitalists to exploit the people/nation.[10] Such an understanding readily opened up a discursive space for interrogating social class injustice in modernity within a framework of nationalism grounded in the claim of the native. Thus class issues became entangled with nationalist sentiments and found expression in the language of the native.

If the conflation of class and nation significantly limits and delimits the oppositional potential of this specific nativist discourse, as detailed discussions later in the chapter will show, its cultural politics is further complicated by the implicit association of ethnicity with class in local perceptions, owing to the particular history and circumstances of the Nationalist rule in Taiwan. On account of this association, the incorporation of a sense of internal colonialism and class injustice into *xiangtu* nativism also brings in the issue of ethnic inequality under the guise of nationalist struggle against colonialism.[11] This threatens to destabilize and disrupt the nation's reference in the discourse's nationalist configuration, and potentially opens the discourse up to postmodern identity politics.[12]

Ethnicity in Taiwan, as elsewhere, is foremost a cultural construction on sociohistorical grounds. Reflecting their particular historical trajectories, two main "ethnic" groups are commonly identified in Taiwan.[13] In everyday parlance, the contingent of mainly Han Chinese who moved to Taiwan with the Nationalist government and army after 1945 are identified as "Mainlanders" (*waishengren*), while the descendants of earlier settlers of Chinese extraction (mainly from the coastal provinces of Fujian and Guangdong) are called the "Taiwanese" or *benshengren* (literally, people from the local province). Strictly speaking, of course, neither the Taiwanese nor the Mainlanders constitute a singular ethnic group. Though mainly from the northern provinces, the Mainlanders include a diverse group of people with different local customs and dialects. Among the Taiwanese, there are also minority populations besides the Holo (Fujianese) majority, notably the Hakka people. These diversities ended up being aggregated into the binary ethnic categories of Mainlanders and Taiwanese largely because of the policies and practices of the Nationalist state, which maintained differential treatment between the two groups.

Inequity was most pronounced in the political establishment as political power under the Nationalist government was concentrated in the hands of the Mainlanders until well into the 1970s, when a process of "Taiwanization" in the government and political institutions began. This prolonged exclusionary practice underscored and consolidated differences between the Mainlanders and the Taiwanese, helping to enhance ethnic identification among the latter. More specifically, from its assumption of control over Taiwan in 1945 to the 1970s, the Nationalist government consistently prioritized the ultimate goal of unification of China over the immediate task of development of the island and privileged the Mainlanders over the locals in state employments and governance. The political, economic, and sociocultural policies it established from the early years—including the installation of a hierarchy of party and government structures run by Mainlanders, imposition of martial law, monopolization of economic assets left by the Japanese, elimination of local intellectuals and elites, establishment of Mandarin Chinese as the official language, and institutionalization of mainland history and culture in the school curricula—all had the effects of intensifying and reinforcing ethnic identification and polarization between the Mainlanders and the local Taiwanese, who found themselves marginalized culturally and politically on the island they had called home for centuries. These policies echoed Japanese colonialism and accentuated the experience of colonial subjugation that some Taiwanese had come to associate with life under the Nationalist government since the bloody military repression in 1947, which decimated local elites and became etched in public memory as the watershed "2–28 incident."[14] What resulted is a social propensity for ethnic-political polarization that can easily be mapped onto class inequality.[15]

Such a mapping was facilitated by the fact that until the 1960s, when export-oriented industrial development brought a boom to small-scale private enterprises that improved the economic opportunities of the local people, the majority of the Taiwanese were excluded from middle-class and nonmanual professions, of which government employment made up a significant proportion. This led to a broad correspondence between class and ethnicity during the first decade or so of Nationalist rule, which in turn fed a general belief in the coincidence of class and ethnicity that has remained largely unchanged even after notable changes in social mobility in the 1960s.[16] Inasmuch as the manual working class was identified with the Taiwanese majority, the evocation of class injustice in *xiangtu* nativism easily implied a critique of ethnic inequality as well. Thus the nativist discourse opened up a covert means of political mobilization on ethnic identity, which contributed to the controversy over *xiangtu* literature and led ultimately to the rise of overt Taiwanese nationalism by the end of the 1970s.

Besides the perceived link with class, ethnicity also found its way into the discourse of *xiangtu* nativism through the figure of the rural village as native soil and homeland. Paraphrasing Wang Tuo, a key writer-critic of *xiangtu* literature, the eventful history of generations of ancestors amassing their hopes and labor to open up arable farmland and establish a homeland on the island makes the rural village a rich symbol of a historically rooted Taiwanese identity for the nativists.[17] Strengthened by the predominance of Taiwanese among the rural population and their continued cultivation of the land, this symbolic resonance easily links references to the rural village in *xiangtu* nativism to the Taiwanese and their claim to Taiwan as homeland. Against the backdrop of Mainlander domination, such a link provided a convenient ground for affirming a native Taiwanese identity that is distinctive from mainland Chineseness.

With this subtle infusion of ethnic identification into the meaning of the native, the nationalism inscribed in Taiwan's nativist discourse becomes deeply ambiguous. The unarticulated yet palpable possibility of Taiwan rather than China ultimately constituting the proper reference of the nation renders all nationalist expressions equivocal and tantalizing. Even if an outright proclamation of Taiwan as a nation, or, in the words of its detractors, "Taiwanese separatism," was still too radical in the 1970s, the implicit ethnic identification of the native raised, at least, the questions of priority and relation between concerns with the native-as-local (whether the rural village or Taiwan as a whole) and with the native-as-nation (China). These questions leave the meaning and significance of nationalist consciousness in *xiangtu* nativism highly contentious and problematic. As Lin Yaofu remarks, "nativism carried within itself two consciousness—Chinese consciousness and Taiwan consciousness" even though the latter was subdued and submerged until well into the 1980s.[18]

These complex issues of class, nation, ethnicity, and modernity inflected with and configured under the sign of the native inform specific works of *xiangtu* literature in the 1970s to various degrees. How they are mapped specifically to contest and to proffer alternatives to the state's vision of modernity, the gender subtext and implications of these mappings, and the limits they pose to the alternative construction of modernity are central concerns for my discussion here and will be addressed in detail later through close analyses of several pieces of well-known *xiangtu* literature. Significantly, besides specific literary works, these issues also shaped the general debate on nativist literature and Taiwan's modernity, which took a course quite independent of the fictional narratives. For this reason, the debate is interesting and illuminating in its own rights, constituting, as it were, a different, but no less important, part of Taiwan's nativist discourse in the 1970s. Waged in an ideologically supercharged atmosphere, the debate yielded particularly revealing statements on different conceptions of the native and its relation to class, ethnicity, nation, and modernity in Taiwan. It is therefore to these statements that I will turn first to assess the parameters and limits of Taiwan's *xiangtu* nativism and its construction of modernity.

NATIVIST LITERATURE AND CULTURAL CONTESTATION

That literature and literary criticism should assume an important role in cultural contestation over post/modernity in Taiwan is perhaps not surprising, given the severe political restraints on social expression of dissent and opposition under martial law, and the traditional Chinese investment of serious social mission in literature. With its adoption of a realist mode, occasional use of the Taiwanese (Holo) dialect (especially in dialogues), and focus on the daily struggles of the "nobodies" as they eke out a living in impoverished environments, particularly in the countryside or small provincial towns, Taiwan's *xiangtu* literature certainly lends itself rather easily to oppositional politics, even though it is not always consciously political. The political connotation of the literature is also enhanced by the historical link of *xiangtu* nativism to Taiwanese resistance literature written under Japan's colonial rule from 1895 to 1945. The term "*xiangtu wenxue*," as literary historians have pointed out, was first adopted in the debate on using the Taiwanese dialect in creative writing and the development of nativist literature in the 1930s. After a period of imposed silence under the oppressive atmosphere of the early Nationalist years, the idea of *xiangtu* literature was revived in the late 1960s by critics interested in promoting the literary works of a new generation of ethnic Taiwanese writers. Implicitly, then, *xiangtu* literature was almost exclusively associated with ethnic Taiwanese writers, as Mainlander writer-critic Ma Sen pointed out.[19] This easily leads to the controversial identification of *xiangtu* nativism with the advocacy of Taiwanese consciousness, though such consciousness did not become open and prevalent until the 1980s.

With its emblematization of anticolonial resistance, the deliberate revival of *xiangtu* literature by the Taiwanese critics suggests definite oppositional intent. Yet, written by a young generation raised under the Nationalist regime's ideology of Chinese nationalism and active repression of local Taiwanese elements, the fictional works that have come to be identified as *xiangtu* literature of the late 1960s and early 1970s do not show a conscious reclaiming of the legacy of nativist literature written against Japanese colonization.[20] Rather, they reflect a deliberate turn to realist representation of ordinary everyday lives, partly in reaction to the domination of the literary scene by "modernist" writings that consciously followed the techniques and thematic concerns of Western modernism(s).[21] Featuring mainly a humanist depiction of rural life, *xiangtu* works of the 1960s remained uncontroversial and apolitical. It was the growing concerns over the neocolonial nature of Taiwan's modernity during the national crisis of the 1970s that dramatically radicalized nativist literature. Nativist works of this period became explicitly critical of the effects of the state-directed importation of Western (capitalist) modernity on the native land and its inhabitants. By focusing on the everyday existence of those who were exploited, sacrificed, and/or forsaken in the process of capitalist modernization, these works insistently reveal the negative sides of socioeconomic and cultural development under a Western-oriented engagement with post/modernity. Through the representation of concrete lives, they weave together issues of national dependence, social disintegration, cultural contamination, moral degeneration, and social injustice. While these fictional narratives are not necessarily informed by socialist aspirations, their focus on the subalterns and social injustice on the native soil highlight the significance of class in constructing alternatives. Interlaced into the native-nation nexus, this class focus sharpens and enriches the narratives' critical reflection on Taiwan's post/modernity. By the same token, it figures prominently in the nativist literature debate.

The nativist literature debate began as a literary argument between advocates of the literature and champions of modernist writings on the social responsibility of literature and the cultural implications of literature's heavy borrowing of Western techniques and thematic concerns. Reflecting the general intellectual atmosphere of questioning Taiwan's submissive following of the West under post/modernity, disagreement over the values of Western-influenced modernist literature has surfaced in the literary circle throughout the 1970s. After the 1972 New Poetry debate, critical attention was turned primarily to fiction, with the literary journal *Wenji* (Literary Quarterly) playing an important role in censuring modernist fiction and galvanizing support for nativist works. By the mid-1970s, a public debate over nativist literature has taken shape. It escalated into a full-scale contestation over the meanings of native and modernity after the Nationalist government orchestrated a series of frontal attack on *xiangtu* literature in 1977.[22] For several months, the public cultural space exploded with discussions and polemical writings on the proper understanding of the native in literary writing, its relation to regionalism, national culture, and nationalism, and the nature and condition of Taiwan's modernity.

Remarkably, despite intractable disagreements and acrimonious exchanges, both sides of the debate left unquestioned the centrality of nationalism and took for granted that the native naturally implies a sense of nation. What was intensely debated under this assumption is what/who constitutes the native-as-nation and who represents, literally and politically, the nation and its relation to modernity. Through these questions, the polarizing issues of class and ethnicity, and their relative importance and priority vis-à-vis nationalism were raised by advocates of the nativist discourse. Intentionally or not, these questions and issues open up the hermeneutic circuit of the native-as-nation, rendering the notion of the native polymorphous and multivalent. Unsurprisingly, it is such opening up of the notion to multiple significations that the state found threatening and sought to suppress through writers and critics in its employ.

Grounding the Native in Chinese Tradition

Keenly aware of the subversive potential of a multiple signification of the native, state-sponsored critics and writers attempted to disarm nativist discourse by fixing a proper referent to the native, a referent which, as we shall see, excludes differences, whether of region, ethnicity, class, or gender. Specifically, they repudiated the *xiangtu* literature advocates' conception of the native for its class and ethnic implications, faulting it for inciting class antagonism and implicitly promoting Taiwanese separatism by advancing regionalism through an emphasis on rural Taiwan. In its place, they sought to establish a proper understanding of the native as national culture defined by the long tradition of Chinese belles lettres. That is, if the *xiangtu* literature advocates' conception of the native is unambiguously place-based and embedded in rich textures of social relations in (rural) Taiwan, the state-sponsored critics' "corrective" undertaking abstracts the native into a pan-Chinese cultural tradition.

The outline of such an abstraction of the native can be seen in Yin Zhengxiong's criticism of three key figures associated with *xiangtu* literature in the 1970s—Wang Tuo, Wang Zhenhe, and Huang Chunming. Central to the criticism is a pointed distinction between good nativism/nationalism and bad nativism/nationalism. According to Yin, the nationalism expressed in *xiangtu* works is "blind, biased, and narrow," and, as such, "dangerous and unhealthy," carrying "negative effects."[23] That the danger suggested here is class consciousness becomes clear as he draws a corresponding distinction between a "broad sense of the 'native' (*xiangtu*) as nation" and "the biased and narrow view of the 'native' as [a particular] region." It is the biased and narrow view, he explains, that turns *xiangtu* fiction into a depiction of "sharp contrasts between the simplicity of the rural people and the baseness of the urbanites," and thus, potentially at least, a "tool for expressing hatred and anger," making it no different from the doomed proletarian literature of China in the 1930s.[24] This reference to proletarian literature reveals that underlying Yin's criticism of *xiangtu* fiction's allegedly narrow regionalist conception of the native is a wariness of class consciousness being expressed through nativism. To counter such a class-based conception, Yin locates the proper literary meaning of the native in an ethos of humble simplicity and pure sincerity, which he attributes to the Chinese literary tradition: "if today we really want to advocate a 'return to the native place,' the only meaningful way is to encourage and revive the humble, simple, pure, and sincere life-force inherent in our literature."[25]

Thus, in censuring *xiangtu* nativism for a narrow nationalism and regionalism, Yin grounds the proper meaning of the native in a cultural configuration of the Chinese nation that is, significantly, dissociated from any reference to land or people. This grounding of the native-as-nation in a particular mode of representation is arguably predictable for official and semiofficial discourses in Taiwan, as making reference to land and people would have been troublesome for the Nationalist regime not only because of the issue of class antagonism that Yin indirectly brought up, but also on account of ethnic-national identification and representation. Given the Nationalist government's competing claim to representation of the Chinese nation against the Communist regime, which controls the vast territory of the Chinese mainland as well as its huge population, any reference to land or people in the constitution of the nation will inevitably expose the Nationalist's weak legitimacy and losing bid. Furthermore, within the island of Taiwan, the native land and people(s) have a distinctive history separate from the Mainlander-controlled Nationalist state that can be mobilized to support an ethnic-national identity other than Chinese. In other words, a place-based focus on land and people may bring out Taiwan's specificity as an ethnic-national entity that is neither reducible to nor subsumable under the Chinese nation. Indeed, it is precisely because the Nationalist government found *xiangtu* literature's attention to the native soil and the little people suggestive enough of a nascent Taiwanese and class consciousness that it orchestrated an attack on *xiangtu* nativism. To neutralize the threat of class and ethnic divisiveness, the nation has to be grounded in the traditional culturalist interpretation of Chineseness to which the Nationalists self-consciously lay claim.

How to reconcile this tradition-based construction of the native-as-nation with the representation of social injustice on which *xiangtu* literature concentrated and to which it owed much of its popular and critical support became a serious issue for state-sponsored criticisms of the literature. An attempt to address this issue can be found in the writings of Peng Ge, one of the top editorial writers for the Nationalist party news organ, *Zhongyang ribao* (Central Daily News), and a key figure in the official censure of *xiangtu* nativism. In a series of newspaper articles, Peng takes *xiangtu* writers to task for their representation of social injustice, accusing them of advocating a "class perspective" that has a tendency to "worsen, rather than correctly reflect society's internal contradictions" as the *xiangtu* writers claim.[26] Writing from such a perspective, he contends, is tantamount to demolishing the foundation of the Chinese nation in the name of social consciousness and concern for the people.[27] On this ground, he objects not so much to *xiangtu* fiction's efforts at social criticism as to its mode of criticism. Maintaining the possibility of "respectable" social critique in literary works, he stresses the need to differentiate between those critiques that are motivated by "love of the nation and humanity" and those that "inflame class opposition and instigate hate."[28]

Underlying this distinction is the notion of a proper mode of representation of social injustice in (Chinese) literature. In his argument, Peng Ge stresses that the standards for judging social injustice should be "human values" as defined in Confucianism, such as "conscientiousness, filial piety, benevolence, love, etc." rather than economic values as indicated in income and monetary wealth, and that the mode of representing social injustice should itself express such "humanity."[29] He justifies this with reference to the need to not only resist the divisive strategies of the nation's Communist enemies, but also continue the Chinese literary tradition as an expression of the national character:

> Geniality and sincerity (*wenyou dunhou*) constitute the mainstream of Chinese literary thoughts. For several thousand years, the Chinese people base their existence on upholding benevolence and kindheartedness and maintaining conscientiousness and altruism. Reflected in literature and art, this national character becomes a style of geniality and sincerity.[30]

For Peng, then, nationalism dictates that the proper meaning of the native be fixed on the nation signified by the traditional mode of representation founded in Confucian ethics. Citing the Tang dynasty poet Du Fu's popular work, "Maowu wei qiufeng suo po ge" (Song of my thatched roof shattered by the autumn gale, ca. 760), he explains how a concern with social justice and public welfare can be included in this mode of representation:

> The broad-hearted extension of consideration and concern for the self to others is the pinnacle of the geniality and sincerity of the traditional Chinese poet. . . . When the poet was in distress and difficulty, he did not think of himself, but of "all the poor *scholars* across the country" (*tienxia hanshi*); and as long as *everybody* (*dajia*) was well, he would not mind that "only [his] own hut was broken" or that he himself might freeze to death. Such extensive love and sympathy are different from shouting abuses both in the mode of expression and in intention.[31]

This explanation zeroes in on a key issue in the nativist literature debate: what/who constitutes the nation and who represents, literally and politically, the nation and its relation to modernity. Just as Peng's predication of Chinese national identity on the Confucian moral code and its literary representation privileges the scholar/intellectual as the subject in literary representation, his reading of Du Fu's concern for "poor *scholars* across the country" as exemplary of the extension of love and sympathy to "*everybody*" also positions scholars to be the (proper) subject of the nation. Such a conception not only excludes the nonscholar commoner, but also elides differences, whether in class, ethnicity, or gender, in the constitution of the nation and national subjects. This is evident in what Peng passes over in his reading of the poem. A few lines before the thoughts on other poor scholars that he focuses on, the poem tells of the poet being cheated by a group of village boys who ran away with the reeds blown off from his roof.[32] In relating this incident, the poem registers the presence of different others whose interests do not necessarily agree with the poet's and whose needs and desires the poet does not unproblematically represent. It is such difference that Peng's reading elides in order to re-present and make present a monolithic culture and homogeneous nation that have continued into modernity in Taiwan. Hence, regardless of its rhetorical tribute to the representation of social injustice, this culturalist construction of the native-as-nation practically denies the significance of social injustice in defining the nation. Sidestepping the issue of neocolonial economic domination raised in *xiangtu* literature, it encodes an understanding of the relation among traditional Chinese culture, the Chinese nation, and modernity in Taiwan that reflects the official Nationalist ideology.

Through the Chinese Cultural Renaissance Movement launched in 1966, the Nationalist government has vigorously promoted a vision of modernity for Taiwan that integrates Chinese cultural traditions with modern

(Western) scientific and technological development.[33] Such integration, it maintains, will enable the Chinese nation as represented by Taiwan to assume a unique role in the world of modernity. The following excerpts from an official text on the Cultural Renaissance give a clear outline of the vision:

> The West's scientific and material civilization has tremendous success in conquering nature, but its spiritual decadence is quite alarming. Its so-called "humanism" and "renaissance" are nothing but liberal thoughts and individualist development which put emphasis on the individual self rather than humanity and thus by no means the true humanism that brings forth humanity . . .
>
> A reconstruction of humanism is necessary in the modern world. In order to rebuild humanity, it is most important for us to cultivate and develop reason. We must allow the spiritual to lead and guide the material, not the other way round. In other words, we should not let life be controlled by science, but make science submit to life. To solve the problem [of modern spiritual decadence], we need the standpoint of human reason and not that of the rational individual (Western culture). Reason is precisely the foundation of Confucian thoughts . . .
>
> We must advocate Chinese culture so that people around the world will revere reason . . . so that human culture will not be destroyed by science and science can become a tool for promoting human culture and advancing human happiness.[34]

Delineated here is a conception of a distinctive Chinese modernity that submits Western science and technology to the control of Confucian ethics and thus redefines modernity potentially for the whole world. In this conception of modernity, exploitative economic relations among and within nations under the global expansion of capitalism hardly signify. Instead, it is material "progress" on the basis of scientific and technological development originated in the West that is accorded primary significance in constituting modernity. In other words, science rather than capitalism is taken to be the powerhouse and motor behind Western modernity. Accordingly, modernity for the Chinese nation is imagined as a struggle to master and control Western sciences with the truly humanistic Confucian ethics. The "renaissance" of Chinese (Confucian) culture is thus central to the Nationalist-led Taiwan's claim to true representation of the Chinese nation and its bid for a different modernity promising the genuine emancipation of humanity through an ethically controlled use of science and technology. Ultimately, it is this vision of Chinese modernity that underlies the effort of state-sponsored writers such as Yin and Peng to wrest the meaning of the native from *xiangtu* fiction and its advocates. In its implicit espousal of capitalism and affirmation of the compatibility between traditional Chinese culture and capitalism, this vision of modernity is arguably a harbinger of the postmodern celebration of capitalist-development-with-a-difference that drove the codification and promotion of an "East Asian development model" in the 1980s. In other words, the vision of modernity expounded in the Chinese Cultural Renaissance Movement may well be seen as a precursor priming the ideological ground for the Oriental articulation of the Pacific Rim discourse discussed in the previous chapter.

Placing Taiwanese Consciousness, Chinese Nationalism, and Social Injustice in Xiangtu Nativism

As the state-sponsored critics reveal in their efforts to disarm *xiangtu* fiction by dismissing, covering over, and displacing social (class) injustice in their construction of the native-as-nation, what distinguishes *xiangtu* nativism's articulation of the nation and modernity is its subversive focus on the working class. If the scholar/intellectual well versed in Confucian ethics and traditional Chinese culture is the presumed national subject in the official and semiofficial discourses, the manual laborer suffering gross social injustice under a Western-dominated modernity constitutes the rightful native/national subject in the nativist discourse of *xiangtu* literature. Yet, between the representation of social injustice and the affirmation of the native-as-nation, *xiangtu* nativism is caught in competing interests. Its attempt to weave class and nation together into the manual laborer's reality and vision of modernity embodies a tension that taxes its cogency. Practically, the tension also threatened the solidarity of *xiangtu* literature proponents and advocates during the debate. How social injustice and the plights of the working class under Taiwan's modernity figure in the native-as-nation, how the native-as-nation relates to class and the native soil, and whether a seamless construct of the native-as-nation is possible or desirable when the native is marked by social injustice proved to be vexing and deeply divisive issues for the *xiangtu* advocates.

If this was an incipient tension between Chinese nationalists and Taiwan-identified nativists that threatened to unravel *xiangtu* nativism's defense against its detractors, it has become retrospectively obvious with the outright articulation of an ethnic Taiwanese consciousness since the 1980s. The faultlines were laid bare in an open disagreement over the appropriateness of claiming, through proper naming, a separate category of "Taiwanese Literature" with its implication of a distinctive Taiwanese consciousness. The disagreement pitted so-called third-worldists who proposed theorizing Taiwan's literature in terms of third world literature (*Disan shijie wenxuelun*) against "Taiwanese nativists" who championed Taiwanese literature as an autonomous and indigenous development (*Taiwan wenxue bentulun*).[35] As the apparent metamorphosis of Chinese nationalists into third-worldists suggests, the disagreement involves not only the obvious question of whether the nativists' primary allegiance lies with the Chinese nation or Taiwanese ethnic (or even national) identification, but also the subtle question of whether class-related concerns of anti-imperialism and anticapitalist exploitation encapsulated in the term "third world" can or should be connected to an ethnic-national Taiwanese consciousness. In short, the disagreement hinges on the issue whether social class injustice should be mapped onto Chinese nationalism or Taiwanese consciousness.

The ideas galvanizing Taiwanese nativists were first put forward in the nativist literature debate by Ye Shitao, a veteran Taiwanese writer who had been silenced for years after the fateful 2–28 incident. In a groundbreaking article titled "Taiwan xiangtu wenxue shi daolun" (An introductory discussion of the history of Taiwan's native literature), Ye implicitly equates the native with Taiwan, as he introduces the notion of "Taiwanese consciousness" (*Taiwan yishi*) into the discourse of *xiangtu* nativism and the discussion of Taiwan's literature. Careful to concede that Taiwan does not have its own language and writing to be completely distinct from Han national culture (*Han minzu wenhua*), Ye nonetheless highlights the "pronounced native style" (*nonghou xiangtu fengge*) that Taiwanese culture has acquired on account of its grounding place, including the Formosa island's subtropical climate, rich natural endowment, multiracial heritage, and history of repeated colonizations.[36] This pronounced native style, he further argues, clearly distinguishes Taiwanese culture from mainland Chinese culture (*Zhongguo dalu wenhua*), even though it remains a tributary of Han national culture.[37] With this subtle differentiation between Han national culture and mainland Chinese culture, Ye takes pain to establish Taiwanese culture as a distinctive *native* culture grounded in a particular place and *ethnic* history that sets it apart from mainland Chinese culture, but he stops short of identifying it as a separate *national* culture.

Significantly, Ye's delineation of the distinctiveness of this Taiwanese culture stresses the specific history of multiple colonization and oppression suffered by the Han people living on the island. In his view, it is none other than the Han inhabitants' common experience of and resistance to imperialism, feudalism, and oppression that constitutes "Taiwanese consciousness," which, in turn, defines Taiwanese culture and *xiangtu* literature. Such a characterization of Taiwanese consciousness and native culture, in effect, incorporates concerns of social class injustice and transforms them into a form of Taiwanese ethnic identity. While Ye was too cautious to openly proclaim an ethnic-nationalism based on this identity in the tense atmosphere of the late 1970s, his ideas broke the ground for a forthright expression of Taiwanese ethnic-nationalism among Taiwanese nativists in the relatively relaxed political climate of the 1980s.

In developing Ye's construction of the native as Taiwanese consciousness, Taiwanese nativists jettison Ye's nominal acknowledgment of Taiwanese culture as a part of Chinese national culture. This is particularly pronounced in the writings of the literary critic Peng Ruijin, who supports his argument for nativization as the primary task of Taiwanese literature with recourse to the vision of a Taiwanese nation: "By stressing 'nativization' . . . we can relax and say that our ancestors really use their own voices, our own sounds, to sing our aspirations. The legacy and continuation of 'Taiwanese Literature' ascertain that we are a nation with poetry and songs; herein we can find the self-confidence of a nation with its own literature."[38] This nascent Taiwanese ethnic-nationalism leads him to criticize the *xiangtu* literature debate for ignoring the real nature of the literature while hammering at the notion of "[Chinese] nationalist literature." Such a notion, he argues, cannot be grafted onto Taiwan's nativist literature, given the literature's distinctive embodiment of a tradition of indigenous consciousness centered on the protection of the native soil.[39]

With this deliberate dissociation of *xiangtu* nativism from Chinese nationalism, the importance of social class injustice in defining Taiwanese consciousness and nativist culture is highlighted. Following Ye's conception, Taiwanese nativists ground the distinctiveness of Taiwanese consciousness in the collective experience of colonization and simultaneous struggle against imperialism, feudalism, and oppression. Accordingly, Taiwanese consciousness is vested in the general working folks on the other side of economic, political, and social domination. The class subtext to this articulation of Taiwanese consciousness is made explicit in Song Dongyang's argument that the Chinese nationalist idea of "China-as-center" is "nothing more than a self-binding emotional knot of the intellectuals and will not trouble the hearts of the manual laborers at all."[40] It is noteworthy that in shifting attention away from the idea of a Chinese nation, this conception of the native as Taiwanese consciousness avoids the Sinocentrism still observable in Ye's equation of Taiwanese experiences with those of the *Chinese* inhabitants. As Li Qiao carefully points out, "the so-called 'Taiwanese standpoint' means the standpoint of the masses of common folks in the specific time-space of Taiwan . . . this standpoint has no connection to the cultural, political, and economic factors of prior residents (*xianzhumin*, meaning the aborigines), later residents (*houzhumin*, meaning Han settlers from South China), and provincial origins (*shengji*, referring to the Taiwanese-mainlander distinction)."[41] Though this construct of a Taiwanese common folk is not without its problem of eliding differences, especially the persistent inequality and discrimination suffered by the aborigines, it nonetheless shows a conscientious step away from Chinese ethnocentrism in imagining a Taiwanese nation. In sum, Taiwanese nativists in the 1980s deliberately excluded Chinese nationalism from their nativist discourse and sought to refigure class issues into an ethnic-national Taiwanese consciousness.

This accent on a Taiwanese consciousness in the delineation of the native is precisely what the Chinese nationalists and later "third-worldists" disagreed with. The most prominent Taiwanese critic of the articulation of a Taiwanese consciousness and Taiwanese Literature is Chen Yingzhen, who penned a pointed rebuttal to Ye Shitao's article even as he energetically defended *xiangtu* literature during the 1977–1978 debate.[42] His point of contention was not so much Ye's association of the native and *xiangtu* literature with class-related resistance against imperialism, feudalism, and oppression as the characterization of this resistance literature in terms of Taiwanese rather than Chinese consciousness. In other words, it is the ethnic-national identification of class-related struggles that was at issue in the Ye–Chen dissension. Whereas Ye (and later the Taiwanese nativists) focused on the *local specificity* of Taiwan's history of colonization and oppression as the ground of a Taiwanese identity reflected and affirmed in *xiangtu* literature, Chen emphasized the *cultural commonality* of Taiwan's literary struggle against imperialism and feudalism with Chinese nationalism on the mainland. Underlying Chen's argument is the assumption that given Taiwan's Chinese cultural and linguistic tradition, its cultural resistance against imperialist domination necessarily constitutes a part of Chinese nationalist resistance. In particular, he contends:

> All resistance literatures produced on the land of weak nations dominated by capitalist imperialism invariably carry the characteristics of the respective nations. Furthermore, reflecting the social reality of these agricultural colonies, the literatures invariably make the economic and human problems of rural villages their focus of concern and resistance. Thus, the particularity of 'Taiwan' '*xiangtu* literature' disappears in the particularity of literature produced in all colonies in Asia, Central and South America, and Africa, and unites with modern Chinese literature under the specificity of modern resistance against imperialism and feudalism all over China.[43]

In the political atmosphere of the 1970s, this harnessing of the social criticism and cultural resistance in *xiangtu* literature to Chinese nationalism could understandably find a wider circle of open acceptance and support than Ye's pronouncement of a Taiwanese consciousness. Confronting the charges of advocating Taiwanese separatism and inciting class antagonism from state-sponsored critics, *xiangtu* literature champions generally put up a front of Chinese nationalism in defense, while those harboring a vision of the native that diverged from Chinese nationalism strategically stayed away from the debate. So, most writers and critics later identified as Taiwanese nativists kept their silence over the matter during this time, and Ye let Chen's criticism stand without a rejoinder. As Zhang Wenzhi notes in her ethnological study of Taiwanese consciousness in literature, the polarized opposition of China-versus-Taiwan and corresponding refiguration of the nation that came to dominate cultural identity struggles in the 1980s did not figure yet in the nativist discourse of the 1970s, though a rudimentary form of the opposition was suggested in Ye's conception of Taiwan's *xiangtu* literature.[44] Not only was Chinese nationalism an unquestioned premise in the *xiangtu* literature debate, but, perhaps more important, major works of *xiangtu* fiction published in this period also harbor Chinese nationalist sentiments even as the native figure constructed therein is marked unambiguously Taiwanese. In other words, contrary to the argument of Taiwanese nativist critics such as Peng Ruijin, the association of *xiangtu* literature with Chinese nationalism was not merely an ideological smokescreen of the literature's advocates during the 1977–1978 debate. A simultaneous assumption of Chinese nationalism and affirmation of Taiwan as native soil was common in *xiangtu* literature of the 1970s. Rather than ethnicizing social injustice on the native soil and making it the ground of a Taiwanese consciousness, as Taiwanese nativists were wont to do in the 1980s, these works tend to locate social injustice in the experiences of the working class and map the experiences onto a construct of the native that is often ethnically marked Taiwanese but ultimately links up with Chinese nationalism. How this mapping is achieved and how it relates to the local specificities of Taiwan's modernity are thus key to the oppositional claims and effectiveness of the nativist works.

REPRESENTATION OF SOCIAL INJUSTICE ON NATIVE GROUND

The centrality of the representation and critique of social injustice to *xiangtu* literature of the 1970s can be surmised from the fact that it was precisely an insistent focus on the representation of social injustice besides the expression of nationalist sentiment that pitted *xiangtu* literature advocates against its state-sponsored detractors during the debate. Its import and connection with nationalist opposition to imperialism are particularly foregrounded by Wang Tuo, one of the prominent writers commonly identified with *xiangtu* literature and the most vocal in theorizing and defending it during the debate. In a seminal article, Wang situates *xiangtu* literature squarely within the historical reality of Taiwan's Western-oriented modernity and in relation to the sociocultural functions of the representation of social injustice and nationalist cultural renewal in such modernity:

> Since 1970, in Taiwan . . . there has been a general awakening and upsurge of nationalist consciousness against imperialism and social consciousness against the unequal distribution of wealth. In opposition to imperialism, it is natural to find, culturally, a demand for a renewed understanding, evaluation and affirmation of the culture in which one is located (*benwei wenhua*), so as to establish a foundation for constructing a new culture to locate oneself (*xin de benwei wenhua de jizu*). In opposition to the few oligarchic capitalists who monopolize social wealth, it is natural to find criticisms and attacks on all the inequitable and unreasonable phenomena under the existing economic system, as well as more sympathy and support for the relatively low-income people in the society. Furthermore, because the imperialists assume a hypocritical posture of economic cooperation in their ugly economic invasion of Taiwan, social oppositions against imperialism and oligarchic capitalists are often interrelated, and even integrated. In such a situation, those literary writings that use rural villages as the social background and village figures as the main subjects of description can simultaneously satisfy the two different emotional needs of the public [that is, their nationalist and social consciousness].[45]

This positioning of *xiangtu* literature in a double grid of nationalism and social consciousness under Taiwan's neocolonial development is significant not only for highlighting the centrality of a critique of social injustice to *xiangtu* literature, but also for its subtle negotiation of the meaning of nationalist cultural resistance between Chinese nationalism and the affirmation of native cultural traditions. Though Wang's emphasis on the Diaoyutai incident in his discussion of the nationalist awakening of the public (including himself) suggests that his reference to nationalist consciousness implies Chinese nationalism, his description of nationalist opposition to imperialism in the cited passage does not specify the cultural tradition to be renewed as Chinese, only "that in which one is located" (*benwei*). This opens up the possibility of conceiving that cultural tradition in terms of local Taiwanese culture rather than Chinese tradition, even as it implicitly assumes congruence, if not exactly equivalence, between the two. The arguably deliberate ambiguity here enabled Wang to skirt the sensitive question of Chinese nationalism versus Taiwanese consciousness that pitted Chen Yingzhen against Ye Shitao and threatened to divide the *xiangtu* literature advocates, so that attention would not be distracted from the other important issue of social consciousness, which detractors of *xiangtu* literature sought to suppress.

Beyond this delicate question of national cultural identity, Wang's dual emphasis on social consciousness and nationalist consciousness further disrupts the hermeneutic circuit of native-as-nation and reterritorializes the native (*xiangtu*) in a discourse of social injustice under neocolonial modernity. In particular, his analytic conjunction of imperialism and social inequity within the national space turns the native into a multivalent, shifting sign of the marginalized in Taiwan's modernity. As he explains, the term "*xiangtu*" has at least three meanings: first, "homeland and native soil" (*guxiang gutu*); second, "the reality and environment in which one grows up and lives"; and third, "the rural countryside as opposed to the city."[46] Though Wang cites this semantic instability as his reason for repudiating the term "*xiangtu* literature" in favor of "realist literature" (*xianshi wenxue*), he nonetheless mobilizes the term's multiple meanings to establish the native as a sociohistorical site of social injustice and (thus) the textual site of an oppositional vision of modernity in "*xiangtu* literature." Under Wang's treatment, in other words, the native becomes a flexible discursive position to critique and contest what he considers the neocolonial modernity of Taiwan. A semantic shift in the term allows him to connect *xiangtu* literature's interest in the rural village to the critique of social class injustice and economic and cultural imperialism:

> Bombarded by foreign capital and foreign culture, cities in Taiwan have already been Westernized to such an extent that they are not much different from the metropolis of Europe and the United States. This is the case with regard to not only the plainly visible physical constructions, but also human thoughts, values and ideas, as well as attitudes towards life. In comparison, villages have retained more of traditional cultural characteristics and simple lifestyles, even though they have also undergone tremendous changes upon the penetration of industry and commerce. At the same time, village people are often sacrificed and neglected in a society changing rapidly under a policy of vigorous promotion of industrial and commercial development. Their incomes are low, standard of living poor, and work strenuous. It is, therefore, easy for the public to find fulfillment of their nationalist sentiments and social conscience in fictions that make rural societies and village people their subject matter.[47]

In connecting the controversial and explosive issue of unequal and exploitative relations within the national space to the conventionally acceptable and justified sentiment of nationalism against imperialist exploitation and oppression, this reading of *xiangtu* literature's popular appeal forcefully disrupts a polar opposition between the imperialist West and the exploited nation. By virtue of the connection, social class injustice not only becomes a legitimate and crucial issue in the debate over modernity, but can no longer be distanced into simply a problem of imperialism and foreign domination, the elimination of which is then quite beyond the power of the national government.

Bringing "home" to the national space the question of social inequity and conflicting class interests, and implicating the state in the perpetuation of domination and oppression within the nation under a Western-oriented modernity, such representation of social injustice accentuates the critical potential of the nativist discourse. As intimated in the state-sponsored critics' broad charges of "incitement of class antagonism" against *xiangtu* literature, this domestic turn of the critique of capitalist exploitation and imperialist domination was not confined to Wang Tuo's theoretical defense of *xiangtu* literature, and its prevalence in *xiangtu* nativism was particularly troubling to the Nationalist government and the established interests it represented.[48] Conversely speaking, the state's effort at suppression suggests that the insertion of questions of social class injustice into oppositional struggles against imperialism commonly deemed nationalist in nature constitutes the most radical element in the nativist discourse of *xiangtu* literature.

Nativist Representation of Manual Labor

For all its critical potential, the dual emphasis on social consciousness and nationalism creates a tension within *xiangtu* nativism that has significant consequences for its claim to oppositionality. On the one hand, its insistent exposure of social inequity within the national space of Taiwan unmasks the myth of unified national interests that the state supposedly represents, and implicitly challenges the culturalist vision of the Chinese nation and the nation's relation to modernity maintained in official discourses. On the other hand, the unquestioned acceptance of nationalism as sine qua non resistance to imperialism pulls the nativist discourse back into an affirmation of national cultural identity and severely limits its construction of alternatives. To resolve the tension between the class concerns of inequity within the nation and the nationalist frame of resistance, Taiwan's nativists resort to a homologization of class and national oppositions. This strategy, however, brings the nativist discourse in line with the official and semiofficial discourses and significantly undermines its critical power.

Specifically, if the nativist focus on exploitative economic relations stands in opposition to the state's conception of the modern in terms of scientific and technological development, its implicit mapping of capitalist exploitation onto a national frame maintains the Western-Chinese opposition in the official discourse. And if the nativist discourse disrupts and shifts the boundaries of the nation with attention to social class differences, it still keeps in place the exclusionary vision underlying the state's discourse on the nation. That is, even as it draws attention to social inequity, the nativist discourse retains the polarization of the educated elites and the subalterns to contest the official culturalist definition of the nation and the neocolonial modernity it masks. This leaves the hegemonic definition of the binary terms unchallenged and obscures the dominant class structure under capitalist modernity, making it difficult, if not impossible, to raise the radical question of who controls the means and ends of production in the critique of social inequity. Thus, corresponding to the hegemonic constitution of elites in and through intellectual/mental work in traditional Chinese culture, Taiwan's official discourse, as well as the socioeconomic hierarchy of Western modernity, the non-elite—variously described as the majority of the people or the "little people"—is simply equated with manual laborers. Then, in a reversal of the hegemonic hierarchy, manual labor is privileged over intellectual labor and affirmed to be the locus of native values and practices for guiding the nation's course of development and reform in modernity. In other words, assuming a position equivalent to that of intellectual elites and their dominant "high" culture in the official discourse of the nation, manual workers and their life experiences become the privileged repository of national culture and native values, and (thus) the source of an alternative (and, by implication, a more just) modernity in the nativist discourse.

One of the clearest articulations of this reversal can be found in Chen Yingzhen's essay of self-criticism, where he faults his own early fictional writings for demonstrating the "melancholy, depression and sense of helplessness" typical of a "small town petty intellectual" (*shizhen xiao zhishifenzi*). In contrast, Chen holds up the example of *xiangtu* literature such as Huang Chunming's stories for "embracing the majority of producers" and making them "figures of trust and identification in the process of transforming life and the world."[49] What it is in the "producers" that the petty intellectual should embrace and learn from is drawn out by Wang Tuo in his article "Yongbao jiankang de dadi" (Embrace the healthy land):

> In the fields, on hillsides, on fishing boats, in factories, on roadsides, in shops . . . in all kinds of big and small places, people work hard, diligently and steadily. With roughened hands, bending down, standing tall, or flexing arms, they all work and struggle, tenaciously and full of hope, for their daily living and a more just and better future for the next generation. They have never suffered my pale melancholy and insomnia, nor experienced the kind of hazy drifting that kept me anxious all day. . . . Their lives may be hard and difficult, but they live healthily, with peace of mind and full of expectations and hope. In this piece of rich land that is kind and warm like a loving mother, they sow love, hope and expectations with their own hands and feet, cultivate, show concern, and care for the land with indomitable will and perseverance. 'This is our homeland!' 'For the next generation, what does it matter if we suffer some more?' they say.[50]

Such tribute to manual labor reveals *xiangtu* nativism's ideological underpinnings in a dichotomization of manual and intellectual labor that obscures the dominant structure of class opposition under capitalist economy. Particularly, in their efforts to overturn discrimination against manual labor, *xiangtu* nativists simply reverse the discrimination and, in effect, keep the exclusionary binarism of manual versus mental intact. If the value of manual labor is dismissed in hegemonic modern and Chinese discourses, it is sentimentally valorized in their writings to be a healthy, productive, and constructive activity, against which intellectual work "pales." The implicit denial of a productive aspect to intellectual work in this opposition leads them to see the role of literature as no more than "*collecting* (*jizhong*) the aspirations and thoughts (*xinsheng*) of the people"[51] or "*reflecting* (*fanying*) the joys and sorrows, miseries, hopes, struggles, and so on, of the healthy people."[52]

Such a conception of intellectual work has the troubling effect of covering over the differences and discontinuities between the political and literary senses of representation. Gayatri Spivak's critique of Michel Foucault and Gilles Deleuze for valorizing the concrete experiences of the oppressed without taking account of their own implication in intellectual history is useful for elucidating this effacement:

> Two senses of representation are being run together: representation as "speaking for," as in politics, and representation as "re-presentation," as in art or philosophy. . . . The banality of leftist intellectuals' lists of self-knowing, politically canny subalterns stands revealed; representing them, the intellectuals represent themselves as transparent.[53]

Bracketing Spivak's controversial formulation of the issue in terms of the subaltern's (in)ability to speak and know herself, the problematization of leftist intellectuals' claim of letting the oppressed speak for themselves in the intellectuals' literary or philosophical re-presentation is crucial to cultural and social criticism.[54] It is a problem to be raised against Taiwan's *xiangtu* nativists as much as leftist intellectuals in the West, their different positioning in the international division of labor and implication in the epistemic violence of imperialism notwithstanding.

The problematic foreclosure of differences between the two senses of representation is clearly reflected in Wang Tuo's use of the term "*xianshi*" (literally, present reality) rather than "*xieshi*" (literally, writing reality) in his proposed alternative to the controversial designation of "*xiangtu* literature." Sung-sheng Chang has suggested that Wang Tuo's use of "*xianshi*" rather than "*xieshi*" serves to "disentangle the confused debate over the Western-imported literary term 'realism.'"[55] It is arguable, however, that in passing "writing" for "present" (with its connotation of presence), Wang's term has not so much disentangled as effaced the complex issues of re-presentation that the literary term "realism" poses, in Taiwan as well as in the West. More important, the choice of terminology is symptomatic of a pervasive problem. The understanding of literary work to be a faithful reflection of reality as lived by the majority of the people was widely shared among Taiwan's *xiangtu* fiction writers and advocates alike. Caught up in their attempt to speak for, and validate the experience of, the exploited and oppressed people, Wang Tuo and other *xiangtu* fiction writers did not acknowledge or recognize the productive nature of their re-presentation and (mis)took their literary production for the self-presence of the oppressed people. Despite their best intentions, they were in effect appropriating the voices and discursive positions of the marginalized and the oppressed to advance their own perspectives and vision for an alternative modernity.

The danger of such blindness lies not only in the intellectuals' denial of their implication in ideological production and reproduction, not to say their own oppressive act of appropriation, but also in its foreclosure of critiques of ideological subject-constitution within state formations and political economic systems. Oppressed and exploited labor is thereby reified into the authentic national subject, whose always already constitution serves to stimulate but remains outside of change. Such reification is evident in the following statement by Chen Yingzhen:

> Altogether, these "native" figures [living and working industriously and attentively in farms, fishing villages, schools, towns, and factories] take on a gigantic and dignified image, especially when they inspire us to see properly in them the great faces of the Chinese people, who were as simple, honest, diligent, and brave several thousand years ago as they are now. Their lives thereby become glorious and extremely inspiring, lives that stimulate us to continually create and innovate.[56]

The attribution of a timeless national character to the "working people," while reversing the hierarchy of the Confucian order, leaves unchallenged the ideological ground and exclusionary structure on which the "working people" are constituted as subjects in the national order. The hegemonic binary opposition between the scholar/intellectual and the unlearned/laborer is maintained; and manual laborers, albeit "redeemed" and even glorified, continue to be construed as physical bodies dissociated from the linguistic and intellectual culture that defines the writing and reading "we." Moreover, it is precisely the maintenance of manual labor's absolute otherness to the culture of the dominant social class, which is deemed heavily Westernized, that allows *xiangtu* nativism to inscribe manual laborers into an indigenous (and authentically national) source of alternative values for reconstructing, discursively and in reality, Taiwan's modernity. National culture and morality thus continue to be imagined as the exclusive property of one homogeneous and self-present social class, and the ground of justification and value orientation for the nation's quest for modernity.

The limiting effects of such a simple reversion on the leftist intellectuals' vision of alternative modernity are discernible in their categorical dismissal of modernist literature written by their compatriots as mere imitation of the West, completely divorced from the social reality of modern Taiwan. Focusing on modernism's Western origins, they considered the bloom of modernist writing in Taiwan during the 1960s as nothing but a cultural manifestation of dependency on the West. With this judgment, they foreclosed the possibility that Western literary techniques and thematic concerns may be appropriated for implicit criticism of and resistance to Taiwan's existing modernity.[57] The Taiwan modernists' textual preoccupation with the "modern" individual was thus summarily rejected for its putative "individualism," "decadence," and, above all, "moaning and groaning without illness in imitation of Western sentiments and thoughts."[58] In asserting the affectation of the modernist writings, however, the leftist intellectuals were not so much denying the existence of feelings of alienation in Taiwan's modernity as rejecting their validity and relevance to the social reality of the majority of the people. Their tendency to conceive discursive opposition in terms of a positive affirmation of the exploited majority leads to an investment of truth in the majority. This blinds them to the possibility that the "degeneration, decadence, apathy, and perversity" they found in modernist literature might well be a form of negative aesthetics contesting the repression and oppression perpetuated in the name of Confucian ethics, which has been reinforced by capitalist social relations in Taiwan's modernity. By the same token, it totally escaped them that such "negative" cultural responses might be useful in calling into question, and thus opening up the possibility of changing the reality of repression and oppression lived and experienced by not only the urban educated elites but the rural and working masses as well.[59]

In their zeal to affirm the presence of an always already opposition, which they located in manual labor, the *xiangtu* literature advocates in effect upheld certain dominant ideologies. What resulted is a conception of alternative modernity that remains trapped within two sets of mutually reinforcing binary oppositions—the West-versus-the nation and mental labor-versus-manual labor. With such consolidation and privileging of the national divide and a correspondingly partial conception of class opposition, fundamental class concerns such as the ownership and control of the means of production remain displaced and unaddressed in the nativist construction of an alternative to Western-dominated capitalist modernity. The issue of ethnic inequality within the national space, especially the discrimination and exploitation of the non-Chinese aboriginals under the developmentalist project of nation-building, cannot be formally taken up either. Furthermore, no matter how critical the intent of Taiwan's leftist intellectuals in valorizing the native-as-manual-laborer-as-nation, their oppositional strategy relies on an uncritical reaffirmation of the hegemonic cultural tradition that maintains and reproduces dominant oppression, marginalization and exclusion in their proffered alternatives. Given the strong patriarchal tradition in Chinese society, this resort to tradition means, in particular, that the nativist construction of alternative modernity continues to be grounded in a patriarchal order. Gender thus constitutes a central axis of the nativist order and, as such, proffers a crucial vantage point for our critical assessment of Taiwan's *xiangtu* nativism.

To further develop and substantiate these arguments, I turn below to close analysis of three exemplary works of *xiangtu* fiction, that is, texts considered representative of *xiangtu* nativism by both its detractors and advocates. The selection is not meant to take account of all notable works by the *xiangtu* writers. Rather than tracing the variation and development of *xiangtu* nativism in the oeuvres of individual writers, close readings of a few key texts allow critical exploration of the textual strategies and ideological assumptions that establish the native as a locus of alternative modernity, and the limits and limitations they bring to the discursive construction of alternatives. My analysis will focus specifically on the textual configuration of the native position and its relation to the structuration of nation, class, gender, and ethnicity, and in the process unpack its opposition to and complicity with dominant ideologies. As will become clear in the discussion, the selected texts not only illustrate common concerns in Taiwan's *xiangtu* literature of the 1970s but also reflect variations, differences, and introspective negotiations within the broad framework of nativist opposition to the dominant construction of modernity based on Western importation.

The Benevolent Patriarch at Work: Wang Zhenhe's Beleaguered Native

One of the most cited examples of *xiangtu* literature in Taiwan is Wang Zhenhe's "Xiaolin lai Taibei" (Xiaolin comes to Taipei, 1973; hereafter "Xiaolin"),[60] though, like many writers being associated with *xiangtu* literature, the author has neither identified himself or his work with nativism nor participated in the *xiangtu* literature debate.[61] The story features an elaborate superimposition of a Western-Chinese opposition onto the culturally dominant mental-manual class division. It is structured around a day of work in an airline company from the point of view of Xiaolin, a young man who, as the title of the story indicates, has recently moved from a rural village to the capital city, Taipei, in search of better prospects, and has found employment with the airline as an office boy. While the narration is in the third person, the narrator stays within bounds of the consciousness of this migrant labor fresh from the rural hinterland throughout his observation of the "reality" of modern Taiwan. Thus, insofar as the story advances a native position and vision, it is Xiaolin who speaks and stands for it. By the same token, the blindness and biases of Xiaolin's observation enable us to gauge the limits and exclusions of this native vision.

Though the title of the story alludes to the rural origin of Xiaolin, it is his position as a manual laborer that is foregrounded in the narrative, as it follows him at work, running in and out of the company's administrative and front offices. If the manual nature of his work keeps Xiaolin at a physical distance from the nonmanual staff, it also calls attention to his distance from the latter's Westernized culture, which he observes literally from an outsider position every time he enters the offices. This cultural distance is central to the textual construction of a native position to expose the "imposed receptivity" of modernity in the margins and to critique the absurdity and excesses of Western importation pursuant on the Taiwan state's complicit accommodation to postmodern capitalism.

In the story, this cultural distance is specifically inscribed in terms of English, which is not merely a language of business transaction in the airline offices, but provides certain idioms of everyday communication among Xiaolin's nonmanual superiors. The interjection of English words into their casual conversations and the choice of identification by English names characterize the nonmanual staff and mark their difference and distance from manual workers like Xiaolin, who, though literate, is not educated or, more precisely, Westernized enough to embrace English as part of his everyday existence. At the same time, it is precisely Xiaolin's unfamiliarity with English that enables him to notice the absurdity of modern Taiwan's slavish imitation of Western culture. Listening to his nonmanual superiors' adopted English names with the ears of a Taiwanese speaker, he perceives the grotesque decadence of these names in a native context: Nancy becomes "decaying corpse" (*lan shi*); Douglas, "shitting upside down" (*daoguolai lashi*, meaning, of course, talking shit); and Dorothy, "dumping rubbish" (*dao laji*). Through Xiaolin's native ear and voice, Wang Zhenhe's narrative associates the beneficiaries of Taiwan's Western-imported modernity and their Westernized culture with decay, corpse, shit, and rubbish, and thus suggests the uselessness, waste, and corrupting effects of such modernity.[62] More important, the implicit contrast in this linguistic play also establishes Xiaolin's perspective to be fresh, not (yet) contaminated or corrupted, vital, healthy, useful, and productive. With Xiaolin as its focal point, Wang Zhenhe's text thus positions itself to be articulating a native perspective that both retains cultural purity and embodies the vitality of/for a different modernity.

What exactly constitutes the native perspective of Xiaolin is complexly mapped in Wang Zhenhe's story. Linguistically, as previously mentioned, Xiaolin is clearly marked as Taiwanese, in contrast to most of the nonmanual employees whose standard Mandarin, spiced at times with English words and Chinese mainland dialects such as Shanghaiese, announce their more privileged Mainlander status. Besides this language-based ethnic identification of the native, Xiaolin's general characterization in the story suggests that his perspective is overdetermined by the related but different oppositions between Western(ized) and indigenous, mental and manual, as well as urban and rural. This native position thus encodes polymorphous differences and can be seen as multivalent to some degrees, with the potential of engaging multiple hierarchical organization of differences. The relations among these various oppositions and their relative importance in structuring Xiaolin's position in Taiwan's modernity are key to determining the specific realization of Xiaolin's native perspective in the story, and they are intricately woven into the story's plot and narrative discourse.

A single theme—namely, the disintegration of the Chinese family under Taiwan's Western-dominated modernity—runs through the story. By juxtaposing various incidents of family breakup, the story figures family disintegration as a symptom of Taiwan's misguided modernity and exposes the causes of national and social decay under such modernity. It begins with an evocation of family separation via Xiaolin's thoughts on his parents, whose rural home he has left in coming to Taipei. Looking longingly at a Boeing 727 model in the office while cleaning its glass showcase, Xiaolin dreams about travelling in such a plane, "just like the Americans and the Japanese," and recalls a letter he has written earlier to his parents, relating his wish to become a white-collar employee in the company and bring his parents to Taipei to view the beautifully made model.[63] The association of the airplane with family separation here gives a critical twist to the familiar use of modern vehicles (be it the railway or airplane) as a trope for modernity. It calls attention to the different meanings the airplane, and thus modernity, have for different people. With its promise of mobility and connection that can turn the world into a "global village," the airplane is nonetheless not equally accessible to everybody. Even as it makes Taiwan a convenient source of cheap labor and exotic entertainment to the Americans and the Japanese, and, conversely, the West (particularly the United States) a possible if somewhat costly "home" to the next generation of well-off beneficiaries of Taiwan's modernity,[64] it symbolizes nothing but unattainable dreams, tantalizing lack, and regrettable separation for Xiaolin. Xiaolin can only look longingly at a scaled-down simulacrum of an airplane, the visibility of which, ironically, he is required to maintain everyday through manual labor. Tangibly seductive yet practically out-of-reach, the airplane has contradictory meanings for Xiaolin. While its simulacrum elicits a desire in him to emulate and assume an equal place with his nonmanual superiors and the Americans and Japanese, it also reminds him of his distance from the real article, a distance that he vividly experiences in his forced separation from and consequent inability to see, not to mention take care of, his parents living in a poor rural village. To Xiaolin, in other words, the airplane is not only a sign of modernity's promise of freedom and (physical and social) mobility, which has so far eluded him and yet continues to entice him to work harder, but also a marker of the destruction of family and disruption of family relations that he already lives as the reality of modernity.

The contrast the story thus draws between what modernity means for Xiaolin and for the nonmanual staff of the airline, the Americans, and the Japanese highlights three sets of broadly corresponding inequality—between manual and nonmanual labor, between the Taiwanese and the Mainlander, as well as between the native and the West/Westernized. Interestingly, while Xiaolin's recent migrant status also brings up the rural-urban divide, its significance in marking Xiaolin's native position is much attentuated by the story's attention to class inequality in the rural village. Rather than the harmonious collectivity with which the rural village is often invested in opposition to the urban city, Xiaolin's ancestral village is laden with class exploitation and oppression, just like the city Taipei. Furthermore, the story suggests that such exploitation is at the root of the dispersal of Xiaolin's family:

> His family has raised some ducks with feeds bought on credit. Recently, seeing that the ducks have grown big, the owner of the feed-shop claimed financial difficulty and demanded his father to clear his debts. Where would his father find money when the ducks were still unsold?! Taking advantage of the fact that his son-in-law worked in court, the feed-shop owner Li forced Xiaolin's father to trade in the ducks which have taken so much labor to raise, each priced at a minimum. In the end, his father still owed Li some two thousand dollars. . . . For some unknown reasons, his father has always been associated with bad luck. Several decades of cultivating the land have brought nothing but financial loss and exhaustion, making it necessary for his children to leave home and seek prospects all over the place.[65]

In this reminiscent account of family decline, the narrative logic clearly locates the root cause of the family's predicament in the capitalist market and class exploitation, contrary to the passing reference to "bad luck." With Xiaolin providing the point of view, the evocation of bad luck hints at a residual rural ideology of luck and fate within Xiaolin's consciousness that, at times, interferes with an emergent understanding of class exploitation. Against this ideological trace, the clear weight given to Xiaolin's nascent class reading of his family situation underscores the ultimate association of Xiaolin's native perspective with a class rather than a rural position.

The story's location of the native standpoint in the manual laboring class is discernible further in Xiaolin's empathetic observation of his fellow worker Laozhang's unfolding family tragedy, which has the effect of consolidating Xiaolin's emerging class consciousness via, significantly, patriarchal identification. Specifically, through Xiaolin's identification with Laozhang and his response to the latter's family tragedy, the story makes clear that the authority of the native standpoint is vested especially in the traditional Confucian moral order still preserved among the manual laborers. It is none other than this moral order that establishes the native ground for critiquing and contesting Taiwan's modernity. In other words, despite the multivalent potentiality of the native position structured in the narrative framework, an overlay of Chinese culture onto the class of manual labor ultimately constitutes the native standpoint delineated in "Xiaolin."

Laozhang, the man in charge of manual tasks in the airline company, is, strictly speaking, not a manual laborer. Yet he is closely associated with manual labor in the story not only because of the nature of his work, but because his circumstances resemble those of a manual laborer, as Xiaolin observes:

> Laozhang is also an office staff, how come he looks so shabby? The others come and go in taxis, whereas he takes the $1.50 bus. The others lunch out [in fancy restaurants], while he always brings a simple lunchbox. . . . Everyone says that all Laozhang lacks is knowledge of Western languages. If he had known Western languages, he would probably have become a section chief by now. . . . Laozhang's salary has been raised only four times in ten years and the last time was already three years ago.[66]

Xiaolin can identify with Laozhang because he is also located on the other side of privilege under the class structure of a modernity dominated by and oriented toward Western interests. This identification is particularly significant given the two's location on opposite sides of the Taiwanese-Mainlander divide. In establishing the possibility of Xiaolin identifying with Laozhang on the ground of class proximity, Wang Zhenhe's story, in effect, downplays the Taiwanese-Mainlander divide in its delineation of the native standpoint. At the same time, the class displacement of "ethnic" differences allows the story to consolidate an opposition between Chinese and Western(ized) culture that Laozhang's pitiful experience highlights. What results is a mutual reinforcement between the manual/nonmanual class opposition and the Chinese/Western(ized) culture binaries through Xiaolin's empathetic understanding of Laozhang's predicament: his lack of knowledge in Western languages bars him from promotion to the better paid nonmanual jobs that, in turn, enable the luxurious and ostentatious consumption that characterizes the Westernized culture of the nonmanual beneficiaries of Taiwan's modernity. Thus, Laozhang's situation brings out a corresponding class and national cultural opposition that structures the native position in Wang Zhenhe's story.

If Laozhang's situation is inscribed negatively in relation to Western(ized) culture in the dominant discourse of "everyone" in the airline office, which reduces the native position he shares with Xiaolin to one of lack, a countersignification giving the native position a positive meaning based on Chinese culture surfaces in the story's elaboration of Laozhang's relation with his family and Xiaolin's identification with him as a father figure. Like Xiaolin's father, Laozhang experiences class exploitation and oppression partly through imposed familial suffering and separation. Despite an urgent need to attend to his young daughter's serious illness, Laozhang is not allowed a day off. Instead, the airline manager orders him to get a departure visa immediately for the wife of Big Boss Ma (*Malaoban*) so that she can accompany her son and his German wife, who have suddenly decided to cut short their visit, back to Germany. In making this order, the manager openly asserts a categorical difference between the family matters of a mere worker and those of a "boss," and naturalizes this view as commonsense:

> "Annoying bully" (*Qisiren*, the manager) takes from his mouth the fuming cigar with its moldy smokes. "How can Laozhang be so muddleheaded!? How can he leave unattended the business of Big Boss Ma's family?"
>
> He sucks on the cigar, which looks just like an erect penis.[67]
>
> "Why does he take the day off? . . . Why can't his wife take care of a sick daughter? The business of Big Boss Ma's family is unlike any others, how can he be so negligent!?"[118]

The manager's explicit hierarchization of families according to social class positions Laozhang as first and foremost a worker at the complete disposal of his boss, not a father with responsibilities toward his children. Through his discourse, the story not only exposes men's degradation into commodified physical bodies under capitalist modernity, but also implicates the exploitative class structure in the destruction of working-class families. In prioritizing economic relations over family ties and denying workers the rights to fulfill their family responsibilities, the story suggests, capitalism wields unrelenting power through its class system to destroy the working-class family and the values embodied therein.

Significantly, this indictment of class exploitation and oppression is explicitly gendered. It is the male workers' disempowerment and displacement from their rightful positions as family patriarchs that embody and stand for the plight of the working-class family. Furthermore, the disempowerment is graphically linked to the threat of emasculation through the image of the manager's cigar.[69] Functioning as a sign of phallic power, the cigar dramatizes the threat of emasculation that works down the chain of power from the capitalist boss through the manager to the working-class males like Xiaolin and Laozhang. If the manager's sucking an "erect-penis-like" cigar reveals the derivative nature of his power and his own subordinate and necessarily sycophantic position in a modern economy dominated by Western capitalist interests, his access to phallic power renders him simultaneously an agent of the emasculating threat of capitalist modernity to his subordinate manual laborers. This emasculating threat, the story suggests through Laozhang's plight, accentuates the oppression of the working class and disrupts the social and moral order embodied in the working-class family.

With such a representation of working-class oppression under Western-dominated modernity, the story prepares the ground for an affirmation of patriarchal authority as the locus of native opposition. Specifically, the contrast set up between the dysfunctional Westernized family of the boss and the filial family of the manual laborer highlights a patriarchal tradition of familial duties and moral responsibilities maintained in the working class that suggests a positive grounding for the native standpoint. This construction of the native standpoint is made clear in Xiaolin's empathetic reading of Laozhang's importance to his family:

> A woman stands in front of Laozhang's home. She looks quite old . . . her eyes, looking levelly ahead, are so dull as to suggest a loss of mind in the face of an emergency . . .
>
> Laozhang comes out, looking flurried. . . . He nods toward his wife: "Go quickly to prepare! I'll find a cab now!"
>
> "Prepare . . . what. . . ." A helpless fear suddenly covers the woman's pale face.
>
> Anger creeps up, turning Laozhang's face green.
>
> "You . . ."
>
> Laozhang cannot continue. He glances at his wife, shakes his head, heaves a sign, and the anger is repressed. . . .
>
> [Xiaolin watches Laozhang tell his wife what to prepare, then steps up to him, informing him of the manager's order. Looking up at Laozhang, Xiaolin sees his troubled expression.]
>
> At this point, Laozhang's wife walks out slowly, holding a cloth bundle and a hot bottle in her left hand while supporting Xiaozhu with her right hand; she is followed by two boys, one about five, the other about seven.
>
> Xiaozhu is about ten, rather petite, with cheeks burning so red that they seem to be bursting with fever. Her whole body leans weakly

> against her mother, even her head rests on her mother's chest. Her eyes are closed tightly, tightly closed, a part of the body hurts unbearably. The delicate, tiny hands surrounding her mother's waist look so much in need of protection!
>
> Instantly, Xiaolin feels a tremendous resentment towards Annoying Bully. With so many employees in the company, why can't he find someone else to handle Big Boss Ma's family matter?[70]

In his observation of Laozhang's family, Xiaolin gradually identifies with the position of the protective patriarch that he sees Laozhang struggling hard to keep. He takes note of and shares Laozhang's exasperation and patience with a helpless wife, and most significantly, assumes a paternal attitude of protection toward Laozhang's daughter, Xiaozhu, which puts him, for the first time, in conscious opposition to the authority figure of the airline company, the manager Annoying Bully. What seems to be an emergence of class consciousness in Xiaolin is thus based on the assumption of a patriarchal identity. If Xiaolin begins as a filial son in the story, through a gradual identification with Laozhang, he becomes in the end a benevolent and caring, albeit rather helpless, patriarch eager to protect dependent females. It is arguably this patriarchal position that positively constitutes the native standpoint in Wang Zhenhe's story. From a filial son to a caring father, Xiaolin's development traces out a patriarchal order of Confucian ethics as the basis of a native culture that the manual class, in their distance from and perhaps even resistance to the Westernized culture of the more privileged classes, manages to hold onto despite adversity.

This grounding of the native standpoint in a Confucian moral order is further corroborated in the negative examples of family disorder among the Westernized classes. As noted earlier, Wang's story paints the ideological landscape of a Western-dominated and oriented modernity by juxtaposing two different scenarios of family disintegration. There is, on the one hand, the working-class family that is being destroyed by exploitative relations of production against the will of its members, who nonetheless continue to embrace filial duties and espouse familial ethics, as in the case of Xiaolin and Laozhang. On the other hand, there is the bourgeois family, such as Big Boss Ma's, which breaks up on account of its unfilial children who, having received a Western education and gone abroad, end up rejecting their native home. Between the self-dissolution of the Westernized bourgeois family and the imposed breakup of the working class family, the story interlaces critiques of both capitalism and the hegemonic Western culture it brings along, indicting both simultaneously for destroying the social and cultural fabric of Taiwan. Yet, belying this dual focus that allows simultaneous narrative exposition of the ills of class exploitation and cultural domination, class issues are covered over and subsumed into a cultural problem of Westernization in the story's advancement of a patriarchal national tradition as available alternative.

The cultural opposition is set up in a resounding linkage between unfiliality and Westernization that is laid bare in the words of an odious "Chinese young man looking like a student studying abroad":

> Tell me, how can I stay?! Our home is so dirty, so untidy; there is not even a speck of hygiene. And then there is my father—such character and such temperament. He looks utterly like a good-for-nothing, worthless nobody! An utter nobody! How can I bear this! Frankly, now everything my father does, every word he says, even his manner of walking is objectionable to me! An utter nobody . . . I may just as well go back to *my* United States.[71]

The seamless flow from rejection of the natal home and birth father to transference of "national" identification from Taiwan to the United States here underscores the homology of familial and national orders, and their common foundation in patriarchal authority. With the young man's emphatic disrespect for his father signifying both his unfiliality and rejection of his native country, this monologue drives home the importance of Confucian familial ethics to the native/national order.

More than such cases of unfilial sons, the link between Westernization and familial/national disorder and the centrality of patriarchal authority to the native alternative are underscored in the examples of failed mothers in Wang's story. Laozhang's wife, as we have seen, is depicted as a thoroughly incompetent mother who simply loses her head under stress in an emergency. Just as the helplessness of this mother serves as a necessary backdrop to highlight the importance of the father to family welfare in a native setting, the complementary failure of a Westernized mother, Mrs. Wang (*Wang taitai*), illustrates the threat of Westernization to the cultural foundation of patriarchal authority. In many ways, Mrs. Wang is the counterpart of Laozhang in the Westernized order. If Laozhang is an illustrative figure of the native position, then Mrs. Wang represents the privileged Westernized class. Indeed, the story tells us that Laozhang could have become a section chief like Mrs. Wang had he known Western languages. As it is, while Laozhang struggles hard to make ends meet, Mrs. Wang dazzles in conspicuous consumption. The different genders given to these two parallel figures of opposing classes are particularly revealing of the gender assumption and implication of the story's construction of Taiwan's modernity. This construction not only entails a loaded feminization of material consumption—a common ideological investment in Western discourses that has been rigorously critiqued by feminist scholars—as a sign of Western-imported and oriented modernity but, in effect, legitimizes and consolidates gender oppression in the native alternative it proffers to such modernity.

As argued earlier, Wang Zhenhe's story establishes an alternative grounding of Laozhang's position in a native cultural tradition of patriarchal morality to counter its signification as a lack of Western knowledge and material possession in the dominant discourse. It is according to this alternative value system that Laozhang's counterpart, Mrs. Wang, is inscribed as a mother lacking in moral values. The gender marking of Mrs. Wang is particularly significant given the absence of a corresponding negative father figure. Throughout the story, even if fathers fail to fulfill their paternal duties, they fail not because of their own lack of a sense of moral responsibility, but because of class exploitation or the unfiliality of their Westernized sons. Mrs. Wang, in contrast, displays an aversion to maternal virtues in her very demeanor: "Mrs. Wang speaks with an unnatural countenance and an affected manner . . . 'Ka-ji-ka-ji,' Mrs. Wang laughs with her whole body trembling so much that she seems to have more than two breasts."[72] Rather than a matronly figure that supposedly befits her maternal status, Mrs. Wang features an oversexualized body, with her seductive laughs and trembling breasts signifying loose morals and a misuse of the female body that prefigure the narrative revelation of her utter failure as a mother.[73] In this configuration of Mrs. Wang, Wang Zhenhe's story reveals a fear of social and moral disruption in the form of uncontrollable feminine sexuality that Elizabeth Wilson has shown to pervade (male) representations of urban life as a marker of modernity[74]—a fear underlined by the story's perverse gaze on the indecently clad female bodies and sexually charged postures of the airline employees. More important, it establishes a concrete tie between such a fear and the ideological investment in native patriarchal motherhood.

While embellishing the disruptive effects of feminine desires unleashed in a Western-imported and oriented modernity, Wang's story unequivocally attributes Mrs. Wang's maternal failure to her adoring submission to Western culture. Her Westernization has not only turned her into an undesirable model of frivolous, materialistic consumption to her teenage daughter, but also prompted her to send the latter to study in an American school in Taipei. The result is "a Westernization of her family by Western rules," leading to the absurdity of the daughter demanding an apology from the mother for hanging up on her after refusing to satisfy her latest whim in consumption.[75] Through Mrs. Wang, then, Western(ized) culture is singled out to be the main culprit of family disorder among the nonmanual class. It threatens the native familial order by undermining patriarchal authority and dignity.

This figuration of parental failure into an immoral Westernized mother makes clear the limits of the story's construction of a native standpoint to critique Taiwan's modernity. Displacing complex issues of class exploitation, social injustice, and cultural domination onto a feminized problem of Westernization and immorality, it completely forecloses the possibility of calling into question the basis of patriarchal authority and its place in a more just and equitable alternative to Western-dominated modernity. As shown in Xiaolin's evolving consciousness, this native standpoint of critique is derived from the identification, by way of his father and Laozhang, with a Confucian moral order that sanctions filial duties and feminine submissiveness. Grounded in such an order, it cannot entertain the possibility of traditional patriarchal values giving way to a more egalitarian gender system under the challenge of Western culture. Nor can it interrogate the gender assumptions of the patriarchal order without eroding its very foundation of knowledge and critique. Thus, it continues to rely on hegemonic female objectification, reducing women to either pathetic figures in need of protection such as Xiaozhu and her loving but incompetent mother, or bodily spectacles of immorality and materialistic consumption such as Mrs. Wang and the other female employees in the airline company.

This maintenance of gender reification and patriarchal oppression calls for a critical reconsideration of the conceptual framework of superimposed Chinese-Western(ized) and class oppositions underlying the story's native standpoint. If the investment of national(ist) cultural resistance in the exploited class of manual labor allows Wang's story to articulate a simultaneous opposition to Western domination and capitalist exploitation, it also precipitates the problematic reclamation of the Confucian patriarchal order and its attendant gender constructions. Indeed, the gender politics reveals a conservative undercurrent in the story's ostensibly oppositional articulation that reaches beyond gender issues, foreclosing any radical critique of class exploitation. In particular, the superimposition of nation and class turns manual laborers basically into the repository of Chinese values under threat, and the story ends up presenting a picture of class oppression in lieu of class exploitation. That is, the plights of manual laborers under Taiwan's Western-dominated modernity are rendered primarily in terms of the blockage and frustration of their desires and efforts to assume their rightful positions and perform the duties of benevolent patriarchs. Class concerns are thereby displaced into a conservative framework of cultural domination and moral degeneration that leaves little room for raising issues of economic inequity and democratic control of the means and process of production.

Thus, even though an affirmation of manual workers as the resilient bearers of the national cultural tradition and familial order seems to enable a concomitant critique of social injustice and resistance to the erosion of national identity and social cohesion brought about by the imposition and importation of capitalist modernity from the West, the desire for an already constituted national identity and community that can withstand the sweeping force of Western modernity, in fact, poses severe limits on the social critique and the formulation of alternatives. Wang Zhenhe's story shows vividly that such a desire can lead to a problematic endorsement of an existing moral order with no space allowed for questioning its own exclusionary and oppressive assumptions and mechanisms. In the end, a real alternative to the unjust and unequal modernity of Western importation is not quite readily available through a refiguration of the national moral tradition in the name of the native and the father, however benevolent.

MOTHERHOOD SANCTIFIED IN SACRIFICE: WANG TUO'S ENDURING NATIVE

In contrast to Wang Zhenhe's location of the native in the benevolent Chinese patriarch in "Xiaolin lai taibei," Wang Tuo presents a sacrificing mother as the native figure in one of his most acclaimed stories, "Jinshuishen" (Aunt Jinshui, 1975).[76] As the contrasting genders of these two native figures suggest, there are notable differences in the stories' mapping of the native onto national and class issues. Yet, even though there is no sign of Wang Zhenhe's benevolent working-class patriarch struggling against Western(ized) culture in Wang Tuo's construction of nativist resistance to Western-imported modernity, the two stories share a similar ideological investment in the exploited and the oppressed as an indigenous moral center to resist the valorization of material wealth in the dominant discourse of modernity. Motivated by the desire to locate and affirm a timeless native ethics for cultural identity and social solidarity, this ideological investment leads to a consolidation of the dominant culture of patriarchy in "Jinshuishen" as well, for all its celebratory focus on a woman.

In a nutshell, "Jinshuishen" is the story of a selfless, hard-working, rural mother betrayed and forsaken by her calculating, money-minded, urban sons. The title character Jinshuishen (literally Aunt Jinshui, or, more exactly, the middle-aged wife of Jinshui) is an uneducated woman married to an indolent and irresponsible fisherman who dumped the burden of raising their six sons all on her. To make ends meet, she has peddled odds and ends in their tiny fishing village for almost twenty years. This has enabled her to miraculously support all her sons through higher education. Owing to her foresight and hard work, her sons have become successful professionals with luxurious homes in the city (Jilong), enjoying all the amenities modernity affords the middle class—"color television, washing machine, phonograph, water heating system, sofa set, etc," the story meticulously lists.[77] In stark contrast, Jinshuishen continues to live in a primitive shed with a broken roof and no electricity. Moreover, she has to not only keep working to support herself and her husband, but also borrow money for her sons' weddings and business ventures. All the troubles and sacrifices she underwent for her sons' sakes remain unreciprocated and unappreciated to the end. When her sons' business venture turned out to be a fraud, leaving her heavily in debt, her husband simply passed away and her sons refused to assume responsibility for any of the debts. Each claiming insolvency and blaming the others for incurring the debts, all of her sons ruthlessly abandoned her. In what is perhaps the story's most problematic and ideologically revealing development, Jinshuishen remains unbroken and self-sacrificing as ever. She left the village to work as a domestic helper in Taipei, harboring hopes that she would eventually repay all the debts and return, "innocent and clean," to offer thanks at the village's Mazu temple.

The contrast between the lives of Jinshuishen and her sons points to a structural inequality between manual laborers living from hand to mouth in rural areas and nonmanual professionals making it in the cities. Here, as in Wang Zhenhe's text, exploitation and oppression are closely linked to formal education and its translation into money, material possession, and proximity to social power under the dominant structure of modernity. The higher education of Jinshuishen's sons affords them a way out of the poor, fixed lot of fishermen like their father into the middle-class world of managers and administrators, with its titillating promise of promotion, material wealth, and prestige. By the same token, this class ascendance co-opts them into the modern machinery of exploitation and oppression, disposing them to abandon, after exhausting all economic values out of, their sacrificing mother and native place, together with the moral values these embody.

Yet, unlike Wang Zhenhe's story, "Jinshuishen" does not construct differences over the importance of material and moral values into a definitive opposition between the nonmanual and manual classes, or between the rural and urban populace. The egotistic materialism exhibited by Jinshuishen's sons is shown to penetrate every social class and remote village, albeit to different degrees. Indeed, the erosion of community spirit in which familial and kin-like relations take precedence over monetary calculations and economic transactions serves as a primary signifier of the ills of Taiwan's modernity in the story. This is conveyed through a sustained irony between the continuation of kindred address among Jinshuishen's fellow villagers and the increasing dominance of economic calculations in their lives and interactions, which intensifies as the story develops. For instance, despite their nominal acknowledgment of near-kin relationship, Jinshuishen's clients started to take advantage of her long-standing practice of selling goods on credit without written records. Later, when their financial woes became known, Jinshui got into an eventually fatal fight with his sworn brothers over money and Jinshuishen's lifelong neighbors not only offered her no support over her sons' betrayal but pressed her to immediately repay her debts. In the final analysis, it is such reification of family and social relations and the consequent breakdown of community even in rural villages that motivate Wang Tuo's critique of Taiwan's materialistic modernity and construction of a native alternative in stories like "Jinshuishen."

In the context of the *xiangtu* literature debate, this representation is remarkable for not valorizing manual labor and putting it on a pedestal of purity, authenticity, and morality. Despite the author's celebration of manual labor in defense of *xiangtu* literature during the debate, the story here does not place manual workers outside the corruptive materialism of a Western-imported modernity. Making even marginalized working-class families in a remote village susceptible to the seduction of Western consumer goods, "Jinshuishen" presents a picture of greed-driven modernity breeding a general ethos of egotistic materialism that leaves no class unaffected. With such attenuation of the connection between manual labor and resistance to materialistic modernity, the native alternative articulated in the story clearly lies beyond the framework of class opposition.

The story's retreat from class in its conception of the native alternative is already discernible in its focus on ungrateful sons and their sacrificing mother in configuring the relation of exploitation under modernity. This configuration foregrounds a dimension of familial ethics and traditional morals that, in effect, covers over the structural inequality and exploitation between the different class locations of manual laborers and professional administrators and managers. The consequent departure from class analysis is accentuated by the narrative highlight of Jinshuishen's exceptionality, which dissociates her from any specific class location and elevates her to the allegorical loftiness of the sacred native mother:

> In this small remote fishing village, Badouzi, there are two names which no one will find unfamiliar when uttered. One is the Sacred Mother Mazu in the Temple of Heaven Access, the other is the peddler Jinshuishen. Jinshuishen is so well known in Badouzi for two reasons. First, everyday, the whole year round, she carries her baskets of household supplies on a shoulder pole to every home in the village, selling cosmetics, household goods, and sweets and biscuits for children. This occupational convenience naturally gives her a thorough knowledge of family matters, big or small, in every single home of Badouzi. . . . So, imperceptibly, her position appears to be extremely important. Second, she has become a subject of respect and envy among most of the parents in Badouzi, not only because her belly gave her credit, having borne altogether six sons, but also because her sons are good achievers, every one of them attaining college education. . . . Jinshuishen's family has initially been extremely poor and her husband happens to be an irresponsible fellow who likes to

> eat but not work. Nonetheless, she surprisingly manages to give every son an education. That is why whenever Jinshuishen is mentioned, people in Badouzi invariably put their thumbs up and praise her from the bottom of their hearts.[78]

Here, metaphoric association with the "Sacred Mother" Mazu (literally, mother ancestor) marks Jinshuishen off from ordinary working-class mothers and turns her into a symbolic figure of the native place and its cultural heritage.[79] Mazu is one of the most important folk deities in Taiwan. According to legends, Mazu was a pious young woman who sacrificed her life to save her father and all but one of her brothers from drowning. After death, she attained supernatural powers to protect seafarers, and fishermen and sailors turned to her for safeguard against the perils of their profession. In such capacity, she assumed great importance to Chinese settlers who braved the stormy Taiwan Straits to find a new home on the island. Local history shows that Mazu temples were set up at the ports of disembarkation early in Chinese settlement. Later, branch temples reputedly carrying incense ash from the original temples were established in inland settlements. As more and more Chinese emigrated and settled into rural and fishing villages in Taiwan, Mazu gradually developed into an omnipotent goddess looking after the land and people's livelihood on it like a kind and loving mother. As such, Mazu symbolizes for the settlers both a continual cultural tie to mainland China and a growing identification with Taiwan as the native place and homeland. Taiwan scholars have argued that the worship of Mazu was instrumental in breaking down ethnic differences among early Chinese settlers in Taiwan and was an important spiritual force in the nationalist resistance against Japanese Occupation.[80]

The effect of Mazu worship in cultivating a collective identity grounded in Taiwan as adopted homeland arguably continues into contemporary times with the annual island-wide pilgrimages to the original temples in Lugang, Xingang, and, most important, Beigang. According to local anthropologist Wang Mei-ying, when people all over Taiwan engage in the symbolic activities of Mazu pilgrimage, a strong sense of native consciousness and collective identification on the part of Han Taiwanese is clearly expressed.[81] The tangible link between Mazu pilgrimage and the development of a native Taiwanese identity has been explained as follows:

> As the focal symbol of the pan-Taiwan pilgrimage community, Ma Tsu [Mazu] brings together again the many groups of Taiwanese settlers who, in their own villages and market towns, worship deities that differentiate them from their neighbors. . . . In the case of Ma Tsu pilgrimages in Taiwan, the entire island is included, but there is an ethnic and potentially political tone to the pilgrimages as well. For while the Ma Tsu cult has an

> inclusive effect among Taiwanese (uniting otherwise competitive Hakka, Chang-chou, and Ch'uan-chou factions), it clearly differentiates Taiwanese from mainlanders who migrated to the island after the Communist revolution. Ma Tsu, after all, is closely associated with the history of earlier Chinese migration to Taiwan from Fukien and Kwangtung, a fact that highlights differences with recent migrants who came primarily from more distant areas of China.[82]

The strong native identification associated with this "Sacred Mother" who spiritually presides over "Jinshuishen" suggests that Wang Tuo's vision of the native alternative to Western(ized) modernity is not mapped onto Chinese nationalism or Chinese traditional culture so much as the Taiwanese homeland and its indigenized Chinese culture. This accords with his nuanced characterization, in critical writings discussed earlier, of the cultural tradition to be renewed for nationalist consciousness against imperialism as "that in which one is located" (*benwei*) rather than Chinese. Without explicitly naming such an indigenized Chinese culture Taiwanese, Wang Tuo manages to emphasize in his fictions and critical writings a local specificity to the culture that makes it irreducible though historically linked to Chinese traditions. By virtue of local traits and customs such as the Mazu worship, the native culture that he inscribes incorporates the historical experiences of Chinese settlers in founding a new home on a strange land, as well as the commitment and determination to put down roots and make the land one's own that these experiences embody.

In "Jinshuishen," particularly, the evocation of Mazu worship situates the story in the larger context of Taiwan's history of development and struggle for survival. The metaphorical link of Jinshuishen to Mazu adds a level of "national allegory" to her experience of betrayal by the sons for whom she has worked hard and sacrificed herself.[83] Through this Jinshuishen-Mazu trope, Wang Tuo's story suggests that the success and development of modern Taiwan, manifested in the urban life of material wealth and comfort enjoyed by her sons, is built on the toil and sacrifices of those remaining in the native place, whom the beneficiaries of modernity abandon without qualms once their uses have been exhausted. By the same token, Jinshuishen's embodiment of the maternal values of Mazu projects her resilience and hopefulness beyond personal and familial survival into the allegorical realm of native resistance and "national" triumph over the forces of reification and commodification under modernity. In other words, she stands for the promise of native values in envisioning and constructing a different modernity.

Both as a peddler who combines manual labor with the circulation of local family stories and hence promotion of a sense of community in the village, and as a mother who maintains, nurtures, and protects the (patrilineal) family line, Jinshuishen manifests trust, faithfulness, reliability, constancy, and, above all, a sense of embeddedness in and responsibility to the collectivity of her native place. Yet, defying the usual connotation of rootedness, Jinshuishen is a figure not of nostalgia but of utopia in Wang Tuo's text. Even as she holds on to timeless values, she does not remain outside of or antagonistic to change. Rather, she is keenly aware of the necessity of keeping abreast of the times. Not only does she have enough foresight to give all her sons a higher education and thus life opportunities far beyond the bounds of a fishing village, setting them on the path of success in modernity, but she also has little problem keeping up with new commodity trends in her capacity as the village's ingenious entrepreneur, arguably the most valorized figure in the self-image of capitalist modernity. In her small peddling business, she is astute enough to boost her sales by actively introducing new, fashionable commodities—flimsy bikini panties, perfumes and cosmetics, and so on—into the remote fishing village. Indeed, it is precisely her embodiment of a possible, even if problematic, resolution of what David Harvey identifies as the central dilemma of the modernist project—how to combine the eternal and immutable with change—that makes Jinshuishen a figure of utopia.[84] In the context of Taiwan's capitalist mode of production and dominant ideological opposition between "timeless" Chinese cultural heritage and Western material "progress," Jinshuishen also constitutes a utopian figure of the negotiation between ethics and capitalist commodification. The terms in which the eternal and change become reconciled in Jinshuishen are then particularly revealing of the limitations and exclusions of Wang Tuo's nativist vision of the modern.

In Wang Tuo's story, what is eternal and immutable, signified especially by the "Sacred Mother" Mazu, is the maternal sacrifice and selfless commitment of Jinshuishen. These qualities stay with her throughout her tragic experience of family disintegration, and are particularly highlighted in the story's conclusion:

> Spring finally returns to Badouzi. Like a mother who is full of life, Spring enables infinite vitality and vivacity to reappear on the earth, nurturing innumerable tiny lives to leap, jump and cheer under the sun, in the wind. . . . After the festive day of Mazu's birthday, Wangsao and other debtors suddenly receive money from Jinshuishen. Soon, it is circulated around Badouzi that someone has run into Jinshuishen in the Xiangong Temple in Taipei. That day, she went to offer sacrifices to improve her sons' fortunes. For she was afraid that this being the year of the tiger and her sons being born in the years of the snake, dog, pig, rooster, and rabbit, they would meet with bad luck. She asked the person to tell the village that she now worked as a domestic helper in Taipei, doing laundries, cooking dinners, and looking after children; and that she would repay all

> the money her family owed. When that was done, she would return, innocent and clean, to Badouzi to offer incense and thanks at the Mazu temple. The person who saw her also said that she seemed very happy again, just like in the past when she was peddling in Badouzi; she loved to joke, was cheerful, and full of hope for the future.[85]

On the surface, the story's naturalization and affirmation of maternal virtues encapsulated in this passage seem to suggest a critical displacement of the center of the dominant Chinese cultural tradition. Chen Yingzhen, for one, has enthusiastically commended such a displacement in his review of the story.[86] In effect, however, the glorification of a naturalized maternity serves only to consolidate and support the continued dominance of patriarchy, whether it is understood to be traditional or indigenized Chinese patriarchy. Jinshuishen's maternity, like the worship of Mazu with which it is constantly associated in the story, is the underside of Chinese patriarchy: it protects and guarantees the continuation of the patriarchal order.[87] Indeed, Jinshuishen's exemplary compliance with the demands of the patriarchal order on female bodies is what makes her such a venerable mother in the text. She is widely respected in the village because of her exceptional ability to endure the abuses of an irresponsible husband and to bear and raise six sons who not only continue but also improve the patrilineal family line. Belying the apparent questioning and undermining of paternal authority in the textual inscription of a useless and irresponsible father, the failure of Jinshui serves only to highlight the exemplariness of Jinshuishen's maternal virtues and consolidate the hegemonic power of the "native" patriarchal culture.

Any critique of the traditional marginalization of female subjects implied in the narrative focus on Jinshuishen is thus undermined by the story's subscription to the hegemonic patriarchal culture in its construction of this mother figure, and its plot development and resolution. Perhaps most indicative of such subscription is the narrative affirmation of Jinshuishen's own ideological understanding of her life and tragedy, without the slightest trace of irony. Confronted with the reality of her most considerate son's refusal to shoulder any of the debts she has incurred for him, Jinshuishen reflects on her life in the following way:

> Every time she suffered from her husband's irrational kickings and beatings, it was always this son who consoled her, giving her infinite hope, even in the midst of pain, for the future and for these sons, as well as the courage to live on in times when she contemplated suicide or running away from the family. . . . But, now—
>
> She thought [about her son's unconcern] over and over again, and still could not understand.

> How come such a filial son changed suddenly like this? If it weren't for someone constantly abetting him close by, how could he have become like this?
>
> While she was thinking these, the quietly smiling countenance of Axiu [her daughter-in-law] crossed her mind and doubts rose in her heart.[88]

Jinshuishen's suspicion of her daughter-in-law for instigating her son's unfiliality is confirmed in a later scene where all her daughters-in-law take an active part in arguing away their husbands' responsibility toward Jinshuishen and her debts. This displacement of unfiliality onto the women serves to recuperate and consolidate the male-centered moral order that structures and maintains Jinshuishen's position as mother. The narrative further consolidates this order by consistently affirming Jinshuishen's propensity to situate and justify her own existence in relation to male family members and to absolve them from blame for her exploited and oppressed life, as the following accounts of her reactions to her husband's sudden illness and death make clear:

> She tucks the cover neatly around him and sits, curled up, beside him at the head of the bed, holding his cold hand tightly in her warm palm. For thirty some years, it has been this man; it is her fate to follow and stay with him. From youth to old age, nothing has changed. He has never given her any good time; it has been either blows or scolds. Still, she has lived with him for over thirty years. Now, here he is, lying at her side, so real and dependable. She has never realized that he is in fact so close to her. For thirty some years, she has worked hard and hoped, looking forward to her sons' growth, graduation from college, and marriage. It all turned out to be an empty dream, they are not hers. In the end, only this man, no matter how many shortcomings he has and how many decades of tears he has brought her, only he is still, indeed, hers. And she is his.[89]
>
> . . . Jinshuishen thinks of Jinshui's dying moment and uncontrollable tears run down her face again.
>
> In money matters, he never went beyond his lot. As poor as he was all his life, he seldom borrowed money from others. This time, he personally went around asking for a loan and met with such results. He knew clearly that he would not be able to repay the debts, and he no longer harbored any hope in these sons. Naturally, then, there was no one but she to take on this cangue for him. He must have been disturbed by this and felt sorry for her; otherwise, he would not have kept thinking about that money till his last breath. After all, only a spouse of thirty some years could understand her hard and miserable circumstances and state of mind.
>
> Thinking this, Jinshuishen cannot help crying loudly again.[90]

Even if we assume these accounts of Jinshuishen's thoughts to be realistic representations of her ideological subject formation under Chinese patriarchy—an assumption that gives a grim outlook for the possibility of cultural resistance—the manner of their inclusion into a text that holds out the promise and proffers a vision of a brighter future gives us cause for much concern. For the narrative nowhere questions or critiques the ideological underpinnings of these thoughts. It thus, in effect, unequivocally affirms the gender oppression that grounds Jinshuishen's subject formation as mother. Indeed, the narrative itself invests in this self-abnegating maternal subject the ethically immutable ground for an alternative modernity, thereby foreclosing any possibility of interrogating the necessary subjugation of women that underlies such an institution of motherhood. In the final analysis, the story's nativist vision falls back on nationalist discourses' familiar gender strategy of turning women into the repository of tradition and the nation's moral and spiritual mission, even as it breaks the mold in making Jinshuishen a remarkable agent in national progress.[91]

The marginalization of issues of gender oppression and exploitation is arguably an inevitable effect of the story's impulse to affirm an eternal ethics in the existing social and cultural order, on which the hope of an indigenous reconstruction of social relations and collectivities necessitated by the introduction of modernity is invested. Insofar as gender is but one, albeit key, modality of oppression under the existing order, this conservative affirmation of entrenched patriarchal relationships and practices has broader implications for the story's vision of alternatives. The investment of an eternal ethics in Jinshuishen-as-sacred-mother-Mazu suggests that the story cannot articulate a basis for imagining and constituting collectivities that is not predicated on a morality of selfless sacrifice. While the patriarchal nature of this moral order especially sanctions feminine self-sacrifice, its logic of selfless sacrifice for the collective pertains not only to women but to all subjects in its purview. In other words, with its affirmation of a patriarchal ethics in a familial order, the story's vision reproduces the prevailing hierarchical ordering of the family (and other collectivities imagined along familial lines) over individual selves and the privileging of ascriptive ties over common interests. It is thus an even more limiting vision than that inscribed in Wang Zhenhe's "Xiaolin lai Taibei." Though the superimposition of a familial moral order onto the class of manual workers limits the potential for social reconstruction in Wang Zhenhe's vision, the story still allows for the emergence of social solidarity on the basis of common interests among manual workers that can transcend differences in ethnic origins, as Xiaolin's growing identification with Laozhang and indignation against the airline manager shows. In comparison, Wang Tuo's exclusive emphasis on the redeeming power of motherhood and its metaphoric evocation of the motherland forecloses any possibility of building collectivities on grounds other than that of familial, ascriptive ties. Despite its critical intent, the story ends up espousing a vision that essentially maintains and supports the state's ideological vision of a modernity with Chinese characteristics in the name of a nativist alternative—the development of material wealth on a capitalist system regulated by Confucian patriarchal ethics.

The Crippled Proletarian and His Deaf-mute Daughter: Huang Chunming's Subaltern Native

Seductive as it is in offering a readily available resolution of the problems of national identity and social injustice arising from post/modernity perceived in terms of Western domination and materialistic corruption, the affirmation of Confucian ethics as the basis of an alternative modernity has not gone uncontested in Taiwan. Within *xiangtu* literature itself, one can find examples in which the investment of a patriarchal moral tradition in the class of manual labor is resisted. There has also been implicit questioning of the idea that the exploited manual class embodies within its family relations a utopian ground on which a native modernity different from that of Western materialism can be built. The most insistent interrogation of this idea appears in the fictional works of Huang Chunming, especially his short story "Pinguo de ziwei" (The taste of the apples, 1972; hereafter "Pinguo").[92]

The storyline of "Pinguo" is quite simple. An urban subproletariat, Afa, who had recently moved from the rural south to try his luck in the capital, Taipei, was hit by the vehicle of an American colonel. For fear of labor protests in Taiwan at a time when U.S. military operations in Vietnam were far from well received throughout Asia, the U.S. embassy in Taipei persuaded the colonel to compensate Afa and take care of his family financially. Thanks to the accident, Afa was free from financial worries for the first time in his adult life, and he and his family at last got a taste of apples, soft drinks, and other Western packaged food that had formerly been unaffordable to them. The story ends with the ironic note that though Afa lost both of his legs, the accident was really the luck that he had come seeking in Taipei.

This plot line clearly suggests that Huang's story can be read as a national allegory of modern Taiwan. Afa's financial gain after becoming crippled and dependent on a military representative of the United States is a vividly telling comment on Taiwan's dependent development under U.S. imperialism in the 1960s. Yet the richness of the story lies not in this loaded image of national dependence, but in its detailed dissection of public and personal reactions to the consequential crippling encounter. If the story of "Pinguo" plots a critique of U.S. imperialism in the form of national allegory and makes the manual laborer Afa an allegorical figure for Taiwan, the narrative itself maps and pursues closely class, ethnic, gender, and generation differences that remain irreducible and are, indeed, amplified within the nation after its unequal confrontation with Western power. In this light, "Pinguo" is a study of the differential impacts of neocolonial modernity on different people in Taiwan and an exploration of their various overdetermined responses. In representing these differences, the narrative attends not only to the unequal relations between the imperialist United States and neocolonial Taiwan on the national level, or the injustice suffered by the manual workers as a class, but also to the interaction of these national and class relations with other lines of exploitation and oppression within the nation, especially those of ethnicity and gender. In other words, the nation is emphatically not one in Huang's story. Nor are the exploited and oppressed in Taiwan's neocolonial modernity configured into a homogeneous site of class suffering and a resilient repository of unchanging morality. Instead, through unraveling the different experiences of and responses to Afa's accident among his family members and fellow workers, the story problematizes the mutually reinforcing nation and class binaries adopted by many nativist works to construct such a site, and thus questions the validity of an alternative vision that is already constituted within the dominant culture.

Unlike the stories of Wang Zhenhe and Wang Tuo previously discussed, "Pinguo" does not idealize the poor working-class family into a native site of moral values and practices to be reclaimed. Nor does it suggest a diametrical opposition between native morality and Western materialism. In the story, Afa's family by no means illustrates ethical plenitude or exemplifies virtuous existence before his brush with American material superiority. As the master of the family, Afa has ignored the reservations and entreaty of his wife, Agui, and autocratically decided to leave their familiar, if impoverished, home in the south and move to Taipei to try his luck. Relations between the couple worsened under abject poverty in the capital city. Financial worries became the cause and context of much quarrelling and fighting between husband and wife, and made it difficult for them to treat their five children with fairness and care. Just as Afa was not shown to be a caring father in the manner of Laozhang in "Xiaolin lai Taibei," Agui was not an enduring and sacrificing mother like Jinshuishen in Wang Tuo's story. Rather, she routinely abused her children with harsh words and violent threats, not only to discipline them but also to vent her own anger and frustration. Thus Huang's story jettisons the nativist myth of the virtuous working-class family valiantly withstanding the trials and tribulations of an exploitative and oppressive modernity.

In place of the myth, "Pinguo" offers a complex depiction of the reactions of Afa's family to his accident, which dramatically exposes the depth and pervasiveness of exploitation and oppression within the family. Gender-based familial exploitation and oppression are made particularly evident in the figure of the eldest daughter, Achu, who is kept at home, together with her sister "Yaba" (literally, the mute), to help with housework and baby care while her brothers attend school. Reflecting the normativization of this gender inequality, Achu immediately accepts and psychologically prepares herself for a necessary sacrifice when she learns of her father's injury:

> now that Father cannot work, the family will be out of money. This time, Mother will definitely sell me off to other people as an adopted daughter. This time, it will not be like ordinary times, when Mother just threatens: "Achu, if you still don't behave yourself, I'll sell you off."
>
> But this time, Achu is not afraid. She keeps thinking that after becoming an adopted daughter, she must behave well, be obedient, and suffer every hardship without complaint. Then her adopted family will not ill-treat her, and perhaps even allow her to come home to see her younger brothers and sisters. By then, she may have a little money to buy her brothers a gun and her sisters a ball and a doll.
>
> She thinks on, without a tiny bit of fear, but her tears flow more and more heavily as she thinks.[93]

The readiness with which Achu imagines a sacrificing role for herself in the case of family emergency bespeaks an insistent ideological interpellation of this subaltern female into the subject position(s) of obedient daughter and selflessly sacrificing sister. Her mother's repeated threats of selling her unless she "behaves" has succeeded in making her internalize the exploitative and oppressive nature of her existence in the family. She, too, sees her value to the family in terms of disciplined labor and monetary exchange. Indeed, she has so accepted her duty of slaving for her brothers that when one asks to be carried, she simply "squats down without saying a word to let Asong climb onto her back."[94] Thus the story reveals how the domination and subjection she experiences in her everyday familial duties have reduced Achu to a willing domestic slave in her parental home even before the American crashed into her family.

That it is gender that structures Achu's position of submissive sacrifice within the family is made clear through the contrastive position of her younger brother, Aji, who is the eldest son in the family. Against Achu's mental preparation for sacrifice, Aji's unconcern over his father's injury suggests a relatively pampered position in the family. Unlike his sister, Aji's life is dominated not so much by familial duties as by the oppressive school system. Accordingly, he is "less grieved" at the news of his father's accident than at his punishment and humiliation in class for not having paid a required fee; he "cannot understand [why Achu thinks that their mother is going to sell her], nor can he imagine what his father's being hit by an American car has to do with their future."[95] Such incomprehension reflects a position in the family that is significantly less subjected to exploitation and oppression than his sister's. Aji suffers their mother's unreasonable vent of anger and frustration as well, but the threat he gets is quite different from Achu's. While the girl is constantly haunted by the fear of being sold, the boy and his younger brother are threatened only with the prospect of working in place of their injured father to support the family. And Aji is secure enough in his position as the eldest son to laugh in the face of such a threat from his mother, while his younger brother "answers 'yes' seriously and obediently."[96]

This keen attention to multiform generation and gender exploitation and oppression in Afa's family, which his injurious encounter with the American brought sharply into the open, effects an implicit critique of the common nativist strategy of valorizing the working-class family as a site of moral harmony disrupted by Western materialism. Indeed, whatever harmony Afa's family has in Huang's story came after the material help Afa gained from being crippled in the unequal encounter. Such harmony, the story tells us, is built on a relief of financial burdens that have hitherto prevented the humanity in Afa from shining forth:

> Afa has an odd feeling, a feeling of being free from all worries, of having no more concerns in his heart. Seeing its expression on Afa's face, Agui finds him somewhat strange. She has never imagined, not even in her dreams, that the Jiang Afa with whom she has had five children has such a beautiful side too. While Afa is not watching, she moves her head back to look fixedly at him. Look! When has he ever appeared so fine before? Today he looks like a human being at last.[97]

Agui's observation foregrounds that humanity is dependent on a basic satisfaction of material needs and, thus, insofar as ethics is an expression of humanity—as Confucianism claims—no ethical order can be built in complete disregard of the unequal distribution of material wealth. In suggesting this, the story fundamentally challenges the dichotomized opposition between a Chinese/indigenous emphasis on morality and a Western/Westernized focus on the material world, an opposition which, as I have argued, underlies both the state's neo-Confucian ideology of Chinese modernity and its critique by many nativist advocates in Taiwan.

Nonetheless, in making Afa realize his humanity for the first time in the eyes of his own wife because of an unusual "luck" under Taiwan's neocolonial modernity, the story supports rather than undermines the nativist advocates' criticism of neocolonial modernity. The accidental nature of Afa's superficially beneficial hit by the American indicates that even if some workers may be hurled into the rank of beneficiaries under neocolonial modernity, they are the exceptions rather than the rule.[98] Moreover, by drawing out the crippling price

Afa pays for his material "gain," the story makes clear that material compensation is no real solution to the problems of dependency, aggravation of social injustice, and loss of social solidarity generated by neocolonial modernity. In the story, Afa is crippled in more ways than physically by imperialist forces, and the harm is spread to his entire family:

> Everyone is holding an apple, turning it over and over, not quite knowing how to eat it. "Go ahead and eat!" Afa says.
>
> "How?" Achu asks bashfully.
>
> "Just like they do on TV!" Aji says; he then takes a bite to demonstrate.
>
> While everyone is still watching Aji take a bite, Afa says: "The cost of an apple can buy you four catties of rice and you don't know how to eat one!"
>
> Following this remark from Afa, the children and Agui all begin to bite into their apples. . . . Those who have a bite of the apples cannot say anything for a moment, feeling somehow that it is not as sweet as they have imagined. Rather, it is sour, rough, and so frothy on the chew that it gives a sense of hollowness. But when they recall Father's words that an apple can buy four catties of rice, the taste suddenly seems to have improved. They take their second bites and chew enthusiastically.[99]

The apples, which are given to Afa's family by the American colonel who crippled him, symbolize the cultural experience of imperialism for the family. This scene, then, dramatizes the crippling effect of what Gayatri Spivak calls the epistemic violence of imperialism. From the moment they bite into the apples, Afa and his family cannot tell the taste of the apples as they experience it. For the taste of the apples is inscribed in a language of value controlled by imperialist power. In their efforts to make sense of it, Afa and his family necessarily find themselves drawn into the imperialist symbolic order. Thus the story vividly suggests that Afa's unequal and involuntary encounter with the American makes his entire family dependent not only financially but also culturally on the imperialist aggressor.

In arguably one of the story's most significant moves, this cultural dependency is linked to Afa's inability to look beyond the superficial kindness of the American colonel and see the more fundamental reason for his financial "gain" from the accident. Indeed, the story suggests, the apparently generous compensation is meant precisely to perpetuate such blindness. What Afa's dependency prevents him from seeing is foregrounded at the beginning of the story. Right after the scene of the accident, the narrative renders in direct speech a fragment of telephone conversation between the American colonel and a Junior Secretary in the U.S. embassy in Taipei:

> "he won't be here in the morning. . . . Um, um, it doesn't matter, as Junior Secretary, I can make decision in this case. . . . Um, um. . . . No, no. Listen to me. Remember, this is Asia! And the fellow is a worker, right? Is he a worker? . . . Indeed a worker! So, we can't afford a provocation. No? . . . Hear me out. This is the only place in Asia that is most cooperative, most friendly, and most secure to us, right? . . . Hear me out please! The United States doesn't want to have both feet trapped in a mire! Our President and our people all feel this way. . . . Ugh! Don't say otherwise, send him there! . . . Um. All right, I'll be responsible for all these . . . okay, I'll call right away . . . Right! . . . Right, that's it. Goodbye!"[100]

With only the embassy side of the conversation made audible, the colonel's initial reluctance to properly treat and compensate Afa for his injury is literally shown to be repressed and covered over by the public relation and diplomatic courtesy of the imperialist state. Significantly, the speech reveals that what is repressed is not only the blatantly exploitative and oppressive face of imperialism, but also the collective power of workers to oppose this face of imperialism. The real effect of collective labor power in curbing the excesses of neocolonial exploitation is covered over by the benevolent and responsible face imperialism puts on to neutralize this power. That such repression is linked to the epistemic violence of imperialism is dramatized in Afa's attempt to conceal his "fortune" from his fellow workers:

> The happy and harmonious atmosphere of the family is disrupted, but not disagreeably, by Grant [the colonel] bringing in [Afa's] foreman and the workers' representative, Chen Huotu.
>
> The foreman and Huoto enter the sick room without even a word of condolence, saying immediately, in the usual joking manner:
>
> "Wow! Afa, now you can live your entire life lying in bed, eating and shitting, while we brothers still need to work like oxen and horses, no different from before. Who can compare with you! Ho-ho-ho!"
>
> "Ha-ha-ha! We brothers will look to you from now on!" the foreman says.
>
> Afa and Agui are puzzled.
>
> "Hey! Huotu, what are you talking about? You've got me confused."
>
> "Don't pretend, you think we don't know? This American feller has told us all. Also, your mute daughter will be sent to study in the United States, and . . ."
>
> "Who said so?" Agui asks.
>
> "All of our hundred-plus brothers at the work site know about it."
>
> "Of course! Otherwise, how would we know that our brother has not been taken advantage of. Isn't that right?"
>
> "Yes, I've got something. *This Mr. Grant is a good person*," Afa says.[101]

If it is the fear of collective labor power that made the embassy secretary push the colonel to be "good" and compensate his victim, the American's superficial generosity led Afa to understand the situation in terms of individual kindness and moral responsibility. Despite his fellow workers' intimation, Afa remains in the end ignorant of the political calculations and his real indebtedness to the collectivity of workers. Unsurprisingly, then, the link between labor power in Taiwan and the imperialist war in Vietnam that played a crucial part in the American calculations is even more remote from this Taiwan worker's consciousness. It is precisely in making visible the repression of such a link in proletarian consciousness by the capitalist/imperialist power's strategy of buying off, or, in other words, materially and culturally co-opting selected "victims" such as Afa (and his national allegorical equivalent of Taiwan) that, I would argue, Huang's story departs most from the critiques of Western-imported modernity in the works of his fellow *xiangtu* writers to deliver its most radical vision of alternatives. For, here, the story is offering not only an incisive critique of imperialism as an integrated cultural, economic, and military force, but also a diagnosis of the failure of radical opposition and alternative in the moral affirmation of an unchanging working class. Through Afa's growing cultural dependency and distance from his fellow workers, the story makes clear that unless the exploited and oppressed see beyond their own (mis)fortunes to recognize their relations to and implications in other exploitation and oppression, just as the imperialists and capitalists see through and take advantage of the multiplicity of exploitation and oppression, no real opposition and challenge to the imperialist project of modernity can be advanced.

Given the story's attention to the gender and generation exploitation and oppression within Afa's family, the vision of opposition implied here is clearly not the orthodox Marxist line of international class struggle. Indeed, the *other* exploitation and oppression that the story suggests Afa and Taiwan's manual laborers need to confront as well is not only neocolonial exploitation in other countries but also gender, generation, and ethnic injustices within Taiwan, injustices in which some of them are complicit. With such complex understanding of social injustices, Huang's story resists any readily available conception of alternatives or oppositional groups and suggests, instead, the need to include diverse voices in an ongoing process of negotiation for change.

The importance of including diverse voices is foregrounded by the story's concretization of multiple injustices in multiple levels of silencing. From the very beginning, the command of speech and the act of silencing stand out as key figures of power in the story. Besides the epistemic violence that renders Afa and his family speechless about their actual experience of the taste of the apples, the story is replete with incidents of silencing within the familial and national spaces. Particularly important in this latter realm of silencing is the language politics of Taiwan under the Nationalist government. With the state designation of Mandarin, the common language of the Mainlanders, as the official language while the majority of the Taiwanese population speak the dialect of Hokkienese (Fujianese), the dynamics of speech and silence within the national space of Taiwan is closely connected with ethnic domination and inequity. Huang's story draws attention to such domination in its description of the encounters of Afa and Agui, who speak only the local dialect, with the Chinese foreign affairs policeman who represents the state in mediating the interaction between Afa's family and the colonel. Understanding and speaking but little of the local dialect, the policeman embodies the linguistic power of the state, which is totally unprepared and inadequate to the task of listening to and translating for Afa and Agui. With such a state intermediary, Afa and Agui would have been totally silenced in effect, had there not been their children, who have learned the official language of Mandarin, and an American nun who has mastered the local dialect to recruit the Taiwanese population into the religion of the imperialist power. Through the multiple levels of translation involved in communication between the colonel and Afa, the story dramatizes the power dynamics of giving voice and silencing among the military and the "civilizing" forces of U.S. imperialism, the Mainlander-controlled Nationalist state and its education apparatus, and generations of ethnic Taiwanese people.

Beyond this dimension of ethnic injustice, the importance of recognizing and including diverse voices in dialogue is dramatized in "Pinguo" through the figure of Yaba, the deaf-mute daughter of Afa named and treated as a mute. In its representation of this female subaltern, the story not only exposes the silencing involved in advancing a homogeneous manual class as the "authentic" and de jure site of alternative modernity, but also problematizes the power relation between the intellectual and the subaltern subjects he purports to represent, a relation that, as I argued earlier, is commonly glossed over by Taiwan's *xiangtu* literature advocates. The gap between Yaba's figuration as a deaf-mute and naming as a mute calls attention to her possession of a voice and ability to speak, which are all too easily overlooked by the more privileged others who are so wrapped up in their own languages and narratives that they dismiss as mute those with no or very limited access to these languages. Indeed, these more privileged others include her own mother, who treats her voice as noise and literally silences her "with hand gestures of sewing the mouth closed"[102]

The most extreme manifestation of Yaba's silencing takes the form of an asymmetrical exchange between her and the Chinese foreign affairs policeman when he accompanies the American colonel to look for Afa's family. And it is in this episode that the narrative foregrounds the importance of listening closely to the muted female subaltern voice. Throughout the section in which the encounter occurs, the narrative clearly follows the policeman's point of view. However, this identification with the representative of state power is disrupted by the encounter with Yaba:

> The policeman and the foreigner . . . meet in the middle of the lane a little girl with a baby strapped onto her back. When they ask her [where Afa's home is], the moment she opens her mouth, the policeman is struck dumb, while the foreigner at his side mutters "Oh, my God!" The little girl turned out to be a mute. The policeman and foreigner have already walked off into a distance but the mute girl is still gesturing and shouting out "Yiyiyaya" as she watches their retreating backs.[103]

A clear break in narrative point of view occurs over the reading and writing of Yaba's voice in this scene. At the end of the encounter, Yaba's voice disrupts the narrative identification with the policeman representing the power of the nation-state. The subsequent account of Yaba's shouts and gestures implicitly questions and counters the policeman's immediate conclusion of Yaba's muteness and consequent inability to tell him the way. It thereby suggests the complicity of the nation-state in practically silencing the female subaltern who, ironically, is most at home with the needed information and most appropriate for showing the way. In other words, the story implies here that had the female subaltern's voice been given due attention, the nation-state could have reached its goal more easily and efficiently.

This point is reinforced later in the story when Yaba shows her ability to communicate with the American using body signs. If her family members and compatriots marginalize her for her inability to speak their languages, her value and worth are demonstrated in her relation to the foreigner who speaks a language totally different from their own. Significantly enough, as in the case of collective labor power, the value of Yaba's repressed and "undeveloped" ability is recognized and strategically appropriated by the American capitalist/imperialist. To demonstrate his benevolence to Afa's family and the civilizing power of the West—or, in the words of the American nun taking care of Afa, "blessings for those who believe in God"—the American colonel offers to send Yaba to be educated in the United States.[104] In the face of such active appropriation of the female subaltern voice by imperialist power, no alternative can be deemed adequate if this voice is excluded.

Importantly, even as Huang's narrative highlights Yaba's possession of a voice and its significance, there is no attempt to interpret and give coherent meaning to her utterance. It is in thus maintaining an irreducible distance from the ultimate figure of the subaltern and her "Yiyiyaya" while registering her ability to speak that the narrative assumes a relation of representation to the subaltern that is more equal and productive than that shown by Wang

Tuo, Chen Yingzhen and other *xiangtu* literature advocates.[105] The refrainment from rendering the subaltern voice coherent and easily interpretable by the intellectual is crucial here not only because it acknowledges the irreducible difference between the intellectual and the subaltern and the former's interested representation of the latter, but also because it leaves space for the intellectual critique of ideological subject constitution within national state formation and the neocolonial regime of political economy even as it affirms the possibility of subaltern resistance. In other words, it takes into account the cultural domination and hegemony of national patriarchy and the crippling effects of the epistemic violence of imperialism, which make impossible any valorization of the subaltern as naturally embodying and giving voice to a just alternative. The existence of cultural domination and hegemony also means that a coherent and intelligible speech issuing from a subaltern in an intellectual text is, in fact, the language of the dominant culture speaking her and her interests. Marking the voice of the subaltern as unintelligible babble, as "Yiyiyaya," enables the intellectual text to acknowledge the possibility of subaltern resistance without underestimating ideological subject constitution under imperialism and patriarchy, as well as the intellectual's own responsibility and limitation in cultural critiques. A truly enabling alternative to neocolonial modernity, then, literally lies outside the boundary of intellectual representation. It can only emerge through active engagement in collective struggles and critical dialogues where the subaltern "Yiyiyaya" is given as much weight as the dominant language.

PLACING THE NATIVE IN POST/MODERN CRITIQUE

In its commonality and diversity, Taiwan's nativist discourse of the 1970s inhabits a post/modern liminality that turned out to be transitory in its sociocultural specificity. While the advance of global capitalism has set the stage for the human dramas of migration and dislocation, exploitation and oppression depicted in the *xiangtu* fictions, as well as fostered the development of critical consciousness among the nativist advocates, the language and discursive framework in which this critical consciousness was expressed and presented still revolve around modernity, especially the dual concerns of class inequality and national dependence under imperialism and neocolonialism. Discursively, of course, the 1970s had yet to see the concepts of postmodernism and postmodernity mustering the hegemonic power needed to travel out of the West to influence critical thinking in Taiwan and elsewhere in the third world. Experientially, at that historical moment, Taiwan's participation in global capitalism still kept it at or near the bottom rung of the economic hierarchy, with its workers bearing the brunt of capitalist exploitation and oppression that made the exploits of imperialism and neocolonialism a fitting diagnosis of the ills of the island-state. By the 1980s, however, Taiwan has managed to achieve the often elusive goal of "economic development" and found itself emerging on the other side of the capital-labor relationship. With this transformation and the importation of postmodern thoughts, the critique of imperialism and neocolonialism that featured so prominently in the nativist discourse of the 1970s became displaced by a playful postmodern celebration of consumer culture and identity politics that was in part spurred by the economic power wielded by the Taiwanese entrepreneurs and businessmen who had capitalized on Taiwan's integration into global capitalism. The historical conjuncture marked by the intersection of global postmodernity and local modernity that nurtured the rise of *xiangtu* nativism on the island-state has clearly come to pass.

Capturing the struggles of this transitory historical moment, *xiangtu* nativism straddles the common divide between modernity and postmodernity in its diverse construction of a native alternative to Western-imported and oriented modernity. As previously detailed, while the *xiangtu* writers were generally motivated by the interlocking concerns of nationalist resistance to Western imperialist incursions and class opposition to inequality and social injustice, their actual realizations of a native alternative in particular fictional works differ significantly. Nonetheless, above all the differences, their nativist discourse arguably shows an affinity with postmodern attention to situatedness and contextual embeddedness in seriously grounding their different conceptions of the native in a specific place, as opposed to the modern focus on the passage of time and the ephemerality of human attachments. Whether it is the airline office in which Xiaolin works, or the fishing village where Jinshuishen lives out her real-life incarnation of the Mother-goddess Mazu, or the imperialist locus of power in the capital Taipei where Afa finds his luck, the cultural criticism and construction of native alternatives in the fictional works are anchored in a meticulously delineated place. Furthermore, this place is not only a concrete environment in which ordinary folks carry out their daily activities, but also a figurative representation of the historically specific Taiwan, whether identified as a nation or not. Significantly, it is not so much the particular geographical or physical location, such as Jinshuishen's fishing village near the city of Jilong, as the embedded social relations that define and delineate this place standing in for Taiwan; and it is precisely the representativeness and general resonance of these social relations that establish and reinforce the correspondence between the place and Taiwan. In other words, it is Doreen Massey's elaboration of the meaning of place as an intricate set of ever-changing, evolving social relations discussed in the last chapter that best explicates the nature of the native-place (xiangtu) as a ground of alternative social and cultural constructions in the nativist discourse of Taiwan's *xiangtu* literature in the 1970s. The native configured in particular *xiangtu* stories is correspondingly a particular embodiment of social relations. Whether and how this particular embodiment of social relations acknowledges and allows for a multitude of differences in its constitution, and/or reproduces dominant social structures and hierarchies are key to determining the oppositional significance of the native alternative expounded in a particular work, and its ultimate position in the spectrum of post/modern cultural critiques.

Given the propensity of Taiwan's *xiangtu* writers and advocates to subscribe to a discursive framework of superimposed nationalist resistance against Western domination and class opposition to social inequality, the native alternatives advanced in most *xiangtu* works end up, unsurprisingly, reproducing hegemonic binary oppositions characteristics of modernity, despite the possibilities of reimagining and restructuring social relations into more open and egalitarian interactions. Wang Zhenhe's story, as we have seen, reproduces essentialized differences between manual and nonmanual labor as well as reinscribes and legitimizes traditional gender norms and hierarchy in its exclusionary investment of the native in a patriarchal moral order embodied by the benevolent working-class father. Similarly, Wang Tuo's affirmation of the sacrificing mother as the virtuous locus of the native alternative to a modernity driven by materialistic consumption and greed reproduces and endorses the gender norms and hierarchy of the patriarchal tradition. It also reinforces a feminization of the ills of modernity that leaves the exploitative class relations of capitalist modernity unchallenged even as the story displaces class oppositions and struggles into gender-coded conflicts between generations within the family. Of the three nativist works analyzed in this chapter, only Huang Chunming's story advances a conception of the native that is expansive, open, and attuned to multiple differences. In (re)presenting the native as a shifting figure of marginality and subalternity at the intersections of multiple axes of power, of which the deaf-mute daughter of a dislocated and crippled subproletariat is but the most poignant place-marker, Huang's story actualizes a nativist vision that is akin to the postmodernist turn to differences to critique and reenvision modernity. Marking the discursive site of marginality as a position of critique, this "postmodernist" inflection of the native predating the codification and institutionalization of postmodernism opens up the possibilities of an alternative modernity that is actively shaped and reshaped by critical discussions and engagements with historical realities involving the silenced no less than intellectuals and social critics. Though this native position is thus not fixed, it is nonetheless firmly situated in a specific place delineated by particular social practices, nexus of social relations, and concrete historical realizations of post/modernity, as well as circumscribed by the differentially marginalized voices to which the society must learn to listen as it collectively strives for a more just and inclusive future. In such a native the best hopes of Taiwan's nativist discourse of the 1970s once lay.

CHAPTER THREE

Beyond the Reach of Roots

Marginality, Masculinity, and *Xungen* Nativism in the People's Republic of China

Nativist Discourse, Cultural Tradition, and China's Quest for Modernity

Inasmuch as an invocation of the native presupposes an awareness of the foreign or the other, without which an identification of the native makes no sense, nativist discourses, almost by definition, emerge and flourish in conditions where contact with the outside world is intensified and the boundaries between the indigenous and the extraneous become highly porous and unstable. As an attempt to reshape and renegotiate boundaries in the face of foreign encroachment, in other words, nativism emerges and thrives in moments of perceived crisis in collective identity. Taiwan in the 1970s constituted such a moment, with the plight of imminent national delegitimation radicalizing intellectual elites and politicizing problems of social inequity and commodification that had been aggravated by a Western-dominated and oriented economic development, thus effecting an oppositional articulation of nativism. China in the mid-1980s presented a comparable but contrasting moment. The sense of crisis in this case was not triggered by a palpable threat to national survival in the international political arena dominated by Western capitalist powers. Rather, it arose from a widespread alarm at the "backwardness" of the nation and the urgency of catching up with postmodernity under Western capitalist hegemony, even as the value of traditional Chinese culture in post/modernity was celebrated in some, notably diasporic, circles with reference to the phenomenal success of the East Asian "little dragons" in blending Confucian values with capitalist development, as noted in chapter one. Consequently, whereas the *xiangtu* nativism that developed in response to the perceived crisis in Taiwan embodies a strong resistance to Western power and influences through an affirmation of native culture, the nativist discourse circulating in China in the 1980s maintains an intense ambivalence toward a recovery of traditional culture to establish the nation's place in post/modernity. This ambivalence is reflected in the foregrounding of a constitutive search (*xun*) in the rubric "*xungen wenxue*" (root-seeking literature), under which writers and intellectuals practiced and debated nativism and its role in the construction of Chinese modernity in the mid-1980s. With an onus on a process of seeking, *xungen* nativism betrays a wariness toward established traditions and a rejection of readily available native grounds, even as it asserts the importance of a native cultural grounding. This ambivalence fundamentally affects the tenor of the nativist claim and its possibility of positing an alternative ground for imagining and constructing modernity.

Like most cultural phenomena in the contemporary age of transnational movements and global connectedness, this ambivalence can be situated in and understood in terms of a complex interaction between Western-dominated global trends and national cultural dynamics. Globally, the value and significance of recovering cultural roots and reclaiming particular traditions found new affirmation in the 1980s, as postmodernism consolidated in the West and traveled worldwide as the cultural paradigm of the day. With their demystification of universalism and celebration of difference and plurality, postmodern theories and practices make space for the assertion of cultural distinctiveness and the imagination of locally specific articulations of modernity. Though postmodernism was but one of many Western theories and "language games" imported in a rush into China during this time and not particularly influential in itself, its decentering disposition toward difference had rather significant effects on discussions of Chinese modernity through the mediation of writings and debates on the "miraculous" East Asian successes under global capitalism, especially the Oriental version of the Pacific Rim discourse.[1]

As explained in chapter one, the exceptional economic growth achieved by the East Asian "newly industrializing countries" of Taiwan, Singapore, Hong Kong, and South Korea prompted a discursive revision of the relation between capitalist development and the East Asian region. While the Euro-American articulation of the Pacific Rim discourse celebrates the dynamism of capitalist advances in the region, the Oriental elaboration of this Pacific Rim dynamism accentuates the cultural contribution of a shared (neo)Confucian tradition. Mediated through the trans-Pacific valorization of a culturally inflected East Asian model of development that productively mobilizes (neo)Confucian traditions to further capitalist growth, the global atmosphere of a postmodern turn toward difference nourished a hope long-cherished among Chinese intellectuals of both retaining a distinctive cultural tradition and achieving modernity, or, in other words, the possibility of a modernity that is not strictly identified with, or a replicate of, the Western capitalist model. Ironically, even as it spurred renewed interests in diverse cultural traditions, the Western-inspired and originated postmodern vision also moderated the perceived threat of loss of identity and cultural distinctiveness in the pursuit of modernity that typically motivates nativist identification of Westernization as the ill of modernity visited upon "developing" countries, such as that observed in Taiwan's *xiangtu* nativism. With the discursive affirmation of the possibility of realizing a modernity congenial to and accommodating of national cultural traditions, cultural resistance to Western modernity is in effect attenuated and the holding power of traditional culture derived from such resistance paradoxically wanes. In other words, the global postmodern incorporation of difference also breeds a certain cultural indifference that erodes the claim and hold of tradition.

Concomitant and interacting with this global postmodern tension, national dynamics and social conditions within China also fostered an ambivalent position of renewed interests in yet reservation toward a revival of traditional culture among the intelligentsia in the 1980s. Throughout the years of socialist rule, traditional culture, particularly Confucianism understood as the ideological expression of feudalism, has been denigrated and blamed for the nation's backwardness and weakness vis-à-vis the West, though it was also preserved as a sign of Chinese national identity precisely in signifying a condemned past.[2] With the postsocialist regime's redirection toward a market-oriented construction of Chinese modernity, such complete negation of traditional culture and the value of its continuation in modernity became untimely and major reconsiderations were called for. While partially spurred by the trans-Pacific celebration of a communitarian capitalism based on neo-Confucian ethic, in which China also participated tangentially through semi official sponsorship of conferences that explored the relation between modernization and Confucianism/East Asian cultural tradition, the reconsideration was driven above all by the postsocialist regime's legitimation crisis. Having repudiated the Maoist emphasis on class struggle and self-reliance in economic development, the postsocialist regime under the leadership of Deng Xiaoping needed a different ideological ground to legitimate its own modernization program, which focused on the importation of science and technology and the advancement of "open-door" policies to attract capital investment and facilitate China's reentry into the global capitalist system. The identity problem generated in such a foreign-facing course of modernization made nationalism almost a necessary recourse for legitimation purposes. The Deng regime's official goal of building "socialism with Chinese characteristics" testifies to such nationalist appeal. Depleted of the substantive contents of socialism, this ideological vision of a different modernity has to lean heavily on the part of national characteristics for justification, channeling renewed attention to cultural traditions that can confer a distinctive national identity while actively engaging with multinational capitalism in post/modernity.

If the postsocialist modernization project thus fostered a revival of (interests in) traditional culture, the materiality of the modernization program itself paradoxically undermined such a revival. The institution of "open-door" policies to attract foreign capital and technology brought China face-to-face with the postmodern West for the first time after decades of isolation. The encounter left the Chinese people, especially the intelligentsia, with a deep impression of their country's "backwardness." The recognition of an enormous gap in material, technological, and even cultural achievements between China and the West made imperative and urgent a comprehensive project of "modernization" that cannot leave traditional culture untouched.

As Maurice Meisner argues in his study of China under the Deng regime, though the open-door policies have not led to a historical repetition of the loss of national autonomy, there was nonetheless a significant erosion of national self-confidence.[3] This was manifested in an acute anxiety that began to surface in China in the mid-1980s, precipitating a general perception that "China was unquestionably beset with crises, with more and more dangers cropping up all the time."[4] Adding to the anxiety were signs of faltering in the state project of modernization launched just a few years ago. By that time, economic growth has markedly stalled after the initial spectacular success of the agricultural reforms, and the difficulty and cost of "reforming" the urban economy and its industrial enterprises to compete in a globalized market have begun to sink in. Most alarmingly, the mirage of economic boom projected by the special economic zones (SEZs), especially Shenzhen, the showcase of the postsocialist regime's open-door policies, has also vanished into thin air. Rather than the much-heralded channels of advanced technology and capital to the country, they were exposed to be illegal entrepots for foreign consumer goods and hotbeds for corruption, severely draining the country's limited capital for productive investment.[5] The burst of the SEZ bubble unleashed a general disillusionment and heightened public awareness of the exaggerated promise, adverse effects, and abuse of power that have accompanied the modernization efforts, even as it made clear the full extent of China's "backwardness." Becoming apparent at the same time were the implications of "market reforms" for urban everyday lives. With their emphasis on enterprise profitability, the creation of a free labor market through the elimination of job security in state enterprises, and the relaxation of price control, the "reforms" resulted in rampant inflation and growing inequality that turned daily lives into a struggle of survival for the average urbanite. To most people, the promises of modernity seemed more remote and the need for change more urgent than ever before, even as the government's charted course of modernization became questionable.

The unsettling recognition of the immensity of China's lag behind Western postmodernity and the urgency of the slippery project of modernization created among the urban intelligentsia a pervasive sense of crisis that made impossible any unreserved affirmation of the value of traditional culture in forging a Chinese modernity. And yet, as noted earlier, there were overlapping global interests, regional drives, and state efforts to assert national distinction and maintain cultural traditions under postmodern capitalist development. Pulled in different directions by the nationalist claim to cultural identity complementing a postmodern global capitalization of local differences on the one hand, and a national obsession with a perceived lack vis-à-vis the West on the other, intellectuals in China responded with an intense exploration of Western and Chinese cultures in relation to modernity. In the fervent cultural discussion (*wenhua taolun*), advocates of Western scientific knowledge vied with champions of various forms of critical reflection on Chinese cultural traditions, especially Confucianism, to make sense of and articulate "Chinese" modernity. Given the pervasive sense of national crisis, however, even calls for a renewed embrace of traditional culture suppressed under socialism could hardly dismiss Western cultural power and espouse a straightforward revival of traditions, as the priority given to the process of searching in *xungen* nativism makes clear. An underlying ambivalence toward traditional culture was readily discernible, though also easily overlooked.

Under the assumption of Chinese backwardness, the imperative to push ahead with modernization and catch up with the capitalist powers spurred an eager importation of much beyond capital and technology from the Western powers. Translation and introduction of Western works encompassing the whole range of sciences, social sciences and humanities saw remarkable increases in the 1980s.[6] Amid such keenness for Western theory and knowledge, nativism can easily be, and has indeed been positioned by its critics as a conservative return to the national cultural tradition in opposition to Western cultural importation. As the above discussion suggests, however, to argue this is to underestimate the hegemonic power of Western modernity and its discourses in a country shaken to its core by a sudden contact with Western technological and material sophistication after decades of relative insulation, or, in other words, to overemphasize the staying power of cultural traditions under the relentless bombardment of economic and technological forces. Such an argument also neglects the strong string of iconoclasm threading through modern Chinese history, from the overture of the May Fourth Movement to the Maoist crescendo of the Cultural Revolution. Indeed, such an interpretation of nativism reinscribes a simple opposition between Chinese tradition and Western modernity, overlooking the complexity of cultural politics crisscrossing the issue of tradition in contemporary China.

Just as the advocacy of nativism does not necessarily entail a full endorsement of traditional culture, the apparently opposite line of espousing Westernization may go hand in hand with a selective continuation of Chinese cultural traditions. As Jing Wang shows in her discussion of the writings of Jin Guantao and Gan Yang, two prominent enthusiasts for Western knowledge, an active incorporation of Western theory and methodology does not preclude implicit ideological references to national cultural traditions.[7] Gan Yang's deliberately provocative formulation that "going against tradition is the most powerful way of inheriting and promoting tradition" perhaps best illustrates the malleability of the notion of tradition in discussions of Chinese modernity and its relation to hegemonic constructions of (Western) modernity in the 1980s.[8] Indeed, woven into an intricate web of China's socioeconomic connection to and cultural reception of (post)modernity in the Euro-American center, evocations of cultural traditions can be found across ideological and political inclinations and alignments in various discourses of modernity besides nativism. Different conceptions of tradition in these discourses arguably suggest different resolutions of the tension between the imperative to modernize and the belief in the unexhausted glory of native/national cultural traditions as a source of identity and distinction in post/modernity. In short, a renewed interest in cultural traditions concomitant with an avid importation of Western knowledge and culture constituted the discursive backdrop rather than the definitive feature of nativism in China under the "open-door" pursuit of modernity.

The intense and far-reaching discussion of Chinese cultural traditions engaged not only academics and intellectuals but also the public media in the mid-1980s, just as nativism emerged prominently in the literary scene under the rubric of *xungen* (search for roots). There was such fervor for East–West comparison and related debates on Chinese cultural traditions, especially their relevance to and effects on the construction of a "Chinese" modernity, that the phenomenon came to be known as the "Culture Fever" (*wenhuare*). Flourishing simultaneously and sharing discursive space with the Culture Fever debates, *xungen* nativism has often been associated with and even credited for inspiring and igniting the fever. Yet, it is arguable that the general correspondence in timing, orientation, and concerns between the two, while significant in illuminating the discursive focus and limits of the time, can be quite misleading when it comes to the specific interventions the two sought and achieved. Like the common conflation of nativism into nationalism, subsuming *xungen* nativism into the call for revival of cultural tradition in the Culture Fever risks eliding its local emphasis and distinctive oppositional possibilities. Admittedly, both privilege traditional culture(s) in their rumination on the problem and prospect of modernity in China, but the evocation of literary/cultural roots in *xungen* nativism and the revival of interests in the national cultural tradition in the Culture Fever differ significantly in their conceptions of traditional culture(s) and consequently their relations to the state's vision of modernity. Focusing largely on the dominant tradition of Confucianism and a venerable Confucian-Daoist amalgamation long accepted into the canon, advocates of a renewal of traditional culture in the Culture Fever aligned rather neatly, though perhaps not intentionally, with the state's ideological valorization of China as a nation with a rich civilization and culture that can be selectively revived to distinguish the nation in post/modernity. In contrast, the *xungen* proponents were significantly less enamored of and confined to the boundaries of a hegemonic cultural tradition and the nation it underwrites. Though often related to a national imagination, the native or "root" that the *xungen* writers actively sought and evoked in their fictions is not automatically mapped onto the nation. Rather, as will become clear in detailed discussions later, "root" is commonly associated with marginalized places in the nation's remote hinterland and the ethnicized cultural traditions preserved therein, which are, furthermore, represented and embodied in figures of pronounced masculinity who themselves inhabit positions of marginality in their social milieu. In short, in place of the nation-centered orientation of the Culture Fever, marginality figures centrally in the discursive configuration and ideological investment of *xungen* nativism and its claim on cultural traditions. With this positioning in marginality, *xungen* literature offers an interesting case study of nativism as a self-consciously oppositional discourse on cultural traditions, national identity, and China's modernity. Against the postsocialist regime's open-door policies that privilege coastal areas in its effort to expedite and facilitate articulation with global capitalism, *xungen* literature's deliberate focus on the remote hinterland and its "archaic" folk culture suggests an implicit critique of the state's modernization project, if not its ends, at least its course and priorities. What underlies and motivates this focus on exoticized, ethnicized places as a critical discursive locus? How does *xungen* nativism construct the masculinized figure of native root on the ground of marginality? How does it mobilize this figure to implicitly critique the official discourse and project of modernity and posit an alternative foundation for imagining and configuring modernity in China? What are the limits, limitations, and gender politics of such a strategy? These are the main concerns of the following discussion. Given their similar concerns but misleading associations, however, a discussion of the (re)turn to national cultural tradition in the Culture Fever first will help to draw out the specificity and import of *xungen* nativism as a critical response to the Chinese state discourse of modernity and the condition of post/modernity in China during the 1980s.

CULTURALISM, IDEOLOGICAL COMPLICITY, AND THE DISCUSSION OF TRADITION IN THE CULTURE FEVER

Renewed interests in traditional Chinese culture and its difference from the Western tradition in the Culture Fever can largely be seen as a "high" cultural response to the problems inherent in China's obsessive "modernization."[9] In the words of Li Zehou, a Marxist philosopher whose works were highly influential during the period, the Culture Fever emerged in a new wave of "learning from the West" as China awakened from the delusional dream of being the "revolutionary beacon for people around the world" under "the highest and most vibrant Marxism," and became painfully aware of its own "backwardness."[10] Though the Culture Fever thus presupposed China's lack and lag, and reflected the state's dominant rhetoric of modernization as a national imperative and goal, the keenness to propel China forward did not preclude a simultaneous advancement of traditional Chinese culture as a privileged site of national distinction and even "advantage" over the West by some active participants in the cultural discussion. Indeed, much of the debate in the Culture Fever flared precisely around the questions of where and how traditional Chinese culture fits in post/modernity. While few in China shared the "New Confucian" confidence in the eventual triumph of Chinese (Confucian) cultural tradition in the global stage of postmodernity projected by Tu Wei-ming and other diasporic academics, the idea that traditional Chinese culture may yet play a significant role not only in "Chinese" modernity, but also globally as a kind of Oriental supplement to Western domination in modernity excited the imagination of many involved in the cultural debate.[11] Thus, a productive tension between accepting the imperative to modernize and believing in the unexhausted glory of Chinese traditional culture marked the discussions of national heritage in the Culture Fever.

In characterizing this tension as productive, I want to draw attention to its departure from the familiar modern paradigm of opposing national traditions to modernization, which implicitly equates modernization with Westernization. Rather than a diametrical, exclusive construction of Western modernity and Chinese tradition, the Culture Fever showed a conscious effort to render more complex the relation between modernization and Westernization and to affirm the possibility of a modernity that retains some forms of Chinese tradition. It reflected, in other words, a "postmodern" spirit of both-and rather than the dominant modern mode of either-or. If such a spirit generated some excessive claims that led Jing Wang to sarcastically align them with "the epoch's unrelieved contradiction between its conscious promotion of the Great Leap Forward and its simultaneous indulgence in an age-old sinocentric vision that gazes back in nostalgia,"[12] it also produced some thoughtful reconsideration and new formulation of the relation between traditional culture and modernization that merit our attention.

That a spirit of creative retention of traditions in modernity underlies the heightened interest in national cultural tradition during the period of Culture Fever is evident in the work of the state-sponsored but independently run Academy of Chinese Culture (Zhongguo wenhua shuyuan) established in 1984. With the expressed purposes of "continuing and developing the fine tradition of Chinese culture through research and education; and promoting *the modernization of Chinese culture* through the comparative study of Chinese and foreign cultures, as well as the strengthening of cultural and academic exchanges with countries around the world," the academy institutionalized Chinese intellectuals' efforts to rethink the vexing relation between traditions and modernity for present times.[13] Its statement of purpose makes clear that even for those who deemed it critical to maintain national cultural traditions in modernity, the dominant theme was not so much the preservation as "the modernization of Chinese culture." This emphasis on modernization and its relation to the continued value of national cultural traditions is spelled out in the academy director Tang Yijie's introduction to the collection of lectures given in the first "study group on Chinese traditional culture" organized by the academy in March 1985:

> It is necessary to have a clear understanding of Chinese traditional culture. We not only have to understand the positive effects it can have on our modernization so as to facilitate its creative transformation to serve modernization. But also, confronting the challenges of Western culture, a nation should maintain a deep national cultural foundation. This will enable a better assimilation and integration of Western culture coming from outside to construct a modernized culture with national characteristics.[14]

Thus, among Chinese intellectuals in the Deng decade of modernization, the "conservative" impulse of an intellectual (re)turn to tradition was significantly modified by a hegemonic national self-positioning as backward and the corollary imperative to modernize. Under such hegemony, the renewed attention to national cultural traditions in the Culture Fever was often understood and represented in terms of "deepening" the process of modernization from the level of science and technology to the structure of the national cultural psyche (*minzu wenhua xinli jiegou*).[15] Instead of questioning the course of modernization in the name of the past, in other words, Chinese cultural traditions were evoked to broaden the scope of modernization necessary for the purpose of national renewal and advancement. In the sense that it asserts the importance of culture, besides social and economic structures, in the process of modernization, this position could be termed "culturalist" (*wenhuapai*), as it often was during the debates. In adhering to the hegemonic discourse of modernization, the culturalists carved out some discursive space in the politically repressive and ideologically rigid environment to question the state's limitation of modernization to economic development and technological advancement crystallized in the so-called Four Modernizations in agriculture, industry, national defense, and science and technology. Yet, the culturalists' assent to the basic premise of China's "backwardness" also limits their possibility of challenging the state's priorities and goals, especially its enshrinement of the nation and elevation of Western modernity into the yardstick of development. In other words, despite a pronounced will to make their space of enunciation "autonomous" in the era of reform, Chinese intellectuals' culturalist intervention into the discourse of modernity stayed significantly within the bounds of the state modernization program's conceptual framework, thus lending indirect support to state ideological work.[16]

The extent of such complicity can be gauged from the notion of *xiti zhongyong* (Western substance, Chinese function) advanced by Li Zehou, who, among those associated with advocating renewed attention to national cultural traditions, arguably commanded the most respect as a prominent and original thinker. Twisting the idea of *zhongti xiyong* (Chinese substance, Western function) proposed by Zhang Zhidong a century ago to resolve the predicament of learning from the West to ensure the survival of China, Li's notion of *xiti zhongyong* is not so much an inversion of the old idea as a conscientious attempt to reconcile Western-originated Marxism and the historical trajectory it underwrites with the contemporary condition and "reality" of China. That Li defines what he means by Western substance and Chinese function precisely in terms of nationalist modernization bespeaks the hegemony of the state discourse:

> So-called "Western substance" is modernization and Marxism, that is, the noumenon of social existence and the consciousness of such. Although they originated from the West, they constitute the common direction of development for all humankind and the entire world. So-called "Chinese function" refers to the necessity of integrating this Marxism-directed modernization process into the Chinese reality (including the reality of Chinese traditional consciousness) in order for it to come to true fruition. What this means, in other words, is modernization as substance and nationalization as function.[17]

In upholding the universalist claims of Western modernity and maintaining the hegemonic frame of reference, this provocative reformulation of the vexing relation between Chinese tradition and Western modernity that has preoccupied Chinese intellectuals for over a century falls short of a groundbreaking critique. For all its radical coinage, the notion not only retains the two key terms, albeit with somewhat revised contents and a modified relationship, but also affirms the ideological foundation of the postsocialist state's dominant vision of modernity. Though its incorporation of Western culture and thoughts—in the form of Marxism—into what can be considered a revisionist understanding of the Marxist notion of base highlights the necessity of "modernization" at every level of social and cultural existence, including traditional sedimentations in the "deep structure" of the national cultural psyche, its conception of modernity differs little from the state's besides reaching beyond the realms of science, technology, and economics. Particularly, its presumption of the significance of *Chinese* tradition in modernization and the goal of constituting a *Chinese* modernity through the nationalization of Western modernity keeps affirming the primary importance of China-as-a-nation and its cultural distinctiveness from the West. What results is a cultural nationalism that, despite the critical pressure it exerts to broaden the scope of the state's project of modernization, is instrumental to the state's ideological mobilization of national traditions to legitimize its power and rule.

The affinity and amenability of such culturalist argument to the state project of modernization are evident in a similar rhetoric of "critical continuation of tradition" (*chuantong de pipan jicheng*) and "modernization of the people" (*ren de xiandaihua*) found in official documents on cultural and ideological matters. The "Guiding Principles" for constructing a "socialist spiritual civilization" (*shehui zhuyi jingshen wenming*) "to raise the ideological and ethical standards of the whole nation as well as its educational and scientific levels in the interest of socialist modernization," for instance, presents its vision in terms of a Chinese "rejuvenation" (*fuxing*) with modernized traditions:

> For a long period in the history of ancient civilizations, the great Chinese nation with its long history and cultural traditions stood in the front ranks. But in modern times it has lagged behind, because of a decadent feudal system coupled with imperialist aggression. . . . [T]he birth of New China ushered in the rejuvenation of the great Chinese civilization on the basis of socialism. The latest period of our historical development . . . has injected a new, powerful vitality into that rejuvenation. The outcome will be a socialist society that has not only a high material level but also an advanced culture and ideology that takes Marxism as its guide, incorporates the best from historical traditions yet fully embodies the spirit of our time, and bases itself on China's actual conditions yet keep the whole world in view.[18]

This central directive on state ideological work shows a strategic recourse to nationalism and national cultural traditions to defuse challenges to the modernization program from both "conservatives" and "radicals." On the one hand, the nationalistic reference to a rejuvenation of Chinese culture served to appease the "economic adjusters" who, favoring the continued dominance of state planning with limited introduction of market forces into the planned economy, were harshly critical of the implemented market reforms for generating problems of "liberalization" and "spiritual pollution" from Western influences. On the other hand, the rhetoric of a necessary cultural improvement of the "qualities of the people" to effect socialist modernization disarmed the "political reformers" and democracy advocates who sought a much broader scope of modernization than the regime's market reforms, especially in the political and cultural-intellectual spheres. Thus the Deng regime found an expedient use of the culturalist argument on the critical continuation and modernization of national traditions. Whether intended or not, the culturalist argument proved to have significant instrumental value and ideological valence for the dominant official discourse.

Obviously functional is the culturalist argument's underlying nationalism, to which the Deng regime has increasingly turned for legitimation, as evidenced, for instance, in the injunction to "love the fatherland" in the long-running "Three Loves" (*sanreai*) campaign launched in 1982, and the concerted government attempts to increase the "patriotic contents" of cultural and educational activities since 1983. Perhaps less obvious is the convenient deflection of attention from social structural and institutional causes to problems surfacing in the process of modernization that an emphasis on cultural traditions and their sedimentation in the "national cultural psyche" can effect. It is far from coincidental that a concern with the "moral qualities" of the people and the need to "modernize" them was expressed at the highest level of the Party-state precisely when the negative effects of market reforms began to hit people's lives hard in the forms of rampant corruption, soaring inflation, glaring inequality, and blatant bureaucratic nepotism. The moralization of these problems into a matter of below-par qualities of the people in need of modernization served to mask their structural causes in what Maurice Meisner has incisively identified as "bureaucratic capitalism" emerging under the market reform policies.[19] In other words, unable and unwilling to weed out official corruption and nepotism, which were (and still are) functional to the emerging economic system, the Party-state found ideological reprieve in the recourse to national traditions and moral modernization. Indeed, the disparagement of people's objection to growing economic disparity as nothing but a continuation of the traditional morality of peasant egalitarianism fostered by a Maoist "mass canteen" (*daguofan*) mentality was repeated again and again in official publications to dismiss criticisms that the reforms were breeding an outlook of monetary greed.[20] However indirectly and inadvertently, the culturalist arguments in the Culture Fever afforded philosophical legitimation to such state-orchestrated detraction and obscuration of views and sentiments questioning the regime's particular course and vision of modernization.

In the end, the culturalist combination of a critical affirmation and selective recovery of national cultural traditions conveniently served the regime's contradictory needs, enabling it to legitimize its rule and modernization program with a nationalist discourse on the one hand, and displace the problems created in the modernization process onto the moral and cultural deficiencies of the people on the other. The possibility of such ideological use reveals the implicit complicity of the culturalist revival of national traditions in the ideological domination of the state's discourse on modernity.

Xungen Literature in Its Diversity and Oppositionality

Insofar as *xungen* literature partakes in the culturalist revival, its potential complicity in the state's ideological domination is inevitably a cause of concern, especially with regard to its oppositionality. However, it is arguable that *xungen* literature is interesting as a cultural response to the construction of modernity under the Deng regime precisely because it engages in a culturalist recovery of traditions without completely identifying with the nation and nationalism. By virtue of its affirmation of cultural diversity within the nation and attentiveness to the local and, at times, even the personal in configuring the native, *xungen* literature partially circumvents an unreflective association of the native with the national, and thus makes possible a critical interrogation of cultural nationalism. Though it replicates the culturalist displacement of social structural and institutional issues in its critique of modernity, the literary search for roots complicates the question of oppositionality to Western cultural domination and the troubling relation of traditional culture to modernity by decentering "national" cultural traditions and calling attention to marginalized, ethnic cultural roots. Thus, as I will argue, it advances a sense of the native that enables it to resist a straightforward identification with China-as-a-nation and question the state's discourse of modernity and traditional culture. Therein also lies its keenest potential of oppositionality.

Arguably because of the dominance of the realism-versus-modernism debate in the Chinese literary circle during the 1980s, Western studies of *xungen* literature tend to discuss it primarily in terms of modernist aesthetics.[21] To the extent that critical attention is given to the literature's focus on culture, the culture is often taken, without question, to be Chinese *national* culture.[22] The picture gleaned from Chinese discussions of the literature, however, is far more complex.

Xungen made its prominent appearance in the Chinese literary scene in 1985, when the writer Han Shaogong published an article entitled "Wenxue de 'gen'" (The "roots" of literature), arguing the vital importance of "rooting" literature in a recovery of national traditional culture (*minzu chuantong wenhua*) so that

China will maintain a distinctive cultural identity in modernity.[23] This intense but rather confusing article soon became recognized as a de facto "manifesto" for a nativist literature in the name of *xungen*, and the idea of searching for roots quickly caught on in the literary circle. As is to be expected with its rapid and heated reception, the notion of *xungen* was made to include a wide spectrum of ideas and practices. Rather than a clearly defined "movement" with particular, shared characteristics, in other words, *xungen* was more of an umbrella term for a series of concerns about literary writing and its relation to culture, identity, locality, modernity, and the nation at a time of tremendous societal changes and escalating interaction with the world under global capitalism.

Indeed, writers and critics have differed significantly in what they perceive and include as *xungen* literature. From works that redeploy the aesthetics of traditional Chinese literature to those that explore the cultural and psychological makeups of characters living in rural villages, and even stories that dwell on urbanites' travel to "primitive" communities in search of personal renewal and vitality, a wide range of fictional narratives have been discussed in terms of the search for roots.[24] Of the writers and works that form the "core" of *xungen* nativism in many discussions, however, most are distinctly associated with a specific region in the rural hinterland and its historically significant "ethnic" culture: Han Shaogong with "Chu culture" in the Xiangsi area; Jia Pingwa with "Qin-Han culture" in the Shangzhou area; Li Hangyu with "Wu-Yue culture" in the Gechuanjiang (a fictional rendition of the Qiantangjiang) area in Zhejiang province. Two other writers often considered central to *xungen* literature, A Cheng and Zheng Wanlong, depart from this with telling characteristics. A Cheng's works are not regionally marked, but are often included as a kind of root-seeking literature because of their strong evocation of Daoist philosophy and aesthetics, and probably also because A Cheng has published an article arguing the importance of culture in constituting national subjects and literature at the beginning of the call to search for roots.[25] In contrast, Zheng Wanlong's *xungen* works are not "rooted" in any particular recognized cultural traditions, but in a distinctive border region of the Heilongjiang province with a mixed Han and Oloqen population. The inclusion of these two writers in *xungen* literature dramatizes the tension between an affirmation of national traditions and an emphasis on regional ethnic culture, and, relatedly, the indeterminate locus of marginality that divides the literature's reception and critical evaluation. To those who were inclined toward a nationalistic reading of *xungen* nativism, A Cheng's creative revival of Daoism shares the same impetus of reconnecting Chinese culture with traditions that have been broken off, marginalized, and suppressed historically as Han's reclamation of Chu culture or Li's recovery of Wu-Yue culture. To those whose attention was drawn to the strong "regional colors" and the focus on local cultures of marginalized hinterlands in *xungen* works,

Zheng Wanlong's imaginative (re)turn to his border hometown resonates with the efforts of Han, Li, and Jia to excavate the cultural endowment of their respective native soils. If the former assessment tends to highlight the aesthetic and philosophical aspects of the revival of tradition in *xungen* literature to cover (over) its regional and ethnic diversity, the latter leans toward emphasizing the substance and content of root-seeking, particularly its affinity for rustic social lives and local customs.[26] Relatedly, if the former invariably affirms and approves the return to Chinese traditions by way of aesthetics, the latter maintains variously critical attitudes toward the possibility and desirability of continuing rustic cultures in modernity.[27] Between these interpretations, the core *xungen* advocates themselves sometimes vacillate, resulting in some gaping discrepancies between their "theoretical" proclamations and actual practices.

One of the most salient issues emerging from the bulk of Chinese critical discussions on *xungen* literature are thus the competing claims of regional ethnic culture and national culture as "roots." It is perhaps testimony to the strength of nationalism in contemporary China that the nation is more often taken to be the ultimate locus of roots. Whether couched in obliquely or directly critical terms, many critics have denigrated as extreme and deviant any inclination to associate *xungen* with "specific regional cultures,"[28] "old, relatively stable, and even primitive and backward social lives,"[29] "social manners, mores, and customs in border areas and exotic lands,"[30] or "admiration for the old and folk-popular."[31] The "proper" impetus of the search for cultural roots is then reterritorialized to the "strengthening of national cultural consciousness" (*minzu wenhua yishi de jianghua*) within the dynamics of concrete contemporary social life. Alternatively, critics have sought to neutralize the implicit challenge that an emphasis on regional ethnic culture poses to the idea of a national culture by characterizing national Chinese culture as "pluralistic" (*duoyuan*),[32] or constituted through an "open mechanism" (*kaifang de jizhi*) that readily takes in and integrates different cultural elements.[33] The regularity and consistency of such attempts to dismiss the regional and ethnic emphasis of *xungen* or to rationalize it into conformity with the idea of national culture, ironically, help to accentuate the critical importance and potential oppositionality of the reference to the regional and ethnic in *xungen* nativism.

Given the nationalist proclivity of the culturalist arguments in the Culture Fever, these critical efforts to realign *xungen* nativism with a recovery of traditional national culture are quite understandable, if not entirely convincing. More important for the purpose of my discussion, it is precisely against this nationalist backdrop that the references and even tributes contemporaneous *xungen* nativism made to regional ethnic cultures marginalized from the geopolitical and cultural center of the Chinese nation merit special attention.[34]

For they effect a decentering of the Chinese nation and a critical interrogation of traditional national culture that distinguishes *xungen* nativism from the complicitous nationalism of the culturalists. As such, they also make possible a different, more critical, relation to the state project of nationalist modernization and its underlying vision of modernity.

XUNGEN NATIVISM, REGIONAL ETHNIC CULTURES, AND MASCULINE SUBJECTIVITY

It needs to be noted that in line with the constitutive stress on searching, the *xungen* advocates never put forward a theoretically cogent notion of "roots." Nor did they offer rigorous arguments on the relation of "roots" to either national culture or regional ethnic cultures. Their vagueness and ambiguity, indeed, contributed to the conflicting critical interpretations of the search for roots discussed above. Nonetheless, inasmuch as core *xungen* writers tend to focus on regions historically associated with particular cultural heritages and highlight their differences from the normative Confucianism that characterizes Chinese "national" tradition, the "roots" being searched for in *xungen* nativism can be understood as intimately tied to a diffuse notion of regional ethnic cultures that relates to the idea of traditional national culture in various ways.

To speak of regional ethnic cultures among the Han Chinese is, of course, deeply controversial. The received understanding of ethnicity codified in the "nationality" policies of all the different, successive state administrations of modern China is that the Han Chinese constitute a single ethnicity/nationality, making up the majority of the Chinese "nation," which is a multinationality entity encompassing Han and certain "minority nationalities."[25] Underlying this view is a conceptual equation of ethnicity and nationality that is consolidated in language. There is no distinction between nationality and ethnicity in Chinese vocabulary. The term *minzu* is used to cover all the different meanings of nation, nationality, and ethnic group, while the English word "ethnic" is often translated as the equivalent of race, *zhongzu*.[36] This linguistic conflation of nation, nationality, and ethnicity has enormous political significance in the development of nationalism in modern China, as Dru Gladney suggests in his account of the historical emergence of the term *minzu* at the turn of the century to forge a Han-Chinese nationalism against the Manchu imperial court and the foreign powers threatening to divide and colonize China.[37] In the interest of political unity against imperialism, such a notion of *minzu* essentially compresses ethnic identities among culturally diverse peoples constituting (orally) different Sinitic linguistic communities in different regions within China and congeals them into a huge nationality group under the name of Han. On account of its overwhelming majority, Han easily becomes synonymous with Chinese, relegating the "minority nationalities" to the anonymity of secondary nationals.[38] Thus fabricated, the Han *minzu* becomes what Etienne Balibar calls a "fictive ethnicity" that naturalizes the community instituted in the modern nation-state.[39] Cultural and linguistic differences among the Han Chinese are duly displaced from public discourses of nationality/ethnicity, while an orthodoxy of Han culture is revered or criticized as *the Chinese* cultural tradition.

Given the unabated importance of this Han-Chinese nationalism throughout the twentieth century, ethnic differences among the Han have remained unnamable and unrecognized as such in public discourses. Its hegemonic effect is so pervasive that the ethnic makeup of the so-called Han nationality stays largely unexplored not only in China but also in Western studies of China. The fact that the only book-length study of cultural diversity among the Han Chinese in English categorizes the various languages and cultures making up the "Chinese mosaic" as "*sub*languages" and "*sub*ethnic" cultures testifies to the extent of this discursive repression of ethnic differences among the Han.[40]

Against such silences and the increased ideological reliance on Chinese nationalism under the postsocialist regime of modernization, the effort to revive historically suppressed regional cultures, such as Chu and Wu-Yue cultures, as "roots" in *xungen* literature takes on the import of a (re)turn to "ethnic" cultural identification, though it may not be openly named as such. Rather than simply an assertion of regional culture and cultural identity, in other words, it assumes the significance of an ethnic identification. As the critic Qian Liqun argues, *xungen* literature differs from previous "nativist literature" (*xiangtu wenxue*) in that it goes beyond the rendition of regional color and culture to "self-consciously seek a kind of cultural consciousness and philosophical consciousness."[41] This self-conscious effort implies an ethnic identification foremost in the sense that underlying the *xungen* advocates' evocation of distinctive regional cultures is an attempt at boundary making, culturally distinguishing "natives" of the particular regions from the dominant construct of Han Chineseness. This boundary making, furthermore, is naturalized through the trope of "roots" with its implication of natural origin, biological connection, and contiguous growth. It is thus invested with the sentiments and emotive force and intensity of primordial attachment, making the cultural identification "ethnic" in the additional sense that the culture with which the *xungen* writer identifies is deemed naturally his own by descent.[42] It is noteworthy that whether actual bloodlines and lineages are involved or not is immaterial here, for the weight of this ethnic identification lies precisely in the realm of the symbolic and emotive.

Such ethnic identification is, of course, not necessarily opposed to the nationalist project of modernization. As Prasenjit Duara shows in the case of late nineteenth-century Chinese intellectual mobilization of provincial traditions and consolidation of provincial cultural boundaries to build an alternative political identity to challenge the existing state and its conception of the nation and its future, those who insist on strong local ties and identification with regional traditions can also be simultaneously nationalistic, embracing a notion of the nation that is inflected with their local identifications.[43] More particularly, not every *xungen* advocate and text emphasizes regional ethnic identification in opposition to national identity. At best, regional ethnic identification operates in tension with the hegemonic discourse of nationalism. Indeed, as will be argued, some *xungen* works fall into the culturalist mode of elucidating the need to modernize traditional culture(s) to facilitate the state's project of nationalist development. However, insofar as *xungen* nativism constitutes a critical response to the state's project of modernization, its distinctiveness clearly lies in the ethnic identification of and with regional cultures as "roots," and the implicit problematization of the state's discourse of nationalism that such identification affords. For this reason, my analysis will focus on how regional ethnic identification enables *xungen* nativism to interrogate the state's project of modernization and in what ways it remains complicit with the dominant ideology and vision of modernity.

It needs to be stressed that the critical potential of *xungen* nativism's focus on regional ethnic identification in problematizing and displacing the state's discourse of nationalism lies in its positing marginalized ethnic cultures within the Han majority nationality. Where *xungen* nativism includes the cultures of minority nationalities in its representation of regional ethnic cultures and affirms their values particularly in terms of preserving the energy, vitality, and authenticity of primitive cultures, as in Han Shaogong's "*xungen* manifesto" and Zheng Wanlong's fictional pieces on Oloqens in the border region of Heilongjiang (to be discussed), the hegemonic conception of the multiethnic and multicultural Chinese nation underlying the dominant discourse of nationalism is confirmed rather than questioned. Officially, China is made up of fifty-five minority nationalities in addition to the majority nationality of the Han. Far from undermining the idea of a unified Chinese nation, the incorporation of the minority nationalities and their diverse cultures into this hegemonic conception of China serves to highlight its cultural richness and consolidate the putative unity and cultural dominance of the Han, not to say maintain the vast territory of China as a nation-state. The inclusion of ethnic minorities who are obviously different in language, customs, and traditions helps to constitute and unify the Han majority nationality by deemphasizing and desensitizing awareness of "internal" differences among the Han. The representation and positioning of the minority nationalities as "primitive" and "backward" further helps to elevate the Han and affirms their self-image as "advanced" and "civilized," leading the minorities on the road toward progress and development. Under the postsocialist regime's continued evocation of a Marxist teleology of development to justify its nationalist project of modernization, such representation accentuates the legitimacy of Han cultural dominance in a unified Chinese nation-state. Insofar as *xungen* nativism celebrates ethnic minority cultures for their primitive energy and naïve vitality, it partakes in and maintains the appropriative inclusiveness of such hegemonic Chinese nationalism.

Yet, if *xungen* nativism's inclusion of minority cultures in its conception of regional ethnic cultures inadvertently reaffirms the ideological structure of a Han-dominated Chinese nation, its evocation of regional ethnic cultures among the Han nonetheless poses a challenge to the hegemonic construct of nationalism sustained by the "myth" of an ethnically homogeneous Han nationality with a great cultural tradition, on which, as previously observed, the postsocialist Party-state has become dependent for legitimation. In conjunction with this challenge, *xungen* nativism's revival of regional ethnic culture and identification critically engages the dominant discourse of modernity by highlighting the significance of place, which tends to be effaced by the universalist temporality of progress maintained in the idea of modernization.[44] In contrast to the "global imaginary of identity" underlying the universalist temporality of modernization, a focus on place underscores differences and the unevenness of historical development, thus bringing forth issues of domination and marginalization in the spatiotemporal configuration of the nation-in-modernity.[45] The attention to regional ethnic culture in *xungen* nativism, then, serves to question not only the temporal schema of universal, linear progress in the official discourse of modernization (a challenge negatively confirmed in criticisms of *xungen* literature's obsession with primitivism), but also the center-periphery hierarchy maintained by such universalist temporality. Particularly, the tendency for *xungen* nativism to focus on rural regions in the hinterland opens up the possibility of interrogating the values and ends of modernization from the vantage point of marginality. By calling attention to native culture in rural regions marginalized from the scientific, technological, and material developments that define modernization in the dominant discourse, *xungen* nativism highlights the existence of different cultural values besides those informing Western modernity or orthodox Chinese tradition, and invokes these values to examine and deliberate the goals of modernity. Thus it promises, at its best, not only a critique of the dominant discourse but also an alternative conception of modernity from the margins.

The self-positioning in marginality is therefore central to *xungen* nativism's critical intervention into the project of constructing "Chinese" modernity, but herein also lies its problem of complicity in dominant ideological constructions. The key issue here is *xungen* nativism's representation of the places and cultures of marginality, as well as the *xungen* writers' relation to them. The problems involved have been voiced by Mo Yan, a writer of peasant origin whose self-consciously nostalgic fiction about his home village in the red sorghum country of Gaomi in northeastern Shandong has often been (mis)taken for *xungen* literature by critics. In an interview, Mo Yan criticizes the representation of peasants and rural lives by *zhiqing* writers, who constituted the majority of the *xungen* advocate-writers. He contends that with their circumscribed experiences as "educated youths sent down" to live and work in rural villages, knowing and hoping all along that they would eventually be able to leave (as indeed many did after a few years), *zhiqing* writers may be able to observe the harshness of peasant lives but they cannot understand peasants' thinking process (*siwei guocheng*), and thus cannot reach into their hearts and souls to bring out their deep essence.[46] Any attempt by these writers to represent peasants' cultural values is therefore doomed to be inaccurate. While this criticism's essentialist assumption that only peasants, or writers of peasant origin, can understand and write accurately about the inner lives of peasants is debatable, to say the least, its questioning of *zhiqing* writers' representation of the cultures and values of peasants with whom they have lived only temporarily points incisively to a key issue in the *xungen* advocate-writers' search for alternative groundings of cultural identity and modernity through a self-positioning in marginality.

Most of the major *xungen* advocate-writers have been *zhiqings* and their experiences of being sent down to live and work in the rural hinterlands in the late 1960s and early 1970s certainly played an important part in shaping their *xungen* nativism.[47] On the one hand, their personal experiences of displacement and the harshness of life in the rural hinterlands sensitized them to the significance of place and socioeconomic inequity derived from geographical differences and spatial distances from urban centers, leading them to a critique of modernity through the focal point of marginalized places. On the other hand, their personal experiences also disposed them toward collapsing significant class differences and eliding political issues in the representation of the marginalized places. Their personal grievances and critical awareness, in hindsight, of the fallacy of the Maoist rhetoric behind the policy of sending down educated youths to learn from peasants and temper themselves into new socialist subjects, which had moved some to volunteer themselves in the beginning, easily led them to downplay and even deny the importance of class issues and concerns in their re-visioning of their sojourn in rural China. In their desires to reclaim the "lost years" and to make sense of and give lasting meaning to their experiences of dislocation and material deprivation, as well as their subsequent difficulties in readjusting to urban lives, the *xungen* writers tended to gloss over the material reality of peasant lives to locate the essence of the rural places in the values and cultures preserved in local customs and traditions. Ironically enough, their formative experiences under the

Maoist era with its fanciful rhetoric of rural superiority also gave the *xungen* writers precedents and lessons in investing symbolic meanings of their own making into the rural way of life. In the final analysis, it is this kind of urban intellectual investment of their ideological needs and personal desires into the rural hinterland that shapes the representation of marginalized ethnic cultures in *xungen* nativism.

Such intellectual investment is perhaps most discernible from the fact that despite the different regional focus of the *xungen* writers, from which significant differences in the ethnic cultures delineated would be expected, the "marginalized" cultural values being affirmed in their writings turn out to be remarkably similar. All center on a masculine subjectivity characterized, to various degrees, by vitality, a free spirit, and moral independence and courage in upholding nonutilitarian and nonmaterialistic values.[48] This can take the form of a positive identification in male protagonists who personify such masculine subjectivity, as in the fictions of Li Hangyu and Zheng Wanlong, or a negative indictment of conditions that stifle and constrain the development and maturation of such a masculine subject, as in the works of Han Shaogong and Zheng Yi. Whatever its form, a preoccupation with masculine subjectivity clearly marks the representation of regional ethnic cultures in *xungen* nativism, suggesting that its "root" lies perhaps in the *xungen* writers themselves rather than in the regional ethnic cultures. The fact that all the core *xungen* advocates and writers are male further attests to this possibility.

Masculine subjectivity is by no means an unusual concern in post-Mao literature, and the strong link between an obsession with masculinity and the search for roots in *xungen* literature has often been noted. *Xungen* literature, for instance, has been situated in "the context of the rise of the macho man" in writings of the 1980s.[49] Given the almost paradigmatic example of Zhang Xianliang's sensational "Nanren de yiban shi nuren" (Half of man is woman), this concern with masculine subjectivity is easily taken to be male writers' response to their emasculation under the oppressive regime of Mao, which deprived them of their own voices and individual identities. Yet, with the *zhiqing* writers of *xungen* literature, who experienced in the Maoist era not so much the political persecution suffered by Zhang's generation as an inculcation of an idealistic belief in collectivism and social mission followed by disillusionment and a sense of betrayal, the concern with masculine subjectivity in the post-Mao years seems to have more to do with the need to re-create themselves in the aftermath of spiritual loss and dislocation than with gendered dispossession of power under political repression.[50] Furthermore, the preoccupation with masculinity in this subject reconstitution cannot be understood solely in relation to Maoist policies, under which differences between the sexes were minimized, leading to a "desexualization" that has been lamented as "*yinsheng yangshuai*" (thriving of the feminine and withering of the masculine) in the post-Mao period.[51] Nor can it be simply attributed to and subsumed under the *xungen* writers' turn to nature for inspiration and the invigoration of a culturally constrained and symbolically castrated subject, as suggested in Jing Wang's remark that "the theme of return to nature in a large corpus of [*xungen*] literature . . . delivers collectively a new hero of raw masculinity and spiritual cornucopia [, who] is, in fact, the very personification of nature itself."[52] Even if the masculine subject in *xungen* literature can be read as "rooted" in nature, the question why nature is masculinized rather than feminized in this literature needs to be raised. Otherwise, the gender specificity and significance of *xungen* literature's construction of subjectivity are naturalized and thus, in effect, erased.

On top of the lingering backdrop of Maoist politics, the concern with masculine subjectivity in *xungen* literature should be situated in the immediate context of the emphasis on economic development as modernization under China's engagement with global capitalism. With its elevation of economic competitiveness and material gains into the ultimate measure of social value, the underlying economism of the postsocialist Party-state's vision of modernity caused tremendous concern among Chinese writers who not only saw their standards of living plummet because of inflation and the introduction of market forces into the economy, but also found themselves suddenly beset with the problems of the volume of sales and market value of their "serious" literary works (*chun wenxue*), as well as the decline in social status, prestige, and significance of their established role as purveyors of culture and social conscience.[53] This led to a keen awareness of the threat of intellectual disempowerment and marginalization that intensified the sense of spiritual loss and identity crisis of the *zhiqing* writers. Aggravating the palpable threat was a feeling of being compelled to enter the realm of the market and consumption, which brought with it the peril of emasculation because of its conventional association with the frivolity and fickleness of femininity. In this context, the privileging of a masculine subjectivity embodying marginalized, nonmaterialistic, nonutilitarian values as the "root" of alternative construction of modernity in *xungen* nativism can arguably be read as an attempt on the part of male *zhiqing* writers who maintain the value of "serious literature" to resolve their complex identity crisis. As such, it constitutes an intimate, personal intervention and investment in the discourse of modernity.

To explore specific ways in which *xungen* literature envisions nativist alternatives to the state's vision of modernity through the construct of masculine subjectivity "rooted" in marginalized ethnic cultures, and their respective limitations and gender politics, I turn now to close analysis of some major *xungen* texts. In view of the sheer diversity of works that have been included in critical discussion of *xungen* literature, and the fact that some writers considered to be key practitioners of the literature in critical discussions have never identified themselves as *xungen* writers or publicized their views on the notion of *xungen* (Jia Pingwa being a notable example),[54] I focus my analysis on the works of three writers who are generally considered central to *xungen* literature and have all identified themselves with the literature by publishing their own "manifestoes" on the search for roots—Han Shaogong, Li Hangyu, and Zheng Wanlong. Together, their nativist writings enable a critical evaluation of the cultural parameters, oppositional possibilities, and common pitfalls amidst significant differences in *xungen* nativism's discursive intervention into the construction of modernity in China in the latter half of the 1980s.

Unsettling Roots: Han Shaogong's Search between Cultures

As the author of the most widely recognized *xungen* manifesto, Han Shaogong is ubiquitous in critical discussions of the literature. Han's "Wenxue de 'gen'" (The "Roots" of Literature) stands out among similar statements on literature and native culture of that time not only because it is the first but also because it offers a pithy overall representation of the diverse issues and concerns that have come to be associated with *xungen* literature.[55] In particular, the essay delineates the meaning of "roots" in a variety of contexts, situates it in relation to national culture and regional ethnic cultures, and makes clear how *xungen* nativism constitutes a critical response to the state project of constructing modernity. As such, it offers a rich and revealing introduction to the nativism built around the search for roots.

"Wenxue de 'gen'" begins with a strong hint of lament at cultural loss and dispossession in the question "Where has the magnificent culture of Chu gone?" and proceeds to argue the necessity of recovering and cultivating the roots of literature in "national traditional culture" (*minzu chuantong wenhua*) to give it a distinctive identity in the modern world. From an invocation of a historically submerged regional ethnic culture to the identification of a national traditional culture, the essay makes an unacknowledged conceptual leap, covering over the discontinuity between regionally specific native cultural roots and a national culture as if the latter is simply a natural extension of the former. Still, an anxiety about the discontinuity is discernible in Han's adamant assertion that the search for roots is not "a kind of cheap nostalgia and regionalism" but "a form of renewed understanding of the nation, an awakening of the historical elements latent in aesthetic consciousness, and a concretized expression of the search for and grasp of the infinity and eternity of the world."[56]

Underlying this rarefied definition is a fundamental concern with remapping the tripartite relation among native cultural roots, the nation, and the world under changing conditions. That such a mapping is a conscious response to China's contemporary efforts to modernize through active participation in the globalized economy dominated by Western capital, technology, and values is highlighted at the end of the essay:

> Taking place here and now are spectacular economic reforms, economic and cultural constructions, "grabbing" from the West everything we can use in science, technology, etc., and moving toward a modern way of life. But . . . China is still China, especially in regard of literature and art, as well as the deep structure of national spirit and cultural characteristics. We have our national identity; our responsibility is to release the energy from modern concepts to recast and galvanize this form of identity.[57]

The seemingly confident pronouncement that "China is still China" is, ironically, most revealing of the cultural anxiety that Han and others like him experienced in seeing, and recognizing the need for, massive importation from the West to make China a strong player in the modern world. Such anxiety is betrayed again in the essay's invocation of the authority of a Western historian, Arnold Toynbee, to propose that with the exhaustion and decline of Western Christian civilization, the future of the world may depend on the revival of "Oriental civilization."[58] The fact that what is privileged here is Oriental civilization rather than Chinese culture per se reveals the depth of Han's concomitant cultural anxiety and cultural chauvinism, as well as the influence of the Oriental version of the Pacific Rim discourse. It is apparently an automatic assumption of the centrality of Chinese culture to Oriental civilization, together with a painful recognition of China's current "backwardness," generating what Rey Chow has eloquently identified as the "paradox of primitivism,"[59] that leads Han to partially allay his anxiety about Chinese identity in modernity by taking comfort in the promise of a revival of Oriental civilization. To Han, the apparent success of East Asian countries in combining spectacular economic development with the promotion of traditional cultural values in so-called Confucian capitalism since the late 1970s heralded precisely such a revival.[60] In this light, Han's call for root-seeking was a symptomatic response to the keenly felt need to recover a native ground on which Chinese cultural identity can be securely anchored even in the changing world of post/modernity. What this native ground is or can be, and how it relates to the nation and traditional Confucian culture are, however, slippery and contentious issues for Han and his fellow *xungen* advocates, as the suppressed tension between recovering regional ethnic cultures and affirming a national traditional culture in Han's essay suggests. The controversy compounds when other concerns of Chinese modernity besides cultural identity are brought up in the course of locating and defining the native.

In his attempt to delineate the native cultural ground, Han Shaogong includes a number of different elements that do not necessarily cohere but are very revealing of the various concerns that occupied *xungen* nativism as a whole. First, Han contrasts native culture to the business-oriented material artifacts (such as splendid hotels, entertainment complexes, and grand trade and commercial buildings) that have shot up in the SEZ of Shenzhen, which is pointedly compared to the "cultural desert" of the then British colony of Hong Kong nearby.[61] Given that Shenzhen served as a kind of centerpiece in the modernization program in the 1980s, showcasing the Party-state's commitment to importation of Western technology and capital to spearhead rapid economic development in a reversal of the Maoist policy of self-reliance, this contrast bespeaks more than a tendency to oppose native culture to materialism which, as we shall see, is rather common among *xungen* writers. It further signals a reservation toward and critical distance from, if not exactly opposition to, the modernization project undertaken and overseen by the state, particularly its extensive reliance on Western importation and emphasis on economic development as the measure of modernity. Implicit in this delineation of the native ground is thus a gesture toward an alternative construction of modernity.

Han's location of the native ground in *xiangtu*, understood as local (home) villages, indicates where *xungen* advocates tend to found such an alternative. Seeing local villages as "the past of cities and the museum of national history," Han considers them rich repositories of traditional culture ready to be reclaimed for modernity.[62] If such a conception of the native ground carries a largely conservative overtone and seems incongruent with the search for an alternative construction of modernity, its conservatism is somewhat mitigated by Han's association of traditional culture in local villages with "folk culture" that falls outside of normative, orthodox culture (*guifan wenhua*). It is precisely the unorthodox nature of much of the traditional culture crystallized in local villages, Han contends, that makes local folk culture a rich and vibrant native force for nourishing and regenerating the ossified cultural ground on which we stand. This stress on the local folk and the unorthodox signals a concern with cultural domination and counterhegemony that gives Han's idea of *xungen* the potential of "opposition" not only to Westernized modernity but also to the nationalistic discourse of the state.[63]

In line with such privileging of the excluded and marginalized from cultural orthodoxy, Han also celebrates historically marginalized regional ethnic cultures as roots for alternative configurations of the nation-in-modernity. It is, above all, this celebration that leads his *xungen* nativism away from its professed interest in *national* identity to a subtle critique of the state's hegemonic discourse of nationalist modernity based on economic and technological advancement. The nature of this critique is made explicit in Han's response to a question about his interest in Chu culture in an interview. Contrasting the "mysteriousness and intuitiveness" of Chu culture to the "rational, logical thinking pattern" of Confucianism, Han argues that Chu culture is conducive to "the necessary liberation of humanity from the rules and orders of the city, the material world, and industrial technology" by offering a "myth-like beauty that is sacred and wild, non-utilitarian, and full of vitality." In the age of science and industry, he elaborates, such beauty can only be found in "primitive" and "semi-primitive cultures" like those of minority nationality groups in western Hunan, which, continuing the tradition of Chu culture, feature a "beauty of wildness" that enables humans to "live authentically and naturally."[64]

This celebration of marginalized ethnic and minority cultures as the core of regionally specific cultural roots promising alternatives to the staleness of Confucianism and the regimentation of modern industrial lives is corroborated in specific examples of potentially fruitful root-searching given in "Wenxue de 'gen.'" Besides the earlier noted opening quest for Chu culture, which Han traces to the cultures of various minority nationalities in Hunan, the essay suggests mining also the cultural heritages of two historically marginalized groups in Guangdong—the "Liren" (literally, vulgar people, who tilled the land in remote villages) and the "Danhu" (boat people)—and the multiple minority cultures of Xinjiang, including the Orthodox Church culture of the Russian descendants, the Islamic culture of the Uygur and the Hui, and the cultures of the Manchus and Mongols. Together, these examples underscore Han's propensity to locate roots in marginalized local cultures as a means of decentering the hegemonic conception of Han culture at the foundation of the Chinese nation and (re)claiming a historically submerged ethnic identity. If such a root-seeking opens up a way of questioning the state project of utilitarian nationalist modernity, the examples also reveal a troubling elision of differences between marginalized "ethnic" cultures among the Han and cultures of non-Han minority nationalities vis-à-vis orthodox Chinese culture. This elision masks Han appropriation of non-Han minority cultures and the power relations underlying such appropriation. With indisputable Han dominance even in remote provinces such as Xinjiang, the seemingly inclusive gesture of such a quest for native roots is, in effect, an ideological obfuscation of cultural domination and appropriation to enrich and rejuvenate Han culture(s). Given Han Shaogong's tendency to represent the native as relics from the historical past, moreover, this attention to marginalized minority cultures is little more than a spatial translation of his temporal frame of historical progress. Relegating minority cultures to preserved remnants from the "less-developed" historical past, his representation cannot escape the imperialistic implications of similar strategies of exoticization and primitivization found in Western discourses of modernity.[65] In this denial of contemporaneity to marginalized cultures also lies the greatest pitfall of Han Shaogong's *xungen* nativism as an attempt to reconstruct China's cultural heritage for the purpose of reimagining "Chinese" modernity. Specifically, if Han's conception of *xungen* nativism suggests in its focus on marginality a critique of the homogenizing effects of nationalistic modernity, it also undermines this critique by associating marginality with primitiveness and subjecting marginalized cultures to the ultimate end of nationalistic cultural rejuvenation.

An Old Boy Story: Fictive Roots and Retarded Future

The tenuousness of such use of marginality to provide viable alternatives in imagining modernity can be seen in Han Shaogong's own fictions. "Bababa" (1985), Han's most noted *xungen* text, for instance, ostensibly makes use of the landscape, folklore, and folk cultures of western Hunan, only to portray an isolated community locked in the murkiness of cloud-clad mountains, clinging to archaic traditions and superstitions even as occasional contacts with the outside world brought tidings of new inventions and tremendous changes in ways of life.[66] From this spiritually deficient and materially undeveloped community emerges not the beauty of wildness and life of authenticity that Han cites as an alternative to the rationalistic utilitarianism of industrial modernity in his interview with Shi Shuqing, but a vicious cycle of violence and retreat into primitive rituals and customs that seem destined to doom the community.

Bearing the brunt of the communal violence is a figure of arrested masculinity and abject marginality, Bingzai, whose retardation locks him mentally in the toddler stage and limits his social responses to two stock phrases, either utterly pliant and submissive in greeting everyone with "Baba" (signifying father to the villagers) or thoroughly aggressive and abusive in hurling what sounds like sexual expletives about mothers at those who agitate him. Significantly, whichever response he gives, the result is always the same: he gets beaten up. Multiply marginalized from the village community, on account of his imbecility, his lack of a father (who reputedly could not stand the birth of such a "sinful spawn" (*niezhang*) and left the mountain for good), and his having an "outsider" for a mother (who came from "outside the mountain" and speaks with a queer accent), Bingzai's treatment at the hands of the villagers dramatizes this mountain community's deep-rooted suspicion and condemnation of anything "foreign," different, or "outside," and its corresponding customs of combating otherness and responding to perceived outside threats with violence.

This is evident above all in the villagers' repeated reference to Bingzai as "sinful spawn," an identification that is simultaneously a verbal violence marginalizing the retarded offspring from the village community and a condemnation of his parents' union, which carries rich symbolic meaning in the story. Delong, Bingzai's reputed father, was the village's de facto bard before he left the mountain, supposedly because of disgust for what he had sired. A superb singer with an unrivaled voice, he was entrusted with singing the history, lineage, and origin of the village community in festivals and special occasions calling for celebration and commemoration. For the villagers, this "singing the past/dead" (*changgu*) renders "detailed and authoritative interpretations of (their) ancestors" that are more reliable than an official historian's account.[67] Delong was thus a conduit of the village's collective voice, articulating the community's self-understanding of its origin and identity. As such, he was also a trusted cultural custodian tending the roots of the community and cultivating a living link between history, lineage, and community. In light of this key communal role, his union with a woman from "outside the mountain" with a "queer accent" is highly symbolic and significant. That this woman then becomes the village's midwife, who is called upon to bring the future (generation) of the community into place, accentuates the symbolic significance of the union. Bringing together the community's cultivation of cultural roots with the outside, the union literally puts into being an intermediary for delivering the community's future. If the union thus encodes a desire to break out of the isolation and stagnation of the mountain village through a productive engagement with others from the outside, the severe retardation of this union's immediate product, Bingzai, whom the villagers condemn and reject as "sinful spawn," bespeaks the community's moral aversion to such desire and the futility and counterproductivity of any attempt to act on the desire. Delong's disappearance underscores this failure, as it severs the tenuous link between such desire and the roots of the community.

The village's inability to engage creatively and positively with the outside is further dramatized in the story by the community's recourse to age-old customs and rituals of violence to deal with life and its many challenges, from the presence of Bingzai to natural disaster and relations with neighboring villages. Both an effect and a symptom of the village's closed-mindedness, violence is sanctified in rituals, woven into the village's social fabric, and practiced everyday in random acts against the marginalized like Bingzai. The village's response to a poor harvest caused by unseasonable weather, which ultimately brings the community to dissolution and destruction, clearly illustrates this culture of violence, its tie to primitiveness, and the doomed future it portends. From the aborted plan to offer Bingzai as human sacrifice to the god of grains, to the rounds of deadly fighting with a neighboring village over a superstitious effort to destroy the landscape believed to have caused the poor harvest, and the cannibalistic ritual to feed common hatred and build fighting morale by eating the enemy, the villagers' progressive steps of dealing with a natural disaster all revolve around "primitive" beliefs and customs grounded in and feeding on violence. In the end, after depleting their scarce resources in the deadly fights, they follow the footsteps of their ancestors to complete the current cycle of violence by sacrificing the old and the weak, leaving the youths and adults to migrate farther into the mountain to cultivate a new community and, in all likelihood, repeat another cycle of violence.

Nothing in this culture bears any resemblance to the sacred, vital, non-utilitarian, myth-like beauty of Chu culture that Han Shaogong affirms in his interviews and essays as neglected counterpoints to rationalistic, materialistic, industrial modernity. In presenting such a culture in his root-seeking tale of western Hunan, Han betrays a primary concern with cultural critique to address the nation's backwardness rather than an attempt to recover alternative values in marginalized ethnic culture. That this critique is driven and informed by contemporary Chinese experiences is made clear in his interview with Shi Shuqing. Responding to a question about the dominant national allegorical reading of Bingzai as Han's version of the Ah Q character monumentalized in Lu Xun's fiction, a form of personified indictment of the sickness of the Chinese national psyche,[68] Han acknowledges that reading's validity but also stresses that the story was motivated by the massive killings Hunan saw during the Cultural Revolution, and Bingzai was modeled on a neighboring child he encountered in his *zhiqing* years. In drawing attention to the Hunan reality informing his fiction, Han seems to want to reassert its regional specificity against the dominant national allegorical reading. Yet, whatever the historical and real-life sources of Han's fictional construction, on the textual level, the historical and regional specificity of these elements is deliberately blurred to give a timeless, mythical portrayal of a remote village trapped in its primitive cultural tradition and self-imposed isolation from the outside world. Whether Bingzai is meant to be an emblem of the degeneracy of Chinese "national character" (*guomingxing*) or not—of which more will be said later—the narrative strategies of this work showcasing Han's professed search for roots in the marginalized culture of western Hunan suggest an implicit association of marginality with historical stagnation and arrested development, and an indictment of its "root" cause in a failure to open up and engage creatively with the outside world. The apparent gap between the concrete effects of these narrative strategies and Han's authorial comments on root-seeking in Chu and other marginalized regional ethnic culture points, once again, to a fundamental tension in his investment of the meaning of roots between the marginalized region and the nation. While his discursive promotion of *xungen* locates roots in marginality as a positive site of alternative, his literary actualization shows a fundamental concern with marginality as backwardness that implicitly shifts the ground of cultural identification to the nation and displaces the celebratory affirmation of marginality with a call for creative engagement with the outside.

This tension can perhaps be understood in terms of the gap between *xungen* as a literary and a cultural project. It is arguable that Han's interest in root-seeking lies ultimately in an aesthetic quest (inspired by the magical realism of 1982 Nobel Prize winner Gabriel Garcia Marquez) for a distinctive literary voice with a rich cultural legacy and regional flavor. What he seeks to reclaim in "Bababa" is correspondingly the mythic aesthetics of *Chuzi—Chu* poetry—rather than any specific cultural content of the Chu tradition. In the context of the post-Mao struggle to open up new modes of literary writing and fictional representation after decades of doctrinaire prescription of socialist realism, this effort at reclaiming a marginalized traditional aesthetics for contemporary writing certainly befits the spirit of searching for literary roots. Yet, as shown in his *xungen* manifesto and other essays, Han was not content with a narrowly focused literary search for roots, presumably because of the hegemonic Chinese tradition of prescribing social relevance for literary endeavors. He tried to broaden the social and cultural significance of the literary search to issues of national renewal, cultural traditions, and Chinese modernity under global capitalism. It is in translating the literary effort into a cultural search for roots for national renewal in modernity that tension and ambiguities loom in Han's *xungen* nativism.

Interestingly, Han reveals a fundamental ambivalence toward the cultural aspirations of his own root-seeking project in "Bababa," where he draws attention to the selectivity and unreliability of communal self-representations reproduced in and transmitted through traditional practices, cultural narratives, and lyrics, from which marginalized cultural roots are supposed to be recovered. As noted above, "singing the old/dead" plays a vital role in the village's self-understanding in the story. Through such singing commemorating communal legacy and connecting the present with the past, the villagers acquire their understanding of collective histories and identity, which subsequently dictates their understanding of and response to contemporary problems. The significance of this cultural representation is highlighted at the end of the story, when those entrusted with regenerating their community begin their migration farther into the mountain with such a commemorative singing of the old/past. The singing is described as follows:

> This kind of songs make you think of precipitous mountains, giant bamboos in woods, and unnecessarily heavy thresholds. Only this kind of climate and environment can ooze this kind of voice. There is even flowery ornamentation, "heiyohei." It is of course a bright and splendid song, like their eyes, like the earrings and bare feet of the women, like the tiny flowers smiling beside their bare feet. There is absolutely no record and narration of war and disaster, no trace at all of the reek and smell of blood. No trace at all.[69]

Here, as in the introduction of this singing of the past/dead earlier in the story, Han draws attention to its complete elision of bloody realities in the community's history. That this bright and splendid song of the past may very well be not only a sanitized but also an imaginative or fictive version is suggested in the story's inclusion of a different account by an official historian, which the villagers soundly reject in favor of their own songs. Of particular dispute between the two versions are the village community's supposed origins and the cause of its migration. According to the official historian, the community's supposed ancestor, Xingtian, was beheaded in a struggle for power rather than accidentally by his own hands while separating heavens and earth, as sung from generation to generation. Similarly, official history has it that the villagers' ancestors were refugees fleeing a war rather than voluntary migrants led by a phoenix in search of green fields for cultivation, as the villagers themselves believe. The contrasts bring out the communal songs' mythical transformation of violent histories into splendid feats of achievement opening new worlds for descendents. Such transformation prevents the community from knowing the gory realities of its past, especially the destructive role of its culture of violence as manifested in the recent rounds of fighting. Repeating the same songs generation after generation, the village community is unable to learn from historical experiences to question the inherited culture and attenuate its destructive power. Thus, the story suggests, the community is doomed to repeat cycle after cycle of violence, driving itself farther and farther into the primitive wilderness.

This critique of the village's songs is significant on two levels. First, with regard to the story, it makes clear the absolute unavailability of alternatives in the village's faithful adherence to the ancestral songs as roots. Being mythic representations that mystify and distort historical realities, these supposed roots of the community have nothing to offer but bright illusions, false hopes, and a doomed future of repeated violence. Second, beyond the specific reference of the story, in revealing the fictive nature of the mythic songs, which are clearly reminiscent and evocative of the "myth-like beauty" of Chuci, Han brings into question his own professed project of searching for roots in the "mysteriousness and intuitiveness" of Chu culture. If the cultural representations and narratives from which one is supposed to recover marginalized cultural traditions to counter the dominant culture of modernity turn out to be unreliable fictive renditions that elide actual practices shaping historical experiences, what good are they for grounding national identities and offering alternative values in contemporary times? Whether a search for roots in marginalized traditions is of any cultural use besides the literary thus becomes highly questionable. Belying the confident advocacy of *xungen* nativism in his manifesto and other essays, then, Han's own root-seeking story reveals a fundamental ambivalence toward the value of such a literary search for roots for national cultural renewal.

Significantly, instead of root-seeking with its inward orientation, "Bababa" ultimately invests the possibility of an alternative future in openness toward the outside. The ending of the story, with Bingzai miraculously surviving the imposed mass suicide and receiving friendly treatment and even imitation from children of the enemy village, underscores this alternative. Focusing on Bingzai's severe retardation, many critics have read the character as an emblem of the "primitive mentality" produced by traditional culture, an allegorical representation of the infantile national character. That the figure of Bingzai is to be read along a national allegorical line seems incontrovertible, given Han Shaogong's authorial statements and the story's deliberate blurring of historical and regional specificities. Yet Bingzai's marginality in the village community and the symbolism of his parents' union do not seem to sit well with a straightforward reading of him as an emblem of national character, or a symbol of the degeneracy effect of Chinese national traditions. Far from a product solely of traditions, Bingzai arguably embodies and signifies an open reception of new elements from the outside. This is vividly suggested in his characteristic adoption of the stock phrase "baba," which is a way of calling father that "was brought into the mountain from Qianjiaping [literally thousand families lowland] and still not particularly popular."[70] In this distinctive association with a nonnative signifier for the central figure of authority in traditional culture, Bingzai himself becomes a sign of the effort to open up to new culture and ways of life beyond the confines of tradition. The villagers' rejection of Bingzai's calling them "baba," which is further rendered meaningless in the community by the absence of Bingzai's father, thus indicates the community's refusal to incorporate and acknowledge the effort as its own, while Bingzai's stunted growth attests to the effort's inability to take hold and flourish in the community. Insofar as Bingzai stands allegorically for China's national malaise, he externalizes the arrested development and retarded future of a tradition-oriented nation that closes itself off to the outside, as well as the symptomatic absence of a mature modern masculine subjectivity in such a nation. In this light, Bingzai's resilient survival and the chanting of "babababababa" by children from the enemy village in adoring imitation and extension of his utterance of "baba" at the end of the story clearly foreground an investment of hope for the future in the effort to open up and creatively adopt new elements into one's repertoire.

With such an ending, "Bababa" makes clear the absolute unavailability of alternatives to the dominant discourse of modernity in Han's representation of the cultures of marginality. The promise of a native cultural revival that motivates his advocacy of *xungen* is blunted by his subscription to the time-space of modernity organized around the idea of progress and its opposite construct of backwardness. In the end, despite his proclaimed effort to search for roots of cultural regeneration in the surviving legacy of Chu culture among the minority nationalities, the roots that seem to take hold in his fictional endeavors are not so much the marginalized ethnic culture(s) as the May

Fourth legacy of nationalistic critique of the spiritual malaise plaguing the Chinese people that C. T. Hsia has influentially named "the obsession with China."[71] Rather than uncovering alternative values that inform marginalized ethnic cultures, in other words, Han's *xungen* story dramatizes a vital need for a reorientation of national mentality toward incorporating the new and the foreign, echoing and endorsing, perhaps not incidentally, the open-door policies anchoring the post-Mao state project of modernization. In (re)presenting a community doomed by its faithful adherence to tradition, the story also suggests a need for opening up, "modernizing" the national psyche that resonates with the culturalist argument in the Culture Fever and shares its complicity in the state discourse of modernity. Perhaps not surprisingly, whatever Han's authorial intentions, the figure of Bingzai ended up enlivening criticisms among Chinese intellectuals that the Chinese people lack a robust masculine subjectivity capable of breaking the cycle of a degenerate, violent culture that ritualizes the sacrifice of individuals for collective survival.

Masculinity Caught at the Roots: Li Hangyu's "Last" Heroes

If Han Shaogong's *xungen* nativism reveals an ultimate identification with the Chinese nation rather than regional ethnic cultures, the opposite seems to hold sway in the works of another *xungen* advocate-writer, Li Hangyu. Clearly aligning himself with the search for roots in an article titled "Liyili women de 'gen'" (Attending to our 'roots,'),[72] published five months after Han Shaogong's *xungen* manifesto, Li Hangyu had put his ideas into practice before the notion of *xungen* was promoted. In the early 1980s, he published a series of works on life along the riverbanks of the fictional Gechuanjiang—which is modeled on the Qiantangjiang, the largest river in Zhejiang Province flowing by Hangzhou, the provincial capital and Li's hometown. Known collectively as the Gechuanjiang series and widely cited as representative *xungen* literature, these fictional works clearly center on a particular region and the ethnic culture "rooted" therein. Yet, in his theoretical articles on the significance of attending to cultural roots, Li still shies away from any direct reference to regional ethnicity and, like Han Shaogong in his manifesto, vacillates between national and ethnic cultural identity. Holding that the retention of national cultural heritage is necessary for literature to have its distinctive characteristics in a world increasingly homogenized by the advancement of Western industrial culture, for instance, he laments in "'Wenhua' de ganga" (The embarrassment of 'culture,' 1986) the "embarrassing" situation that confronts a Chinese writer, given as he is a national cultural heritage that he considers "awful" (*zaogao*) yet has to acknowledge for his own identity in modernity.[73] Li's "solution" to this embarrassment, as suggested in his fictions and essays, is to turn to marginalized and repressed regional ethnic cultures as an alternative source of cultural heritage and identification.

In his essay on attending to roots, Li not only distinguishes between the cultures of the Han and the minority nationalities, favoring, as is typical of *xungen* advocates, the latter for their romantic imagination, harmony with nature, and unaffected vigor. He also differentiates among the Han traditions, juxtaposing the "shallowness and mediocrity" of the Confucianism-based orthodox culture originating from the northern "central plain" to the "glory" and "mysticism" of the historically marginalized cultures of ethnic communities in the northwest (Xia), southwest (Chu), and southeast (Wu-Yue). Revealingly, what stands out in Li's characterizations of these various Han cultures is not so much distinctive differences among the marginalized cultures as their common difference from the orthodox Confucian culture, which Li repeatedly criticizes for its emphasis on the practical, pragmatic, and functional (*shiji* and *shiyong*).

Pronounced in the midst of reforms overseen by Deng Xiaoping, who was famed for and himself took pride in a pragmatism neatly captured in the signature statement that white or black, a cat that catches mice is a good cat, Li's criticism of pragmatic functionalism in the orthodox Chinese tradition cannot but suggest an implicit critique of the value system underlying the modernization program of the Deng regime. By the same token, his evocation of marginalized ethnic cultures within the Han nationality needs to be read not simply as an attempt to recover alternative "national" cultural traditions that can spare the writer some embarrassment, but, arguably with broader significance, as a subtle intervention into the dominant state discourse of modernity by highlighting an alternative value system that remains repressed and marginalized. This alternative value system is concretized in the ethnic culture of the Gechuanjiang region (whose real-life counterpart lies in historical Wu-Yue area) lovingly depicted in his fictional works.[74] That Li chose to fictionalize the name of the region though it was closely modeled on the area around his hometown, Hangzhou, underscores the status of the depicted regional ethnic culture as an imaginary construct of alternative values rather than a social reality.[75]

Risk in Abandon: Masculinity and the Gechuanjiang Culture

The most direct representation of the Gechuanjiang culture can be found in Li's early story, "Gechuanjiang shang renjia" (Families on the Gechuanjiang, 1982).[76] Through the accident of a runaway boat hurtling along in the Gechuanjiang's gushing waters, the story offers a vignette of the people who, for generations, have made their living by navigating the dangerous river. It focuses on Sishen, a widow toughened and worn beyond her age raising five daughters on her own by assuming the traditionally male job of transporting goods along the river after her husband's untimely death; her eldest daughter, Qiuzi, whom she has arranged to marry into town to escape a repetition of her harsh life and ensure a better future for the whole family; and Dahei, who, for the love of Qiuzi, is willing to risk his near new boat and his life to come to the help of Sishen and Qiuzi when their boat was torn from its moor. As made palpable by the accident, these people's lives are intimately tied to and determined by the river that both provides for and takes away their livelihood and, at times, even their lives. In this light, Li's choice of the river rather than the more common farming community in rural China as his focal native place is significant. The river, in its nurturing and threatening duality, constitutes an environment where risk-taking is the very essence of life for the people living on it. What results is a culture that is antithetical to the pragmatic functionalism deplored by Li. The people living on the Gechuanjian River, Li's story notes, have always frowned upon cautious, calculative behavior; they live lives fully for the moment, drinking heavily and spending money as quickly as it is earned.[77] What they value most in a man is vigor (*jin*) and courage (*dan*); and they take pride in the struggle they put up against adverse forces, whatever the outcome.[78]

If this depiction of the Gechuanjiang culture encodes a value system opposed to pragmatic functionalism, it also reveals a significant gender subtext to the opposition. With its emphasis on the manly show of reckless vigor and courage, this oppositional culture and value system is clearly based on the experience of men toiling hard for a living on the river. Insofar as Sishen is included in the depiction, she does so as the exceptional woman who has no choice but to take on the male responsibility of providing for the family. Still, her dismissal of Dahei's love for her daughter and her calculative decision to marry Qiuzi into town, however sympathetically rendered as coming from her own bitter experiences of life as a boatman's wife, clearly mark her difference from the spontaneous, passionate, risk-taking character of the men, exemplified in the story by Dahei. This implicit association of women with pragmatic calculation and men with passionate spontaneity is reinforced by the story's characterization of Qiuzi. Seemingly an ingenuous young woman with a happy-go-lucky disposition, Qiuzi, the story tells us, in fact puts on such a face deliberately to lighten up her mother's life.[79] Though she apparently cares for Dahei and finds her prospective husband falling somewhat short of her native-bred Gechuanjiang idea of manliness, she acquiesces in the marriage plan, not only because she wants to please her mother but also because she herself is seduced by the material attractions in town. As if to highlight the unnaturalness of such calculative and pragmatic behaviors to the Gechuanjiang culture, however, the story shows Sishen and Quizi, who, after all, have immersed in the culture all their lives, reacting spontaneously in a daredevil manner to the challenges the river hurled their way, like true scions of the

Gechuanjiang. Thus, even as the story systematically deploys gender differences to dramatize the alternative value system of the Gechuanjiang, positing a nonutilitarian, noncalculative, passionate alternative in the native masculine subjectivity, it also covers this gender subtext with an overarching construct of regional ethnic culture governing the conduct of natives in the area.

Be that as it may, the gender investment of the story has far-reaching significance. With women adopting an attitude of pragmatic calculation that is antithetical to the local culture, the reproduction of this ethnic culture is in jeopardy, literally and figuratively. This threat is made concrete and palpable by Dahei's inevitable loss of Qiuzi to urban material comforts and the value system they encode, even after he shattered his boat and source of livelihood to save her. Indeed, the story intimates throughout that the Gechuanjiang way of life embodied by men like Dahei is fast becoming a relic of the past that will eventually be eliminated by the progression of modernity. The tragic fate of this way of life is foreshadowed not only in the almost routine deaths at work of the Gechuanjiang boatmen, including Dahei's father and grandfather, but also in the curtailed life of Laosi, Sishen's husband, a fine specimen of Gechuanjiang manhood who drank himself to death.

In its representation of the habit of drinking among Gechuanjiang men, Li's story betrays an ultimate ambivalence toward the culture it ostensibly eulogizes. Rhetorically, heavy drinking is positively presented as an everyday manifestation of the masculine Gechuanjiang culture of daring and living to one's utmost capacity. Yet, drinking is also shown to be a self-destructive refuge from disappointment and frustration for Gechuanjiang "heroes" like Laosi. Albeit a superb navigator, Laosi was overburdened by his harsh lot in life. To escape the financial strains of a handful of daughters and frustration over the lack of a son to continue the family line, he took the manly habit of drinking and daring to extremes and turned from a loving husband and father to an irresponsible drunkard.[80] Thus, his life and transformation highlight a precariousness of physical and cultural reproduction for the Gechuanjiang men, and foreground their potential self-destructiveness in following the dictates of their culture. Such danger is reenacted in a different form in Dahei's heroic struggle to rescue his beloved, only to lose both his boat and her to the relentless forces of nature and modern development. Through the different courses but similar fates of Laosi and Dahei, then, the story draws out a tragic fate for the masculine culture of the Gechuanjiang. It suggests that this ethnic culture, while admirable in its passion, vigor, and zest in seizing the moment and living life to the full, especially as a counterpoint to pragmatic functionalism, may nonetheless be self-destructive and have difficulty reproducing itself in a modern world where traditional manliness is no longer an effective defense against adversity, and calculative behavior rather than vigor and courage is increasingly important to ensure survival and prosperity. In short, the culture of heroic masculinity is at most a valiant but questionable antidote to modernity in "Gechuanjiang shang renjia."

Sweeping Tide: The Passing of Nostalgia and Demise of Masculine Subjectivity

The sense of an imminent loss of the Gechuanjiang culture to a modernity characterized by pragmatic functionalism makes Li's story almost a farewell tribute to a native culture that the author seems reconciled to losing more than recovering. Indeed, the farewell overtone to his evocation of the Gechuanjiang culture is accentuated in the title of his most celebrated story, "Zuihou yige yulaoer" (The last fisherman, 1983). As the title suggests, the story portrays a lone man who insistently continues a life of "freedom" as an individual fisherman when others have all left the no longer sustainable, not to say profitable, livelihood.[81] The critic Li Qingxi (who happens to be Li Hangyu's brother) has noted that such a figure of "the last one" is characteristic of Li Hangyu's *xungen* orientation, embodying as he does a complex reflection on modern civilization that recognizes the necessary erosion of individual spiritual freedom under material and scientific progress, and thus the tragic grandeur of an ultimately unviable insistence on maintaining an independent spirit through an adherence to a preindustrial mode of living.[82]

Such ambivalence toward the passing of a traditional way of life highlights the departure of Li's *xungen* nativism from nostalgia, to which representations of the native are often linked. Rather than straightforward nostalgia, which, in its history and etymology, is characterized by mourning and longing for an idealized past that is conventionally tied to the home and maternal plenitude, Li's nativism as realized in his stories' construction of the Gechuanjiang culture as roots features a determination to celebrate surviving traces of an exuberant yet flawed culture centered on a male struggle to meet the challenge of nature, with the acknowledgment, however, that this culture is largely outmoded in modernity. Not only are longing and mourning not the structure of feeling here, but an idealized past is missing from Li's representation of a native culture on the wane. If, as Rita Felski has convincingly argued, nostalgia is part and parcel of the self-constitution of modernity rather than an anachronistic sentiment in the West, such departure of Li's nativism from nostalgia can perhaps be understood in terms of the hegemonic Chinese obsession with China's "backwardness" or "premodernity."[83] In other words, the absence of nostalgia in Li Hangyu's nativism is arguably symptomatic of an anxiety over China's backwardness perpetuated by the state's dominant discourse of modernization as the national imperative. To the extent that intellectuals like Li were convinced of China's lagging behind in modernity, it was difficult for them to indulge in an idealization of and longing for the past, however much they felt the need to ground themselves in native culture. Furthermore, whereas nostalgia usefully embodies a utopian vision of prelapsarian unity to counter modern alienation in the West, the significance of such utopianism is much deflated in modern China, given its history of compulsory collectivity and prolonged struggle for individual freedom and rights. Thus, even as a romantic vision of an aesthetic and sensual alternative to instrumental rationality in modernity informs Li Hangyu's nativism, little in it suggests nostalgia for the past or primordial unity and its conventional association with the maternal.[84]

That Li's evocation of the Gechuanjiang culture as native roots is mediated by an ambivalent subscription to a "forward" vision of modernity that is antithetical to the possibility and even desire of returning to a native past is made particularly clear in the story "Shanhusha de nongchaoer" (Shanhusha's tidal waves players, 1984).[85] Focusing on the physical, mental, and psychological experiences of a man, Kang Da, who returns to the hometown of his childhood to visit his mother, whom he has not seen ever since his parents' divorce decades ago, "Shanhusha" has all the necessary makings of a work of nostalgia. Yet, this is decidedly not the path taken. Rather than a web of nostalgic feelings of loss, yearning, and homesickness, Kang and the narrative voice, which stays close to the protagonist's consciousness, are marked more by detached observation and apathy, seldom exhibiting feelings of any kind. The extent of Kang's apathy is registered in the story not only by an involuntary coldness toward his wife, but, significantly, by his inability to feel anything toward his mother, not even in their first meeting after thirty years of separation. This diminution of the maternal is so thorough that apart from a brief remark about the old crooked woman she has become, no further reference is made of his mother throughout the entire text, as it follows Kang in his reunion (or the lack thereof) with his native home. Thus distancing Kang from the feeling of nostalgia, the story seeks to establish apathy as a symptom of modernity's malady, of which Kang is a living embodiment. In following primarily Kang's point of view and adopting a tone of rational reflection, however, the story itself weighs in heavily on the side of modernity despite its malady. So, even though it offers the Gechuanjiang culture as an emotive alternative in the figure of an old native who retains his vigor and passion, this ethnic culture never gains the status of a real alternative to apathetic modernity, serving rather as a device to tally its cost.[86]

"Shanhusha" sets about reckoning the cost of modernity by establishing a persistent contrast between the past and the present, and a parallel opposition between the Gechuanjiang and Xian, where Kang now lives and works. If, as mentioned above, Kang's mother does not figure at all in his remembrance of the past, what takes her place and manages to rouse Kang somewhat from his apathy is the Gechuanjiang, especially the opportunity it has given him to distinguish himself. Where Kang's hometown lies along the Gechuanjiang is a beach called Shanhusha, which features an ideal setting for local males, or the "tidal waves players," to brave the tremendous waves backing up from the sea to grab home sizeable fishes swept in by the waves. As a child, Kang was a formidable tidal waves player, earning his very first glory in life in the waters of the Gechuanjiang. In retrospect, it is to his feats in the tidal waves that Kang attributes his once possessing a distinctive character (*you le xingge*) that has since been lost, as he remembers the Gechuanjiang waves fondly as a venue where "a person employs all his abilities, and where heroes and good-for-nothings can immediately be told apart."[87] Rather than the maternal, in other words, the Gechuanjiang signifies for Kang a quintessentially masculine proving ground, offering him and other males an opportunity of self-constitution and individual distinction.[88] As such, it is also a site of emotional richness and investment, "preserving the numerous dreams and fantasies of childhood" and "resembling the woman of one's first love."[89]

The kind of masculine subject such a Gechuanjiang would nurture into being takes the concrete form of an unnamed old man (*laotou*) who, past sixty, still possesses the energy, passion, self-confidence, and assertiveness to try himself and his luck in the Gechuanjiang. Epitomizing the title role of "Shanhusha's tidal waves player," the old man embodies the essence and fate of the Gechuanjiang culture, in sharp contrast to the person Kang has become since leaving his hometown. Whereas Kang has degenerated from a wildly energetic (*ye*) boy into a "hollow radish" (*kongxin luobo*) both physically and emotionally, retaining only the appearance of health and youth, the old man is still full of vigor and zest, commanding enough of his faculties, skills, and will to battle the tidal waves year after year. Yet, reflecting the story's pessimistic outlook on the unstoppable tide of modernity, it is Kang who survives while the old man perishes in the end. Though a superbly experienced wave player, the old man drowns after giving up his two chances of going onshore with the tide, first in giving the fatigued Kang a hand and then for the "superstitious" belief that such an escape would bring bad luck the following year. What kills the old man, then, is his own belief, which, Kang surmises, originated in the old-time wave players' desire to show off their true manliness (*cheng haohan*). Despite his passion and zeal, in other words, the old man's fate is a tragic death brought about by a heroic adherence to a cultural principle that defines who he is but, from the "modern" point of view of Kang and the narrator, has become archaic and even dangerous to himself.

Insofar as the old man embodies the masculine subjectivity that defines the Gechuanjiang culture in Li's story, his fate also implies the eventual demise of the impassioned and heroic Gechuanjiang culture, as well as the masculinity it nurtures, in the new world of modernity. Resonating with the farewell overtone in "Gechuanjiang shang renjia," this portent of demise is reinforced in the rhetorical question with which the story ends: "In ten years' time, will there still be tidal waves players on Shanhusha?" The overall tone of the story makes the answer a resounding no.

Underlying this contrast between Kang and the old man is a broader opposition between the cultures of the Gechuanjiang and Xian, where Kang has been living since he left the Gechuanjiang area. Xian, the ancient capital of the Chinese empire unified under the Emperor Qin, constitutes an absent center of the story. As the capital of the crucial Qin-Han period during which the Chinese empire and its bureaucracy and ruling ideology took shape, Xian symbolizes the historical consolidation of northern China and its culture into the political and cultural center of China, effectively marginalizing and ultimately repressing from Chinese orthodoxy other regional cultures such as the Chu and Wu-Yue cultures along the Yangtse River in the south.[90] Associated in such capacity with the bureaucracy and pragmatism of China's ancient regime, Xian is the antithesis of the spontaneity and romantic freedom invested in the Gechuanjiang (as part of Wu-Yue culture) in Li's story.[91]

To this historical cultural opposition between Xian and the Gechuanjiang region, the story superimposes a contrast between the present and the past as experienced by Kang that clearly takes on the connotation of modern bureaucracy versus robust, creative living. Through this contrast, Li's story implicitly critiques the bureaucratically engineered and controlled project of modernity in contemporary China, castigating it as a continuation of the bureaucratic and pragmatic tradition of dominant Chinese culture. The undesirable effects of such a project are suggested in a deliberate link of the weak, "nondescript" (*meiyu xingge*), and emotionally deplete man Kang has become in Xian to his job as a general office director in the Party-state bureaucracy. In the story's most direct reference to the "reforms" implemented by the Deng regime, Kang's promotion under the policy of "rejuvenating the cadre ranks" (*ganbu nianqinghua*) is attributed precisely to his loss of youth in reality:

> In the recent round of promotion, "rejuvenation" was of course a condition, but the fact that the superiors picked only the "juvenescence" of him, Kang Da, was, in the final analysis, because he was no longer young emotionally. To a general office director, such a thing as emotion does not have much meaning; it is at most a kind of embellishment in his personal life.[92]

That this cold routinized way of bureaucracy is not only the defining structure and ethos of Kang's life but a general phenomenon pervading all aspects of social existence in modern times is highlighted in the past-present contrast that repeatedly crosses Kang's mind as he revisits his native Gechuanjiang. For instance, wondering whether his seven-year-old son watching the tidal waves would have the same desire to battle the tidal waves as he had at that age, Kang observes that nowadays children are raised differently: "everything follows scientific formulae"; in kindergartens, they have thorough, collective routines, down to even the bodily function of defecation, and their education is standardized and regulated, to the effect that children like his son find their glories not in the tidal waves as he once did, but in the paper flowers given out weekly to award students who follow the disciplines.[93] The upshot, Kang continues dryly, is that children nowadays have a poor digestive system and cannot stomach anything that is different. In the same vein, Kang further reflects, with the "modernization" of neighbor relations in urban cities, reduced contacts lead to fewer conflicts among the adults and eliminate any chances of fights among the children. Thus, through Kang's mental contrast between the past and the present, Li's story firmly associates modern times with "sanitized" and routinized disciplines enshrined in the structure of bureaucracy or, in other words, the Weberian "iron cage."

A Fishy Affair: Class, Gender, and the Limits of Alternatives in Ethnic Culture

If the superimposition of an opposition between the Gechuanjiang and Xian onto a contrast between an ebullient past and an apathetic, mechanical, modern present in "Shanhusha" implies a critique of the postsocialist vision of modernity, which dovetails with the bureaucratic and pragmatic-minded orthodox Chinese culture rooted in the north, it also unequivocally relegates the Gechuanjiang culture to the past and an eventual extinction, making it impossible for this ethnic culture to constitute any kind of viable alternative or make any significant difference in modernity. The hegemonic understanding of modernity as what Max Weber called the "iron cage" of bureaucracy is thereby affirmed to be an incontestable trend of development, even as its negative effects are highlighted against the vivid vitality of the Gechuanjiang. This reveals significant limits and limitations in Li's figuration of native ethnic culture into a critical site for interrogating the state's discourse of modernity. By localizing the critical site in an ethnicized geographical place, Li renders a static opposition to modern bureaucratic culture, offering, at best, an ahistorical indictment of modernity imagined as a universal phenomenon. Such a critique cannot probe the particular historical effects that socialist construction under Mao Zedong had on the vision and project of modernity in post-Mao China. Nor can there be any consideration of the specific ways in which China's modernization engages modern bureaucratism under the authoritarian rule of the Communist Party. What is especially obfuscated in this static ethnicization of the locus of critique is the issue of class and its relation to modernity in China.

Class is of course the pivot of Maoism that has been much maligned under the postsocialist regime. It is perhaps testimony to the depth of the trauma Maoism created in the Cultural Revolution decade that reference to class became associated with unruly excess, violent radicalism, and destructive extremism in the post-Mao era. Yet, however much havoc the Maoist discourse of class struggle wrought, class concerns are what distinguished the Chinese socialist construction of modernity, which sought to give proper representation to and institute justice and equality for the exploited and oppressed under capitalist development. As Maurice Meisner has insistently pointed out, Maoism envisions socialist modernity in terms of both economic development and the progressive attenuation and eventual elimination of the "three great differences" between mental and manual labor, between workers and peasants, and between cities and the countryside, even though Mao himself was unable to resolve the contradictions between development objectives and socialist aspirations.[94] The repudiation of class as an inalienable concern in the building of modernity that prevailed in the post-Mao era (and continues into present days) is thus tantamount to a rejection and denial of the legacy of socialist construction of modernity under Mao, however much lip service continued to be paid to upholding the vision of socialism in official ideology. With its emphasis on wealth and strength for the nation-state administered by a bureaucracy of technological and managerial experts, Deng's program of modernization clearly sidesteps the relevance of class equity to the vision of modernity. More significantly, the rejection of class concerns as ultraleftist among intellectuals makes it impossible for them to question such modernization on the grounds of democratic control of production and equality and justice for the exploited and oppressed, notably poor peasants from whom much extraction have continued to be made, albeit in different forms, throughout the period of socialist construction and beyond.[95]

In making an ethnic culture rooted in a native place associated with the past the discursive site for critiquing bureaucratic modernity, Li's Gechuanjiang stories partake in this intellectual denial of the legacy of socialist construction and obfuscation of class issues. This is evident in "Shanhusha," where the historical change to modernity is described in terms of people's shift from tidal waves players in keeping with the native tradition to tidal waves watchers joining in a popular pastime of modern affluence. As part of Kang's past, the story relates that in the early days, tidal waves players on the Shanhusha beach included not only offsprings of the tea farmers native to the land, but also children of state employees relocated from different parts of the country to work in the sanatoriums the Communist government built in the area. Though strictly speaking not quite Gechuanjiang natives, children of state employees like Kang in those days adopted the native practices of local farm boys, including the ritual of battling the tidal waves for fish. Such rustication and nativization, however, are no longer current in modern times. Nowadays, the story observes, "human lives have become precious as there is more money to spend day to day, so the number of tidal waves players on the Gechuanjiang banks has dwindled while the number of tidal waves watchers increases year after year . . . and that is why no children from the sanatorium employees' quarters can be seen on Shanhusha today."[96] While this observation seems to subtly register class difference and inequality between the state employees and local farmers, the class element is in fact effaced in the temporal framework of past versus present structuring Kang's perspective discussed above, which glosses over the radical social and economic changes between the times with a brief reference to the current availability of money. It is particularly indicative of such effacement of class that the existing disparity between the state employees and the local tea farmers reflected in their children's different positions as wave watchers and wave players is largely imagined away when the story concludes with Kang's rhetorical question about whether there will still be wave players in ten years' time. Extrapolating from Kang's observation of the changed conditions for children of the state employees, the question assumes a progression of modernity that will ultimately transcend the structural differences between the classes and eliminate the ground for continuing native practices even for the offspring of local farmers. How and why that would be the case, however, are questions that could not be raised, let alone answered, within the story's construction of an ahistorical contrast between a native culture rooted in the past and a modernity promising material richness but emotional and cultural impoverishment.

It is, of course, the intention of *xungen* writers not to let their literature be confined within the imperative of socialist realism to reflect only socioeconomic realities and class struggles, but, instead, to "deepen" their literary imagination to the level of culture. Nonetheless, pointing out the elision of class concerns in Li's narrative reflection on the cultural costs of modernity is more than an exercise in naming the obvious. It needs to be stressed that by making ethnic cultural tradition a class-transcending standpoint from which to critique modernity, Li's story not only excludes what are irreducibly class issues of economic equity and control over one's labor and production from its envisioning of alternatives, but also renders its interrogation of modernity essentially static. By this, I do not mean to suggest an orthodox Marxist privileging of class struggle as the motor of history. Rather, my contention is that insofar as economic development and related social changes constitute a central axis of modernity, especially in latecomer societies anxious to "catch up" with the West, a critique of modernity without attending to class issues necessarily obscures the dynamics of agency in the construction of modernity and, with it, the possibility of positively intervening in the course and direction of modernity.

Such obfuscation is evident in the opposition between an ethnic culture historically on the wane and a bureaucratic modernity shaping and breeding passive and apathetic figures such as Kang in "Shanhusha." Rendering unquestionable the historical inevitability of the advent of bureaucratic modernity, this opposition in effect covers over the active agency involved in such a historical transformation. Thus the old man and his native culture seem destined to be swept out by the tidal waves of modernity and Kang finds himself propelled into the rank of apathetic bureaucrat and its mechanistic culture without the possibility of resistance. Significantly, to the extent that agents implicated in the process of modern transformation are identified, all are women. It is Kang's wife, for instance, who keeps prodding him into the proper behaviors and demeanor that befit his cadre status, and who eventually steers him back to the rank of wave watchers rather than players. Likewise, teachers who, together with mothers, oversee the regimentation and routinization of the lives of children like Kang's son are clearly marked with female pronouns. In short, just as the story makes men the embodiment of an ebullient Gechuanjiang culture that is destined to be a casualty of modernity, it feminizes the force of pragmatic rationality and prudence that propels men into the cold disciplines and routines of modernity. What this gender investment suggests is that, unwilling and unable to confront the class nature of the bureaucratic modernity being promoted and instituted in contemporary China, Li's story makes women the convenient culprit of a historical development that restrains emotion, spontaneity, and individuality, as well as denies self-determination to labor. Put differently, the grid of gendered opposition between native Gechuanjiang culture and bureaucratic modernity serves to cover over important class issues underlying China's modernization efforts, and makes it impossible for a viable alternative to emerge in Li's story. Herein lies the ideological effects and limitations of the story's gendered ethnic cultural configurations in contesting the meaning of modernity.

These ideological effects and limitations are crystallized in Li Hangyu's most famous story, "Zuihou yige yulao'er."[97] Through the fictional character Fukui, the story's namesake who insists on fishing for a living in the Gechuanjiang when others in his village have all turned to farming in view of the polluted river's vastly dwindled yield, this story portrays an embodied resistance to bureaucratic capitalist modernity and the particular problem of official corruption that infests contemporary China in the course of economic reforms. The story focuses on Fukui's relation to two figures, Dagui (literally, the highly ranked and valued), who is a distant nephew of Fukui and a member of the commune affairs committee, and Aqi, a widow who has had a long affair with Fukui but has lately taken up with a better-off man living securely on a state pension. Planning to marry this man, Aqi has decided to quit her cleaning job in a commune-run factory manufacturing MSG—the chemical flavor enhancer symptomatic of modernity's inherent blandness and reliance on artificiality—and, in a token of her love, arranged for Fukui to take over the job. All Fukui needs to do is to "beg the favor" of the job from Dagui, the occasion for which Aqi also orchestrates when she chances upon Fukui catching a special fish that has become almost extinct in the river. Telling Dagui to go to Fukui's home and savor the fish in her place, she hopes the job transfer can be settled over the rare treat. Fukui, however, has little interest in a routine factory job. Furthermore, he has long borne a grudge against the opportunistic Dagui, who once extorted a lot of fish from Fukui for some old fishhooks that he himself no longer needed after seizing the moment of "reforms" to contract the extremely profitable fishery from the commune. This time, rather than letting Dagui take advantage of him again, Fukui decides to sacrifice his own pleasure. Throwing over to his cat the fish that could easily have gotten him a fair sum of much-needed money in the market, had he not decided to keep it for his own enjoyment, he defiantly asserts his independence from the circuit of calculation, exchange, and power that controls contemporary social lives. In character to the end as a primary producer who treasures his freedom to dispose of his labor and its products in whatever ways he likes, Fukui rejects Aqi's "good intentions" and stays on as the last fisherman on the Gechuangjiang.

In creating the opposition between Fukui and Dagui, Li's story indirectly reveals the opportunism, greed, and corruption of the bureaucratic establishment in taking advantage of the reform policy of rural decollectivization to enrich itself. However, even though the story's figuration of Dagui contains elements of a possible critique of China's emerging bureaucratic capitalist modernity along the lines of class inequality, exploitation, and commodification, such a critique is undercut by the story's romanticized representation of Fukui as the last holdout to a life of freedom under the sky rather than a poor fisherman straitened by the state policy of modernization. Like Li's other stories, the "opposition" embodied by Fukui is not so much a viable alternative to the path that has enriched the likes of Dagui as an outmoded way of life that seems poignant and memorable precisely because it is giving out its last sparks. Moreover, it is again a woman, Aqi, who dramatizes the sterilization of this once virile way of life of Fukui's, as well as personifies the force of pragmatic calculation and cold rationality that, in Li's overall conception, defines modernity, emasculates men, and drives them away from their native cultures and ways of life. With Aqi openly admitting material comforts as her reason for deserting Fukui, whom she apparently still loves, and her misguided initiative to induct Fukui into the "security" of waged labor, the story foregrounds a gendered coding of modernity-as-calculative materialism that obscures the critical importance of class inequity in structuring Fukui's relation to this modernity. Given such mystification of Fukui's relation to modernity, the "opposition" that Fukui embodies in the story is necessarily ideological in the Althusserian sense that it is a representation of imaginary relations to real conditions of existence.

This is amply revealed in the story's persistent association of Fukui with the "freedom" and limited self-consciousness of a "natural" existence. Not only does Fukui appear in the story almost in the state of nature, naked except for a loose bit of underpants that, tellingly, once belonged to Aqi, but his characterization is also replete with animal images, the most significant of which is his metaphoric connection to the almost extinct fish that he catches and gives to his cat in order to spite Dagui. The naturalness of his existence is described as follows: "Fishing in the Gechuanjiang gives [him] the great expanse of sky and earth, and freedom. . . . He is used to this life, so used to it that he seems to be born a fisherman, having already learned how to cast nets and set hooks in his mother's womb. . . . It is impossible to make a dog eat grass or a cow eat meat."[98] Such naturalization of Fukui forecloses any possibility of conscious resistance to the modernity Aqi presented to him. Thus, his insistent continuation of a fisherman's life is attributed to a failure to understand the complexities of the contemporary world: "he honestly cannot ponder such things as 'science,' 'pollution,' 'primitive' . . . all he can ponder is eating, sleeping, setting hooks, and extortion by others at certain times."[99] Whatever alternative values Fukui's life embodies in modernity are thereby primitivized, and their oppositional potentialities severely undermined. Between his primitive, natural existence and a calculative, disciplinary materialistic modernity, the possibility of an alternative modernity, particularly a socialist modernity that Maoism has sought to capture in however circumscribed a form, is erased; and the impacts of collectivization and related class struggles on the consciousness and understanding of a fisherman like Fukui are completely denied. What remains is an elitist intellectual representation of a primitive, rustic figure and way of life that gives vent to the male intellectual's romantic imagination of and desire for the freedom and spontaneity of a "native" masculine culture and existence. Bearing hardly any resemblance to the real conditions of a fisherman's life in contemporary China, this representation reveals the largely escapist tenet of the male intellectual's evocation of a regional ethnic culture as an alternative (to) modernity. It further reflects Li's ambivalent acceptance of the necessity and universality of a modernity defined by the disciplinary coldness of bureaucracy and pragmatic rationality of materialism, a modernity that fits in well, if not identical, with the vision of modernization promoted in the official reform programs of the 1980s. With such a representation of the native, the ideological limitation and complicity of Li's nativist engagement with the prospect of modernity in China become fully evident.

Masculinities in Exile: Zheng Wanlong's Imaginary Roots

In contrast to Li Hangyu's romanticization of a native place at the margin of orthodox cultural China into an ethnic alternative doomed to extinction under the onslaught of modernity, which constitutes a telling example of the use and limits of regional ethnic culture as a critical site in *xungen* nativism, Zheng Wanlong attempts to create a more dynamic basis of critique in his imaginative revival of native roots at the margin of Chinese territory to counter the dominant values underlying the state-promoted vision of modernity. Rather than a static opposition between an ethnic culture and modernity, Zheng focuses on the dynamics of masculine subject constitution in marginality to question the dominant values of modernity. In other words, what is an implicit association between alternative values and masculinity in Li Hangyu's nativism becomes foregrounded in Zheng's works in which the coding of alternative values as masculinity is not mediated by a definite ethnic culture.

Set in the border area of the northeastern Heilongjiang province, where native Oroqens live side by side with Han migrants who have come in search of gold, Zheng's series of *Yixiang yiwen* (Strange tales from other homelands) tell stories of both the Hans and the Oroqens that could have dramatized ethnic cultural differences and cultural domination.[100] Yet, while the stories certainly embellish on the different sociohistorical and cultural contexts in which the Han and Oroqen populations live, what stands out in the stories is not so much contrasts between the Han and Oroqen cultures as the commonality of struggles that constitute male subjectivity for members of both nationality groups. Unlike Li's stories, which focus on exemplary figures of a particular ethnic culture, Zheng's stories portray individuals who are essentially exiles from their respective ethnic communities. Not only are the Han golddiggers and golddiggers-turned-hunters who populate the stories practically exiled from their native communities within proper Han territories, but the native protagonists of the land also share a similar situation. Whether it is Shenken in "Xiagu" (The gorge), Zhebie in "Huangyan" (Yellow smoke), or Molitu in "Zhong" (Clock), the Oroqen protagonists all suffer banishment from their communities because of some transgression against local taboos. Marking these Han and Oroqen men off from their native, communal identities and cultures, the exile state also makes them individual-subjects-in-formation who, at times, can better appreciate and preserve the values of their native cultures in marginality. In this sense, Zheng's *xungen* stories advance male subject constitution in marginality as the site of cultural resistance. As such, they prioritize cultural struggles at the level of the individual over that of either ethnicity or nation, representing a *xungen* nativism that tries to keep as far a distance from cultural nationalism as imaginable.

Zheng's interest in individualizing rather than nationalizing or ethnicizing "roots" is made clear in his version of *xungen* manifesto.[101] Entitled "Wo de gen' (My roots), Zheng's manifesto highlights the specificity of *his* individual roots in the remote Heilongjiang borderland "considered by many to be the boundaries of nations and the limits of civilization in history," making no reference whatsoever to national culture as the ultimate ground of his root-seeking.[102] Emphasizing the opportunities offered by this land of "uncultivated wildness" (*huangman*), Zheng characterizes the locus of his roots as a place for "pioneers" (*kaituozhe*) where they "create themselves in the very process of creating material wealth for themselves"; the place, to him, is thus "full of warmth, desires, feelings, life and vitality, and longing."[103] This characterization reveals that however much Zheng stresses individual subject constitution, his root-seeking is fundamentally Han-Sinocentric in that it obliterates the cultural presence of the Oroqens from their homeland, relegates them to primitive savageness, and absolves the Han "pioneers" of their undeniably colonizing moves in the name of civilization.[104] Ironically, it is at the point where Zheng endeavors to clear his roots of the trappings of national and ethnic culture to imagine new subjects-in-constitution that his ethnic-national identity (and bias) is most manifest. Zheng, however, persists in downplaying the ethnic-national ground of his representation by individualizing it as inextricably tied to the "sense perceptions and feelings" (*ganjue*) he has of the place from his childhood years.[105] Stressing that his fiction is not a re-presentation of his childhood experiences of the place but a projection of his "ideal and experiential worlds," he professes that his objective in deploying myths, legends, and customs is to "establish [his] own sense of ideals, values, ethics and morality, as well as culture."[106] By his own account, then, what Zheng seeks to achieve through his fictional construction of the native place is his own self-constitution through an imaginative and imaginary rooting of himself in a world marginalized from conventional Han-Chinese culture and modern civilization.[107] In a nutshell, the root that Zheng lays claim to is a legacy of Han Chinese seeking the opportunity of reinventing masculine subjectivity in a "native place" of marginality.

The appropriation and primitivization of the homeland and culture of the Oroqen minorities involved in such a root-seeking project are troublingly reminiscent of the use of non-Western lands and cultures in modernist cultural productions against bourgeois philistinism and artificiality in the West during the high tide of colonialism, and Zheng's focus on masculine subjects in exile in his *xungen* stories should undoubtedly be seen in this light.[108] Yet, insofar as Zheng's stories constitute a specific nativist response to the construction of modernity in China in the 1980s that cannot be dissociated from his ethnic-national grounding, our critique of the stories needs to go beyond a general comparison. It is important to explore the specificities of the stories' construction of masculinity in marginality, its connection to Han ethnic culture(s), and its relation to the critique of modernity envisioned in the heat of modernization in China. This is so, particularly since the Oroqen women in Zheng's stories are not especially sexualized, as is often the case in Western modernist representation of primitive women and in mainstream Chinese representation of non-Han cultures.[109] Furthermore, Oroqen male protagonists share in many ways the struggles that constitute masculine subjectivity for Han men in the stories. To discuss these specificities, I turn now to some close analysis of the "strange tales from other homelands."

Other Homeland: The Moral Order of Masculinity

The clearest embodiment of the masculine subjectivity Zheng invests in the wild Heilongjiang borderland can be found in the figure of Chen Sanjiao (literally, three kick Chen) in "Laobangzi jiuguan" (Old Stick's wine shop), one of the earliest stories in the *Yixiang yiwen* series. Known only by a nickname referring to his legendary killing of a wolf in three kicks, Chen Sanjiao embodies the essence of the Han men roaming the wilderness of Zheng's "other homeland," who all left behind past histories to remake themselves in the "frontier of opportunities." To highlight this self-constitution, Zheng takes pain to clear Chen of any conventional social markings: "Nobody knows how old he is, whether he has ever been married, what women he has loved, or whether he is Han or Tahur."[110] With this complete erasure of personal history and ethnic identity, Chen assumes the form of a totally self-made man, shaping and distinguishing himself with nothing but his own extraordinary physical prowess, unsurpassed skill with the knife, and exceptional courage. The actions of such a man, especially his decision to take his chances with an ultimately fatal wound in the snow-covered wilderness of winter rather than expose his vulnerability by recuperating in Laobangzi's wine shop, easily lend themselves to a reading of the character as what one critic calls the typical "macho man."[111] Yet, if fighting, killing, and risk-taking mark Zheng's masculine protagonist, perhaps predictably given his life as a hunter in an untamed land, they are not what the story dwells on. Nor do they constitute the core of Chen's self-projection and active shaping of his legacy. Rather, the story centers on an economy of moral debt and gratitude that Chen establishes to counter and supersede the monetary economy of debt and profiteering among the transplanted populace.

It is to this moral economy that Chen calls Laobangzi's attention when he pays his last visit to the latter's wine shop to essentially settle his account and dictate his legacy before walking off to his death in the wintry snow. In anticipation of Laobangzi's demand for the wine money he has never paid over the years, Chen asks Laobangzi to put in his account the money and goods others owe him. His purpose is not to make Laobangzi claim his wine money from these people, as Laobangzi initially thinks, but "to let these people remember that they are all indebted to me, and that they should do less wrong in future."[112] As to the wine money he owes, Chen assures Laobangzi that it will be repaid in future. Upon Laobangzi's questioning how, childless as he is, Chen points to the forty-three wounds on his body and states, "the gold is right here."[113] The wounds are apparently trophies of Chen's fights with local thugs on behalf of those victimized and too weak to defend themselves. In naming these wounds the gold he needs to pay his wine debt, Chen is, in effect, supplanting the monetary economy with one of justice and moral obligations. Not only is he implying that the acts of selfless justice behind his wounds are as valuable as gold, but he is also positing the possibility of a different system of reckoning necessary human exchanges than monetary calculation and, with it, a different way of understanding interdependence among people. Instead of profits and debts, needs and a sense of moral obligation to be just and to repay help and generosity with kind deeds to others are the driving force of this system.

The meaning of this moral alternative is brought home to us through money-minded Laobangzi at the end of the story. When Laobangzi seeks out the person whom Chen designates to pay his wine debts, that person turns out to be a boy whose worth lies solely in his apparent inheritance of Chen's moral spirits, besides his debts and personal accoutrements. Showing the same readiness to take care of others' needs as Chen, the boy accepts Chen's wine debts without any hesitation. He gives his words that the debts will be honored when he is old enough to make money and, as a pledge, let Laobangzi keep the ring Chen left him. The boy's words and demeanor revive Laobangzi's remembrance of Chen and his legacy, which moves him to step out of his usual greed and obsession with money to write off the debt. Through Laobangzi, the story dramatizes the effects of Chen's labor to establish an alternative to money-driven relationships, and suggests that the moral economy Chen works hard to initiate may have a chance of becoming a lasting legacy.

The transformation of Laobangzi highlights the importance of an alternative moral order to Chen's masculine subjectivity crafted in the marginality of the "other homeland." It makes clear that central to Zheng's imagination of new subject-constitution is the possibility of individuals having sufficient autonomy and control of their lives to go against the prevailing monetarization of human relations and forge new ties that are grounded in the ethics of social justice and mutual help. While this possibility is inextricably linked to the "freedom" that Chen's exceptional physical prowess affords him in the undeveloped space of wilderness, the masculine subjectivity so constituted is, significantly, marked not by naked force but by strong compassion and sensibilities. Indeed, the story takes pain to show a compassionate core inside Chen's cold and stoic appearance, and to emphasize the strength of his feelings and attachment as a key part of his legacy circulating in legends and rumors. He is said to have suffered almost suicidal grief over his dog's death at the hands of his enemies, while his scarred body testifies to his selfless compassion in helping the vulnerable. His last act—that of arranging provisions to the widow for whose welfare he has fought and received the fatal wound—crystallizes the compassionate core that gives inner strength to this legendary man of the "other homeland."

In short, Zheng's characterization of Chen's masculine subjectivity highlights three interrelated elements: individual autonomy that allows him control of his own labor and way of life; an insistence on a moral order to counteract the reduction of human relations to monetary concerns; and strong feelings and compassion, especially for those who cannot defend themselves, which serve to bridge individual autonomy with the moral order. With its emphasis on individual autonomy and moral order, this characterization can be read as encoding a two-pronged critique of the Party-state's discourse of modernity. On the one hand, its affirmation of the individual challenges the collectivism underlying the state's nationalistic rationalization of its pursuit of modernity. By allowing his male protagonist the freedom to live his own life and create his own social world, Zheng overturns the state's prioritization of the nation whose collective will and needs for modernization it claims to represent, and makes individual freedom a necessary component of the envisioning of alternative modernity. On the other hand, the privileging of a moral order over an economic order of exchange defies the Party-state's stress on the accumulation of wealth in its program of modernization. At a time when the state ideological apparatus was vigorously promoting the principles of efficiency and profitability as necessary measures of modernity, such privileging clearly suggests an oppositional stance toward the economism informing the state's vision of modernity.[114] In particular, it directly contests the state ideology's denial of any contradiction between morality and moneymaking. What Zheng endorses in his portrayal of Chen is, in fact, a principle of "valuing moral righteousness and devaluing profitability" (*zhongyi qingli*) that the state ideological regime has repeatedly denounced as a Confucian remnant hampering China's economic development.[115] Zheng's implicit critique of the state's economistic vision of modernity is thus partially informed by a moralism that is akin to traditional Han-Chinese moral culture. Yet it is not a conservative recovery of the culture in that moral righteousness is dissociated from the hierarchical order of Confucianism and linked to individual autonomy and rights. Furthermore, the persistent absence of historical and temporal references in the story confers timelessness to the moral order. This combination of individual autonomy with a timeless affirmation of the traditional privileging of morality in Han-Chinese culture makes Zheng's characterization of male subjectivity forged in "other homelands" a critical reconstruction and spatialization of tradition that establishes a nominally "nativist" ground for questioning the state construction of modernity.

Doomed (in) Exile: Interethnic Masculinity and the Critique of Modernity

Associated as it is with male subjectivity, Zheng's reconstruction of moral tradition is, unsurprisingly, grounded in a problematic gender ideology and representation, as will be discussed in detail later. For the moment, the "ethnic" grounding of the reconstructed morality needs closer examination, given its setting in the homeland of a minority nationality. Interestingly, though the moral emphasis in Zheng's characterization of masculine subjectivity can be traced to the Confucian tradition, this model of masculinity is not limited to Han migrants in Zheng's stories. The deliberate blurring of Chen's ethnic identity in "Laobangzi jiuguan" suggests as much, and the fact that other stories in the series featuring Oroqen protagonists spot a masculinity similar to Chen's reinforces this cross-ethnic claim. The similar figuration indicates that Zheng's representation of Oroqen male subjects is also structured by the two principles of critique against the state construction of modernity—individual autonomy and the priority of morality over economic and materialistic considerations. This means that, like most writers from dominant cultures, Zheng projects his own needs, desires, and political and cultural conceptions onto the minority ethnic groups, though he does not demonize them according to a Manichean logic of othering. Thus his Oroqen protagonists act out a familiar drama of moral individuals standing against materialistic modernity, only in a different social context marked by stereotypical images of "primitive societies."[116] (Re)Presenting the Oroqens as living in a backward social formation that is farther away from modernity than Han Chinese society, Zheng's Oroqen stories particularly dramatize the oppositional values that the masculine protagonists enact against both the oppressiveness of communal culture and the materialism and economism of modernity.

A significant example of this can be found in "Xiagu" (The gorge), where the protagonist, Shenken, is a telling Oroqen counterpart to Chen Sanjiao in "Laobangzi jiuguan." Expelled from his community for artlessly laughing at the sight of the shaman's pants dropping down in the middle of a religious dance, Shenken is essentially an uprooted individual like Chen throughout his adult life. Yet, he remains spiritually rooted in his native culture. While his seemingly blasphemous offense suggests an independent spirit against the rigidity of codified traditions and rituals, he is shown to have a genuine understanding and appreciation of the spiritual inheritance of his people and the history of his native place. This is expressed specifically in a deep compassion for the young and the defenseless, and an empathetic connection to the world of nature that opposes human exploitation of it for materialistic ends and monetary gains. Thus, though apparently situated in a different ethnic culture, Shenken features the same qualities of individual autonomy, moral/spiritual opposition to materialistic greed, and strong compassion that characterize Chen's masculinity.

That this masculinity in marginality encodes an alternative to a modernity defined by materialistic pursuits is suggested in the contrast between Shenken and two adolescent boys from his former community, Bieerdan and Enduli, who are set on hunting a bear on their own to prove their manhood. Shenken runs into the youths on their way to the bear cave armed with borrowed guns. Objecting to the use of guns to hunt bears and aware of the utter inexperience of the boys, Shenken insists on accompanying them to the cave and seizes the opportunity to teach them the history and spirituality of their community in the native land. According to Shenken, guns, which the Oroqens have increasingly depended on in their bear hunts, are in fact an aberration to the native way of living in harmony with the natural world. He laments:

> Bears cannot be indiscriminately hunted. They will come to you when it is time for them to die. . . . How many hunters these days know that the earliest bear was human too, that it was transformed from a woman wearing red bracelets? None of them is a good hunter. . . . One cannot use guns to hunt bears. . . . If guns are used, no more bears will be found in the Lele Mountains; the trees there will wither, grass will not grow. Our livelihood depends upon it.[117]

Contrasting sharply with this ecological vision of human dependence on the gifts of nature is the consumption-driven, materialistic preying on nature that the two adolescents, especially Bieerdan, represent. To highlight the foreignness of the modern value of materialistic preying and the warped sense of manliness it cultivates, Zheng's story draws a significant difference between Enduli and Bieerdan. An accomplished fisherman and sculptor at his young age, Enduli has already gained recognition as a brave and capable fellow in their community's time-honored ways and does not really need to prove his manhood. He is simply led on by Bieerdan, whose knowledge of the urban world outside proves quite persuasive to his peers. Bieerdan, in contrast, has not acquired any special skills from his middle school education to distinguish himself in the local way of life, and is particularly keen on establishing his manliness by gunning down a bear. That a mistaking of callousness for courage and a crude destruction of life for material gratification underlie his sense of manliness becomes clear in his disagreement with Shenken over the killing of the bear. Upon discovering that the bear is with cub and ready to deliver, Shenken compassionately appeals to the youths to spare two lives and let the cycle of life continue. The two, however, summarily dismiss Shenken as a coward. Going after the bear with his gun, Bieerdan thinks not of the spirits of life but of the material pleasures that money from the sale of two bears can afford him in the market-town: visiting the public bath, watching a movie, eating in a restaurant, having his picture taken, and perhaps even a trip to Harbin. In relating this, the narrative highlights Bieerdan's education, suggesting that outside knowledge has inculcated in him values and desires that are antithetical to the native masculine culture embodied by Shenken, and "books have given him a lot of knowledge that makes no sense in talking to persons like Shenken."[118]

This contrast between the native spirituality of Shenken's masculinity and Bieerdan's crass materialism learned from the modern world outside reaches a crescendo at the end of the story, as Bieerdan and Enduli grapple with the "heroic" death of Shenken and the meaning of his life. After Shenken has angrily disarmed the unrelenting youths, the infuriated bear makes a sudden attack on the trio. In defense, Shenken single-handedly kills the bear with his knife, but dies, too, rolling down the hill with the bear tightly clasped in his arms. Carrying his dead body out of the mountain, the deeply moved Enduli and Bieerdan open their hearts to each other:

> "I want to die like Shenken," Enduli says.
>
> "Me too, but I," Bieerdan—this young fellow who has attended middle school—pauses, sighs deeply, then says, "but I don't want to live like Shenken."
>
> "He's lived quite dauntlessly as well."
>
> "He's not even been to Harbin."
>
> "That's true. He's lived alone all his life."
>
> "I don't want to be alone, I want to marry a city girl."
>
> The two become silent again. The farther they go, the lighter the load on the stretcher feels. It is as if they are walking unburdened, even the birch stems on their shoulders weigh nothing.
>
> "Have you ever heard about human souls?" Enduli breaks the silence.
>
> "I have, but I don't believe in souls," Bieerdan says confidently.
>
> "Shenken and the bear's souls are still in the mountain, that's why it feels so light."
>
> "That's to say souls are the weightiest?"
>
> "Yes, otherwise why is there no weight to our stretcher?"
>
> Harboring an inexpressible sorrow, they disappear into the darkness.[119]

In highlighting Bieerdan's rejection of Shenken's soulful way of life despite being moved by his heroic death, this ending puts in doubt whether Shenken's native spirituality will survive to influence the young generation after his death, Enduli's dubious appreciation notwithstanding. The tragic irony of Shenken's death further reinforces this doubt. Despite his impassioned plea for human restraint on their materialistic greed to sustain the natural cycle of life, it is he himself who ultimately has to break that cycle and kill the pregnant bear. In the end, even he cannot escape the effects of others' greed and live his own life in the wilderness. The story thus reveals a resounding pessimism over the possibility of alternatives to materialistic modernity that resonates with Li Hangyu's elegiac celebration of native culture. This is arguably the deeper meaning of Zheng's "exile" of masculine subjectivity to the marginality of his professedly imaginary homeland in the wilderness. Such a masculine subjectivity, he seems to suggest, has no place or chance of survival in the world of modernity, not even among the "primitive" Oroqens who, as Bieerdan observes after Shenken's death, all use guns to hunt bears nowadays.

Morbid Speaking: The Gender Politics of Masculinity in Nativist Critique

Exiled into an imaginary homeland, the masculine subjectivity of Shenken and Chen Sanjiao projects a "native" value system that suggests not so much a return to a specific tradition, whether Han Confucian or Oroqen, as a critique and revisioning of modernity. While informed by Zheng's own Han ethnic cultural background, this "native" value system is constructed largely in a logic of opposition to the supposed materialism of dominant modernity. Underlying its critique is a culturalist conception that figures modernity primarily in terms of a prioritization of materialistic values and monetary concerns over spirituality and morality. Though it differs in particulars from Li Hangyu's depiction of modernity's pragmatic, calculative, and bureaucratic stifling of spontaneity and vitality, it similarly focuses on culture and values in delimiting modernity. As such, it shares many of the limitations of Li Hangyu's ethnicized critique discussed earlier. Above all, in positing his native alternative in a masculine subjectivity rooted in a "primitive" mode of production and existence, Zheng's critique of modernity necessarily occludes the complex social and political economic relations constituting the material realities of different modernities. With its deliberately ahistorical setting, there is no way of addressing issues of exploitation and class inequities that are central to the Maoist effort of building an alternative modernity, and from which the post-Mao regime has insistently distanced in its program of modernization. While this ahistorical design arguably allows Zheng's *xungen* nativism to go beyond the immediate politics of the Maoist and Dengist visions to explore the relationship between traditional culture and modernity, it also limits

Zheng's envisioning of alternatives to a timeless morality and spirituality that is implied to be native, but with a specific content that is not based on any ethnically distinctive cultural tradition besides a formal opposition to monetary greed in line with Confucianism and other precapitalist cultural systems. When native morality is so dehistoricized and decontextualized, it is perhaps unsurprising that the "universal" ground on which it is constituted and signified turns out to be gender relations. Herein lies the particular significance of masculinity in Zheng's construction of individual subjectivity in marginality.

The moral/spiritual alternative grounding the subjectivities of Chen Sanjiao and Shenken, as we have seen, hinges on a different male–female relation than that prevalent in the dominant social order governed by materialism. Whereas the likes of Laobangzi care only about making profits from and taking sexual advantages of women, Chen Sanjiao acts out his moral difference by risking his life to help a widow. Similarly, Shenken shows his moral difference from Bieerdan not only in cherishing the pregnant bear as a descendant of a woman wearing red bracelets and a carrier of life, but also in harboring a lasting love for a woman whom he can never possess, while Bieerdan desires to marry a city girl for urban material attractions. A nonmaterialistic, affective regard for the female thus marks the moral constitution of masculine subjectivity in Zheng's protagonists.

The significance of woman in this moral constitution of masculine subjectivity is, ironically, revealed in the fact that neither the widow in "Laobangzi jiuguan" nor the woman Shenken loves in "Xiagu" makes even an appearance in the stories. Far from active characters, they serve only as objects of material, moral, and linguistic exchanges among the men. Specifically, as signifiers of the reification of human relations in a materialistic economy, women are no more than bodies of objectified passivity on which Zheng's protagonists construct their masculine order of morality. In other words, inasmuch as a nonmaterialistic, affective relation to women constitutes the distinguishing moral factor of the protagonists' masculine subjectivity, women in Zheng's stories are bound to the world of materialism against which the masculine subjects define and distinguish themselves. They are denied any subjectivity or agency to transcend their status as objects of exchange and to change their own lives so that the male protagonists can demonstrate their moral difference. Confined within the economy of material transactions, they constitute a common inert medium for the male protagonists to express their yearnings for, and (re)form themselves in, an alternative public space of morality. In such capacity, female characters in Zheng's stories are basically recurring representations of an abstract notion of Woman, as the Chinese critic Chen Mo has pointed out.[120] The above discussion suggests that this abstract notion of Woman has two interrelated sides. On the one hand, through the repeated motif of women equaling certain pieces of gold, Woman becomes a signifier of men's alienation from their humanity in a materialistic economy. On the other hand, as the object of care and love for the male protagonists, Woman symbolizes men's aspiration for the affective, nonmaterialistic dimension of life that confers humanity and promises transcendence.

This dual signification of Woman and its crucial importance to the moral constitution of masculine subjectivity is thematized in the story "Yedian" (Wild lodging). The reduction of women to passive objects on which the masculine subject projects his own desires and acts out his moral difference is glaringly clear in this story, where the woman character, Dazhenzi, has literally become a corpse over which the male protagonist, "he," and her husband, Fugeng, fight to assert themselves and the values they represent. Having sold herself for six pieces of gold to Fugeng while loving the male protagonist, who, at that time, had disappeared into the wilderness trying to find enough money to buy her out of prostitution, Dazhenzi was so distressed in her marriage that she died before "he" could find the sixteen pieces of gold that her husband subsequently demanded as her price. The story opens with the male protagonist discovering her shabby grave, a few days after her death, in the mass burial ground where the dead bodies of the impoverished and the homeless are dumped. In the eyes of the protagonist, the shabbiness of her grave, which is but a small mound of freshly dug soil unmarked even by a little piece of wood, testifies to her husband's mean treatment and valuation of her, namely, "no different from a dog."[121] What Fugeng represents in the story is precisely the utilitarian and materialistic view of human relations signified by the equation of Woman to certain pieces of gold. Dazhenzi's body, which he has bought for sexual release and reproduction, is worthless to him after her death, since it has lost its utilitarian and exchange value.

The protagonist, in contrast, shows increased appreciation of Dazhenzi's value after the demise of her body. His treatment of her corpse reflects this appreciation, especially in opposition to the callousness of her husband. Digging her out of the shallow grave, he takes the body to a "wild lodging," a man-made cave by the river where navigators and wayfarers used to take their rest, and "where people act according to their conscience . . . and money has no use."[122] There, he lovingly cleanses her corpse with spirits, preparing it for a proper burial, complete with a formal tombstone in a cemetery for natives of her home province down the river. Such elaborate rites are meant not only to show the protagonist's regard for the woman as a distinctive person irreducible to the exchange value of her body, but, more important, to dramatize his moral difference from her husband, Fugeng. As the story follows his actions, it also enters his consciousness to reveal his different valuation of the woman than Fugeng's. Early on in the story, he reflects that both he and Fugeng "should know how to cherish a woman; what a woman wants is not gold bangles."[123] Later, as he holds her corpse in his arms, he laments that "he has not lived a day that makes him feel a bit human! He thinks she should have turned him into a human being, but he has missed the opportunity."[124] Before his final confrontation with Fugeng, he curses Fugeng for "not understanding that a woman is a goddess in this place of ours."[125] All these reflections suggest that the woman symbolizes for the protagonist his aspiration for a life beyond material and monetary concerns, a life of affection and spiritual fulfillment that can make him human. It is this different understanding of the value of a woman that ostensibly marks his difference as a moral/spiritual being from Fugeng's utter embeddedness in the world of materialism and utilitarianism.

Yet, precisely because this moral difference acquires meaning only against a prevailing materialistic and utilitarian conception of human relation, it necessarily maintains the commodification and objectification of women as its condition of possibility. Put differently, the male protagonist's moral difference is produced only on the ground of denying women subjectivity and the capacity of choosing how to live and change their own lives. This is revealed in the story when "he" recalls the time Dazhenzi left Fugeng to visit him and proposed to stay regardless of his inability to provide her with a permanent home or material security. He refused and made her go back to Fugeng, thereby obliterating her will and desire to take the initiative in changing her own life. Far from any concern about maintaining her livelihood, his reason for refusing is that he "cannot break [his] word to a bastard like Fugeng."[126] Thus his assertion of moral superiority over Fugeng requires him to treat Dazhenzi, in effect, as an object and a commodity, to be bought from Fugeng with sixteen pieces of gold. Whatever spiritual and emotional values he projects on the woman, she is, in the final analysis, nothing but an objectified vehicle for him to assert his moral difference from the dominating men in the material world, to constitute himself against the materialistic distortion of humanity. As such, the woman is categorically exiled from humanity as well as subjectivity.

It is not difficult to see from this construction of masculine subjectivity in moral opposition to materialism and utilitarianism that no viable alternative is offered on its ground. The dominance of materialistic exchange is maintained while the masculine subject and his morality are marginalized and contained within the deserted "wild lodging." Like all of Zheng's male protagonists in the *Yixiang yiwen* series, "he" in "Yedian" cannot escape the fate of a tragic, liminal figure, harboring a moral difference that never has a chance of being realized in the world of materialistic values. In the end, the story leaves him seriously wounded by Fugeng, hanging between life and death, alone with the corpse of Dazhenzi in the "wild lodging." With such an ending, the prospect of a viable alternative masculine subjectivity is dimmed, if not yet completely doomed. Insofar as the native root that Zheng seeks to re/discover lies in such a construct of alternative masculine subjectivity, this also spells the feebleness and inherent failure of Zheng's nativism in imagining a positive alternative to the state's materialistic and economistic construction of modernity.

The Limited Oppositionality of Imaginary Roots

From Han Shaogong's Bingzai, Li Hangyu's Dahei, Laotou, and Fukui, to Zheng Wanlong's Laobangzi, Shenken, and nameless "he," exiled or marginalized masculine subjectivity figures centrally in the roots that *xungen* nativists creatively searched for among diverse regional locations and ethnic cultures. This re(dis)covery of substantially common roots from a diversity of search loci reveals *xungen* nativism's essentially negative oppositionality. That is, the root(s) on which the *xungen* nativists projected their hope for a different modernity and identity are primarily structured in opposition to dominant constructions. Rather than the marginalized ethnic traditions supposedly recovered in the act of root-seeking, it is this opposition that gives discursive coherence to the concrete configuration of roots. The similar characterization of the various *xungen* "heroes" further corroborates this negative oppositionality. Though placed in different milieus, the heroes in the stories of Li Hangyu and Zheng Wanlong all feature a masculine subjectivity that exudes autonomous individuality and an independent spirit against incorporation into a circuit of calculative materialism and economic exchange based on monetary values. What makes such a masculine subjectivity clearly an abstract oppositional figure is its simultaneous representation as rooted in traditions, as even the true custodian of traditions that the ethic community to which the masculine subject (once) belongs has itself forgotten or forsaken in the pursuit of a materialistic modernity. Through the figuration of a marginalized masculine subjectivity that is at once autonomous and culturally rooted, in short, *xungen* nativism posits a mythical traditional culture that supports individual freedom, independent judgment, and autonomous expressions in a moral economy free from the trappings of Western individualism. Underscoring its mythical nature, the (various) local places in which this tradition is supposed to be located are rendered outside of history, locked in an ahistorical past bearing little if any real links to contemporary social relations. Removed from concrete social, historical grounding, its specific contents are determined by the dominant construction of modernity to which it is opposed, particularly the privileged figure of a collective-minded subject devoted to material progress and economic development as the goal and ultimate value of modernity that is common to both the postsocialist state project of modernization and the Oriental version of the Pacific Rim discourse.

By virtue of this negative opposition, *xungen* nativism incorporates the dominant discourse's assumptions and conceptions of modernity even as it seeks to articulate alternatives. Specifically, as we have seen above, in displacing individual freedom, spontaneity, passion, compassion, and moral integrity onto a marginalized masculine subjectivity, *xungen* stories maintain the hegemonic understanding of modernity as a universal teleology of rationalistic standardization and materialistic economic development. The historical link of such a conception of modernity to capitalism and its logic of exchange values and maximum profits is thereby occluded, while the foreshadowed demise and necessary doom of that masculine subjectivity further affirm the inevitability of such modernity. Thus, despite the *xungen* nativists' conscious efforts to envision an alternative modernity for China through an exploration of the devalued rural local and individual, the oppositional potency of their *xungen* constructs is neutralized by the universalized capitalist paradigm of modernity in which they are inscribed and circumscribed. A vibrant masculine subjectivity as oppositional roots ends up being relegated to an imaginary realm of negative projection, neither linked to the particular history of China's socialist and postsocialist wrestling with modernity nor mapped to a utopian future.

This exile of alternatives to the imaginary realm reveals a deliberate myth-making underlying the *xungen* nativists' efforts to intervene in the discourse of modernity. While this discursive strategy serves the dual purposes of decentering cultural traditions reclaimed in post/modernity and challenging the legitimation of the state project of modernization on nationalistic grounds, it also lays bare the immaterial nature of the nativist space of countermodernity inscribed therein. This may well be the ultimate meaning of the constitutive component of searching in *xungen* nativism. In foregrounding the act of searching, *xungen* nativism reveals its conscious design as a literary intervention that articulates "tradition" to present concerns through the imagination of a native place and indigenous cultural roots that exist nowhere and everywhere. The native in *xungen* nativism, then, is no more than a fictive, imaginative projection of oppositional politics determined by an abstract, deterritorialized understanding of (capitalist) modernity. As such, it not only reproduces common Western modernist tropes of primitivism, the noble savage, and the self-making masculine subject, but also significantly limits the range of concrete social relations of power that *xungen* nativism can engage and contest in its mapping of marginality onto the native, not least class and gender hierarchies.

Particularly remiss in *xungen* nativism's oppositional politics is a reflexive engagement with the power relation between intellectuals and the marginalized figures they represent in their writings. The representation of the rural subaltern has been a central concern of nativist writing in modern China, and Lu Xun's moving rendition of the almost unbridgeable gap between intellectuals and the rural subaltern has brought the issue to life. Yet, arguably because of its deliberate myth-making, *xungen* nativism shows little concern over the issue, blithely overlooking the gap between intellectual representation and the experiences of marginalized others and the ensuing problem of intellectual appropriation of marginality to consolidate their representational authority. It is as if the admittedly mythic qualities of the marginalized ethnic culture and the characters cultivated therein give license for an intellectual freehand in representation in the name of imagining alternatives. What results is an unacknowledged generalization and substitution of the male intellectual writers' interests and concerns in post/modernity for the marginalized perspective and vision of alternative modernity. Thus the threat to their customary subject position of relative power and privilege that male intellectuals experienced under the extension of capitalist market relations into everyday life comes to stand for all marginalization under capitalist modernity, further silencing the subaltern peasants and women. Though this male-intellectual-centered strategy does effect some forms of critical intervention in calling attention to and challenging the combined economistic developmentalism and cultural nationalism in the state's project of modernization, it completely elides class issues and maintains a masculinist construction of alternative that closes off rather than opens up radically different possibilities of modernity.

Problematic as it is, this nativist attempt at imagining alternatives turns out in historical hindsight to be precisely the valiant yet doomed resistance to the sweeping power of global capitalist modernity that is so passionately depicted in the *xungen* works. With the full-blown development of mass consumerism under the Party-state's active promotion of market economy in the 1990s to disarm and neutralize the silenced discontent of the populace over the 1989 brutal suppression of demonstrations at Tiananmen Square, the reference to a "native" realm of moral values and idealistic adherence to tradition-based individual principles that drives *xungen* nativism's contestation of the rationalistic materialism of bureaucratic capitalist modernity became obviously anachronistic and irrelevant. The increasing dominance of the market and consumption in everyday life brought forth a different discursive construction of the historical conditions and ideological constitution of Chinese modernity in terms of the postmodern. *Xungen* nativism's negative opposition to capitalist modernity and abstractly utopian imagination of alternatives could not but give way to a rising tide of consumerist celebration of market choices and differences that calls for a more historically grounded and socially contingent mode of contestation.

CHAPTER FOUR

Gendering Natives, Engendering Alternatives

There is a wealth of evidence to suggest that, for women, the "modern" is always perilously close to the "alien," particularly when contemplated codes of behaviour can be identified as an outright betrayal of the expectations of their own communities.

—Deniz Kandiyoti

The category of consumption situated femininity at the heart of the modern. . . . [T]he idea of the modern becomes aligned with a pessimistic vision of an unpredictable yet curiously passive femininity seduced by the glittering phantasmagoria of an emerging consumer culture. No longer equated with a progressive development toward a more rational society, modernity now comes to exemplify the growth of irrationalism, the return of repressed nature in the form of inchoate desire.

Rita Felski

Women have an uncanny (*unheimlich*) presence in *xiangtu* and *xungen* nativism. On the one hand, they are triply absent: first, from the league of established and/or self-proclaimed nativist writers; second, from the conceptualization and theoretical articulations of nativist concerns; and, third, from the debates on *xiangtu wenxue* and *xungen wenxue*. On the other hand, women are ideologically central to concrete narrativizations of post/modernity in nativist stories, even as or precisely as they are materially absent or marginal on the textual level. This uncanny presence encapsulates the gender politics of *xiangtu* and *xungen* nativism, which are tellingly similar despite significant textual and contextual differences in the two discourses. Tracing women's relation to the discourses thus affords an illuminating comparison and critical evaluation of the promise and limits of oppositionality and alternative vision of modernity encoded in *xiangtu* and *xungen* nativism.

Women, as the opening epigraphs suggest, are a key discursive figure of modernity in being linked to at least two important loci of modern signification: national/communal identity and consumption. Women's centrality to national identification in modernity is discernible in the ubiquitous nationalist rhetoric and trope of nation-as-women, especially women to be protected, and the concomitant preoccupation with female sexuality and codification of women's proper sexual conduct, which is in turn often linked to the feminization of consumption common to analytic accounts and cultural critiques of modernity.[1] By virtue of such intricate discursive connections, women constitute a rich and complex site for constructing and contesting modernity across different historical and social contexts. A specific instance and instructive discussion of this complex discursive site can be found in Rita Felski's study of woman as a key figure for expressing ambivalence toward the modern in nineteenth-century Europe, which encompasses various articulations of longing, and temporal and spatial displacements in search of meaning elsewhere.[2] In particular, Felski's delineation of the relation between an increase in feminized representation of modernity and the rise of a culture of consumption provides useful clues for exploring gender politics in nativist critiques of dominant discourses of modernity. Yet, her analysis of the European experience also leaves out issues that are particularly important in the postcolonial contexts of the non-European world. Notably absent from her list of significant issues in theorizing cultural representation of women and modernity—commodification and consumerism, the private/public distinction, female sexuality, politics of avant-garde aesthetics and mass culture, the organizational power of historical narratives, and simultaneous differentiation and contamination of political, religious, and scientific vocabularies—is national/ communal identity, which, as we have seen, is a core issue in the construction of modernity in China and Taiwan. Given that the state's promotion of nationalism to legitimize its policies of modernization through Western importation makes national identity a key issue in modernity for these two social formations, we cannot examine the gender politics of *xiangtu* and *xungen* nativism as counterdiscourses of modernity without taking into consideration women's representation in the discursive construction of national/communal identity in post/modernity.

Alternatively speaking, insofar as nativist discourses partake in debates of modernity through the figuration and representation of communal identities and cultural heritages, thus inevitably engaging nationalism (if only as an alternative or contesting formulation), nationalist significations of women also play an important part in the discursive politics of nativism. By the same token, unpacking the different representations of women in *xiangtu* and *xungen* nativism may highlight their distinctiveness as oppositional discourses. For comparative purposes, Deniz Kandiyoti's summary characterization of various portrayals of women in nationalist discourses offers a convenient point of departure.[3] To paraphrase Kandiyoti, precisely because nationalism involves a Janus-faced self-representation as both a modern transformational project forging new identities and a timeless affirmation of cultural traditions conferring authenticity and rooted community in a time of change, its signification and ideological investment in women are chameleonic and at times even contradictory. Among various portrayals, Kandiyoti identifies three main types: victims of social backwardness; icons of modernity; and privileged bearers of cultural authenticity. Each of these representations puts women in a different relationship to modernity, yet almost invariably makes them a sign of some vexing concerns or controversial issues in the nation's (construction of) modernity. It is precisely such signification of contestation and ambivalence toward modernity that structures the gender politics of *xiangtu* and *xungen* nativism.

With reference to Kandiyoti's three types of nationalist portrayals, a review of the representation of women in *xiangtu* and *xungen* nativist works discussed in earlier chapters reveals interesting differences. First, there is remarkably little representation of social backwardness as a national condition and hardly any signs of women as victims of social backwardness in either nativism. Though nativism's general orientation in affirming and reclaiming a native realm may make this unsurprising, given the inextricable link of the idea of native to some form of historical grounding in traditions, the pervasive absence of textual signification of social backwardness is still telling. It suggests a general reservation toward a progressivist understanding of the project of modernity and a corresponding refusal to dismiss traditional elements of society and culture as outdated and irrelevant, even if their survivability in modernity is questionable for reasons of power and hegemony. In the exceptional case of Han Shaogong's *xungen* story, which breaks this mode to feature social backwardness in its representation of the meaning of modernity and modernization for the nation/community, the specific gender coding of backwardness is no less telling. Rather than a woman like Bingzai's mother, it is the retarded male subject, the old boy Bingzai himself, who embodies the victimizing effects of social backwardness. Such a gendering highlights *xungen* nativism's difference from the collectivism of the state nationalist discourse in accentuating the repression of (masculine) individual subjectivity as the paradigmatic sign of China's malaise, which may indeed be intensified and reinforced in the dominant form of modernity underwritten by state bureaucratic power in the name of the nation, as Li Hangyu's stories, in particular, illustrate. With the focus thus trained on masculine subjectivity, women are either banished from the stage of modernity altogether or displaced from the sign of victimization by the young, defenseless male.

A similar gender politics is apparent in the absence of representation of women as privileged bearers of cultural authenticity and repositories of native values in *xiangtu* and *xungen* nativism. If nationalist discourses tend to lodge cultural authenticity and traditional values in women so as to free men for the active role of modernizing agents or modern subjects in the fashion of dominant (masculine) Western conceptions of modernity, the frustrated development of masculine subjects—on significantly different accounts—in *xiangtu* and *xungen* nativism's representation of (the failure of) the state project of modernity completely unhinges this particular gender(ed) system of modern signification. In the nativist narratives of alternative modernity, it is not women but men struggling to maintain their masculinity who are the privileged custodians of native values and cultural authenticity, and thereby the genuine subject of a congenial modernity based on indigenous culture. Here, a difference between *xiangtu* nativism and *xungen* nativism is noteworthy. Whereas individual subjects holding onto the local culture of manliness that is threatened with extinction by the onslaught of "alien" modernity on their marginalized ethnic community constitute the quintessential bearer of authentic native values in *xungen* nativism, the native heritage and cultural authenticity in *xiangtu* nativism are vested with the class of exploited and oppressed manual workers who struggle to uphold their patriarchal values and codes of conduct against the corrupting effects of a Western-oriented capitalist modernity. With individual masculinity as the ultimate locus and measure of cultural vitality and autonomy, not only is the native tradition gendered masculine, but its custodian is also male by default in *xungen* nativism. Indeed, inasmuch as *xungen* nativism's attempt to validate the autonomous subjectivity of a culturally rooted man as the authentic native hinges on representing his principled challenge to traditional authority, which is lodged in the figure of the father-patriarch-state, as a faithful espousal of the genuine spirit of tradition, patriarchy is not a constitutive part of the *xungen* native, and there is a corresponding absence of valorization of the mother or motherland. In *xiangtu* nativism, in contrast, the native resides ultimately in the patriarchal culture of the manual working class, which entails both male and female paragons of virtues and may at times be best represented by mother figures such as Jinshuishen, even though women are still not the privileged bearer of cultural authenticity and marker of native identity. In their supportive role of sacrificing mothers and symbols of the motherland, women figure in *xiangtu* nativism as feminine keepers of traditional culture in need of protection by their native sons, on whose and no other's heads the laurel of authentic collective identity squarely rests.

Though both rest on masculine concerns and authority, the particular gendering of the native as the patriarchal tradition in *xiangtu* nativism, and as masculine subjectivity harboring the authentic spirit of native culture in *xungen* nativism highlights differences between the two discourses. Similarly arising from a conscious effort to contest the respective states' project of modernity and construct indigenously grounded alternatives to a Western inspired and oriented modernity, the differences can be related to the particular conditions and circumstances under which the states carried out their projects of modernity at the time of the nativist challenge. A key difference is the states' relative position and power differentials in the international world order and their different relations to the development of global capitalism. These differences and their underlying power structures, in part, determine the uncanny presence and specific representations of women in the nativist works.

Feminizing Modernity and a Nation of Whores

If Taiwan was to become part of a celebrated model of development that inspired confidence in a culturally inflected "Chinese" modernity and thus contributed to the rise of *xungen* nativism in the 1980s, its international status was much more precarious in the heyday of *xiangtu* nativism. Displaced by the PRC at the United Nations, Taiwan in the 1970s had to struggle for even a slight footing in the international political order, just as economically, it began to carve a role for itself in the postmodern development of global capitalism as a link of cheap labor in the multinational manufacturing chains controlled by globally mobile capital. Yet to yield the economic capital that would make the island-state a "little tiger" of development in a decades' time, the subordinate nature of such a participation in global capitalism reinforced the political weakness and vulnerability of the state internationally. Particularly, in generating a stream of young, largely female, poorly paid, and ruthlessly used rural migrants into the assembly lines of foreign-owned and/or controlled factories, this mode of economic development carries a feminine connotation that easily lends a gender coding to the state's relative powerlessness in the international order. The state project of modernity may then be correspondingly seen as feminizing and the nation as feminized under a foreign-oriented modernity.

Such a gender coding is made further plausible by a strong and highly visible American presence in the island-state, not only in the form of capitalist investment but especially in the form of the military. As a strategic foothold in East Asia for the United States, Taiwan was a regular "rest and recreation" site for American soldiers posted to the Pacific, especially during the Vietnam War. Besides a vivid display of imperialist domination, this brought to Taiwan American consumer goods that, by virtue of their limited availability at exorbitant prices, fostered conspicuous consumption as a sign of modernity and class privileges. Together with a strong contingent of Japanese businessmen who doubled the gains of their lucrative economic activities on the island with lascivious adventures, American soldiers also spawned a bustling sex trade that made prostitutes a particularly resonant symbol of the nation-state's position in and relation to (Western) modernity. In heightening the visibility of consumption and prostitution, which are clearly gendered practices associated with femininity, American military presence made palpable a gendered reading of Taiwan as feminized and its state project of modernity as feminine and feminizing.

That such a gendered reading of the state project of modernity underlies *xiangtu* nativism's attempt to articulate a native alternative is apparent in the spectacle of feminized consumption and sexualized, objectified female bodies in Wang Zhenhe's story discussed in chapter two. In a more subtle manner, Wang Tuo, too, locates the problem of Taiwan's modernity in women's frivolous consumption and its corrupting effects through his representation of Jinshuishen's daughters-in-law and customers. On one level, this use of feminine consumption to signify problems and concerns with the dominant construction of modernity is little different from a long line of critiques of capitalist modernity in the West, including the influential writings of Horkheimer, Adorno, and other thinkers associated with the Frankfurt School. As Rita Felski and other feminist scholars have shown, the identification of women with consumption, which is ideologically positioned on the negative side of modernity conceptualized in terms of binary oppositions such as production–consumption, authenticity–artificiality, individuality–conformity, and rationality–fantasy, has consistently been central to Western theorizations of the relation between femininity and modernity, and related critiques of the feminizing—objectifying and commodifying—effects of capitalist modernity.[4] In contrast to the dominant masculine conception of modernity as the rebellion of an autonomous, individual subject creating and defining himself against tradition and conventions, this conception of feminized modernity focuses on the problematic areas of commodification, massification, and the generation of artificial, irrational, and excessive desires, with the prostitute as the paradigmatic figure. Motivated by negative critiques of modernity, such a mapping of women to modernity and consumption necessarily reduces the complexity and variability of women's implication in modernity in general and consumer culture in particular.[5] As Carolyn Steedman shows, there are multiple, contradictory ways in which women relate to consumption, notably as commodified objects and signifiers in narratives of exchange; as consumers of commodities and fantasy; as both objects of desires and desiring subjects; and as producers of goods for consumption.[6] In making women stand for commodification in a mass culture that propagates excessive desires and irrational fantasies manufactured according to the logic of profit and standardization, critiques of feminized modernity reduce women to passive objects of consumption, even in the role of desiring subjects, where their very desires and fantasies turn out to be none other than inauthentic consumer products.

Representations of women in the nativist stories of Wang Zhenhe and Wang Tuo unambiguously enact a similar construction of women's relation to consumption and modernity. Yet, instead of universalizing the relation, *xiangtu* nativism maps it onto class to articulate a particular indictment of an "alien" corrupting modernity oriented toward and motivated by alienating desires of foreign origins. Whereas Western critiques of capitalist modernity implicitly base their universalized conception of women's relation to consumption on the experiences of a particular class of women—bourgeois women—whose lives are principally structured by the dominant ideology of public–private separation that limits their "work" in modernity to the realm of reproduction, *xiangtu* nativism foregrounds the class affiliation of women seduced and objectified by consumption. In other words, if consumption is linked to women in general in Western critiques of modernity, it is clearly associated in *xiangtu* nativism with a particular class of women who identify with the state's construction of Western-oriented capitalist modernity. It is this very mapping of class and gender to form concrete figures of middle-class consuming women such as Mrs. Wang in Wang Zhenhe's story, and sacrificing working-class women like Jinshuishen in Wang Tuo's story, that enables *xiangtu* literature to offer a nativist critique of and alternative to modernity directed and dominated by foreign interests. Through the bifurcated representation of women, whereby middle-class women are identified with the artificiality, alienation, objectification, and immoral desire of compulsory consumption to signify an "alien" feminizing modernity linked to Westernization, and working-class women come to symbolize the undue burden, exploitation, and oppression suffered by the motherland under such an alien modernity, *xiangtu* nativism figures the native alternative as a restoration of the benevolent patriarchal tradition, which the urban middle class jettisons under the seduction of consumption and the working class is prevented from observing under the double exploitation of a Western-dominated capitalist modernity.

Masculine State, Effeminate Subjects, and Bureaucratic Modernity

In contrast to Taiwan's disempowerment in the international order, which, together with the dominating presence of foreign capitalist interests, allowed a gender reading of the nation as feminized by Western (capitalist) power,

China occupied a relatively strong position vis-à-vis the capitalist West even as it actively sought foreign investment in capital and technology in the 1980s. Though there was a pervasive sense of national backwardness, which was skillfully exploited by the Communist Party-state to promote its program of modernization, China did not experience or perceive the kind or degree of foreign domination felt in Taiwan. Boasting a huge potential market coveted by Western capitalists, boosted by East Asian economic "miracles," and buffered by a socialist legacy that had yet to completely lose its legitimating power, the country maintained a national strength and independence far from effeminate in relation to global capitalism. Yet, though the nation-state was not subordinated under the capitalist West in a power hierarchy that lent itself to gender symbolism, the experience of the nation under the modernization program forcefully implemented by the authoritarian Party-state could still be represented in gendered terms owing to a perceived threat of commodification with the introduction of market mechanisms into the running of the country in the name of modernization.

A significant part of women's identification with consumption, as we have seen, is the prevailing feminine coding of commodities with their connotation of standardized objects for market exchange and mass consumption. On account of this gender coding, even though conspicuous consumption was not (yet) an issue of modernity in China in the mid-1980s—unlike Taiwan in the 1970s—a similar representation of the nation being feminized under the state's project of modernity can be found in *xungen* nativism as in *xiangtu* nativism. Without a boisterous consumption scene linked to Westernization, however, the agent and mechanism of feminization are differently conceived in *xungen* nativism. If it is the corrupting effects and exploitative tactics of Western (capitalist) modernity exemplified in the consumption craze of middle-class women that account for the nation's feminization in *xiangtu* nativism, what threatens masculine identity in *xungen* nativism is the bureaucratic rationalization and standardization of an administered society that advances a modernity of materialistic calculation reducing individuals to commodities for exchange in an economic circuit. In other words, rather than the feminine mode of modernity associated with problems of consumption that *xiangtu* nativism opposes, it is a masculine modernity of disciplines, rationality, and utilitarianism in production that is critiqued in *xungen* nativism. Belying the differences, however, these two modes of modernity may be seen as intimately related, like two sides of the same coin, as Horkeimer and Adorno suggest in their influential critique of Western capitalist modernity.

In *Dialectic of Enlightenment*, Horkeimer and Adorno unmask the disciplined male bourgeois individual's repression of the body and the feminine to achieve domination of nature and the world through rereading the Greek myth of Odysseus and the sirens. As Douglas Kellner usefully summarizes:

Culturalist Critique, Gendered Alternatives, and Nativist Oppositionality

Despite significant differences in the specific gendering of the native they posit, the limited capacities in which women figure in *xiangtu* and *xungen* nativism make clear the discourses' characteristics as culturalist critiques of modernity by male intellectuals. Whether cast as Westernized urban whores or exploited rural mothers in *xiangtu* nativism, or as feminizing agents of bureaucratic, rationalistic modernity in *xungen* nativism, women are key to the ideological representation of the problems of dominant modernity in terms of cultural and moral issues from a masculine intellectual point of view. By the same token, such representation occludes the multiplicity of ways in which women actually partake in the production, reproduction, and, indeed, interrogation of modernity. Particularly revealing of this masculine culturalism is not only the glaring absence of women from the nativist practices and debates, but also the nativist discourses' elision of the significance of women as industrial waged laborers and the specifically gendered exploitation and discrimination that female workers experienced in Taiwan and China's economic development under global capitalism. For instance, the large number of young women drawn from rural villages to work in foreign-owned and/or run factories in the export processing zones or special economic zones because of their supposed docility and nimbleness hardly figure in the two nativist critiques of (capitalist) modernity. Nor is there any critical representation of the sexual commodification of women under such modernity beyond its moral condemnation as an erosion of traditional values. That the emergence of a sizeable contingent of sex workers is also a political economic issue of exploitation simply lies outside their ideological purview.

These exclusions and elisions suggest a filtering out of women's experiences of the everyday realities of post/modernity that do not fit the cultural and moral framework of opposition in *xiangtu* and *xungen* nativism's representation of dominant reality. Such ideological representation casts the problem of dominant modernity in the light of cultural subordination and dispossession, enabling the discursive advancement of a revival of masculine subjectivity or patriarchal traditional order as the basis of an (alter)native modernity. In this sense, the two nativist discourses constitute a culturalist critique of modernity from the standpoint of male intellectuals.

This unpacking of *xiangtu* and *xungen* nativism's gender and cultural politics makes clear the particular limits of their oppositional possibilities. Their commonality as masculine intellectual culturalist critique suggests definite oppositional shortcomings on the ground of gender and class rather than or as well as a nationalistic recourse to primordial origins that is often charged of nativism. In the case of *xungen* nativism, though national identity is arguably a de facto concern, reflecting the dominant ideological landscape of the time, concrete works are not primarily circumscribed by nationalism or a valorization of primordial origins. Of the works considered in this study, Han Shaogong's "Bababa" shows the most preoccupation with the Chinese nation, but only in terms of national modernization, which ironically makes it most critical of the national tradition and affirmative of an open-minded learning from outside. The stories of Zheng Wanlong and Li Hangyu, on the other hand, skirt national identity to inscribe different cultural identifications on the margins of imaginary ethnic traditions to affirm masculine subjectivity against commodification. To the extent that they effect conservative identity politics, it is due not so much to a reification of established traditions or communities rooted in a particular place as to a masculine intellectual appropriation of the marginality of women and ethnic others to imagine and establish the heroic (alter)native modernity of resisting individual subjects. While understandable in light of the compulsory collectivism of the postsocialist regime's nationalistic ideology, this privileging of masculine individual subjects undercuts the possibility of constituting meaningful collective identities and solidarities across differences in gender, ethnicity, and class to build an enabling alternative modernity. The intellectual culturalist critique of commodification further closes off the conceptual openness of an imaginary ethnic identification in marginality to produce a lone "heroic" resistance that is doomed from the start.

To a greater extent, nationalism structures the politics of *xiangtu* nativism in Taiwan and limits its oppositional possibilities, but still falls short of defining it or circumscribing it in conservatism. The crisis in "national" identity Taiwan faced in the 1970s made nationalist sentiments almost unavoidable in *xiangtu* works. Yet, whatever conservative impulse nationalism channels is interrupted by a comparably powerful class identification with manual workers that leads to a politically mixed representation of the nation and complex conception of (alter)native modernity. This is evident in both Wang Zhenhe's "Xiaolin lai Taipei" and Wang Tuo's "Jinshuishen." Though nationalism ultimately compromises the two stories' critical interrogation of class exploitation under capitalist modernity to reconsolidate patriarchal identity and power, their identity politics is not reducible to nationalist conservatism. An empathetic depiction of manual workers in both allows for variable conceptions of native identity that embody emergent possibilities. Wang Zhenhe's story suggests the need and possibility of cross-ethnic class solidarity between Taiwanese and Mainlander workers in the constitution of a native standpoint to critique dominant modernity and construct alternatives, even if its textual rendition of the solidarity is currently based on patriarchal identification. Wang Tuo's national allegorical representation of Jinshuishen as the motherland figures in women's contribution to a creative transformation of the nation into modernity in the capacity of economic providers, putting critical pressure on the story's affirmation of patriarchal ideology in Jinshuishen's native point of view. The incorporation of concerns of gender and class inequity and marginalization into that of national subordination thus wedges open the narrative recourse to nationalism for imagining (alter)native modernity in both stories, making space for the potential emergence of alternatives in the margins of the traditional patriarchal order currently recuperated for the conservative narrative resolution of the problems of dominant modernity.

More than nationalism or place-based identity politics, then, the oppositional possibilities of *xiangtu* and *xungen* nativism are limited by an intellectual rendition of place and nation in terms of ahistorical and already fully constituted traditional values and cultural orders that are grounded in and maintain gender and class hierarchies. Conversely speaking, their particular oppositional potentials rely precisely on the various ways in which the established order is disrupted and native and/or national traditions and cultural values are interrogated and wrested open by concerns of social inequity along the lines of gender, class, ethnicity, and so forth. This critical displacement of readily available (alter)natives to situate the native in a complexly mapped nexus of marginality in constant negotiation with the center is exemplified by Huang Chunming's rendition of nativism. The native in Huang's story "Pinguo de ziwei" is not constituted by any particular national, ethnic, class, or gender position. Rather, it is a variable oppositional term engaging different power structures from the critical position of marginality. If the deaf-mute daughter of an urban subproletariat crippled by American military forces and silenced by imperialist welfare dole stands at the extreme of marginality in the story, she still does not constitute the native position so much as marks contingently the place of multiple marginalization and oppression that affords intellectuals a vantage point to articulate a complex critique of dominant modernity. Without a definite, positive identification of the native, Huang's story offers no readily available alternative either. In place of such an alternative, it locates radically different possibilities literally outside of and beyond intellectual discourses. Enabling possibilities are to emerge contingently from genuine dialogues and practical negotiations in which the subaltern female's "yiyiyaya" are no longer unintelligible but articulated into a collective vision of difference.

Huang Chunming's work thus makes clear that nativism is most productive as a negative critique interrogating the power structures underlying hegemonic conceptions of modernity from the position of marginality rather than a positive construction of native identity as the site of alternatives. In this capacity of negative critique, nativism acknowledges the necessity of engaging Western culture in the effort to construct alternatives without reifying its opposite into native values that in effect continue the ideological dominance of Western culture. While such a critical stance does not posit a native realm completely outside or independent of Western hegemonic culture, it also does not occlude power dynamics or gloss over the incommensurability of cultural values and visions by embracing hybridity. Alternatives, in this critical view, lie at the liminal space of contestation and negotiation where differences are confronted in full recognition of their constitutive power relations to forge new contingent possibilities in actual praxis.

POSTSCRIPT

Place-Based Politics in China and Taiwan Today

In 2001, Han Shaogong returned once more to Hunan to settle in the place where he had experienced rural life as a sent-down youth in the 1970s and imaginatively revisited in his root-seeking writings in the 1980s. This premeditated return after a stint of very successful entrepreneurial-cum-critical ventures in cultural publishing in the special economic zone of Hainan, one of the new "frontiers" of the 1990s, is rich in symbolic meaning and cultural politics, eliciting much attention and discussion. Set at a time when rural China has seen a precarious exodus of labor into urban centers and coastal areas where the jobs, wealth, and future seem to be, Han's travel in the reverse direction calls attention to the question of native place under global capitalism. Significantly, the return of this veteran *xungen* advocate to a place suggestive of native identification is no longer couched in the nativist terminology of roots. Though his personal historical connection to the place clearly matters, he refers not to history or cultural traditions but to human and natural ecology in explaining his latest choice of home. To him, this is a place of familiarity where he understands the local dialect and humanistic background.[1] It is also a place of nature where he can live peacefully far from the city, observe the richness of life, farm organically, and enjoy fresh air and unpolluted water.[2] Moreover, despite its physical remoteness, this is by no means a place of isolation. Upon the naturally endowed environment not yet contaminated by the man-made malaise of modernity, Han has built a place of local and global connections that reach beyond the physical boundaries of his new home. Locally, he has in a sense gone "native" in following the tradition of opening his house for all who care to drop in for a chat and socializing on equal terms with the local peasants, to the extent that he is well known among villagers miles away and addressed like a native in the local idiom as "Handie" (father Han).[3] Beyond this community, he has taken advantage of the technological advancement under global capitalism to build a web of digital connection that allows him to plug into national and global networks to continue performing his duties as president of the Hainan Provincial Federation of Literary and Art Circles and communicating with people around the world. By virtue of these networks, Han's chosen "native place" is traversed by complex global-national-local circuits of routes even as it is rooted in an ecologically delimited and historically constituted place. In such a place, he purports to lead a way of life that balances nature and civilization, and integrates physical and mental labor, in search of a healthier modern civilization.[4]

In once again calling attention to the question of native place and the significance of marginalized rural hinterlands in modernity, but without the culturalist trappings of roots anymore, Han's discussion of his resettlement reflects how much has moved on since *xungen* nativism and how much remains at issue. If, as argued in earlier chapters, nativist discourses like *xungen* and *xiangtu* nativism thrive as critical interrogations of modernity only in times of national ideological instability, when global capitalism has yet to assume hegemony within the nation, enabling an articulation of place-based politics onto a foreign-native oppositional structure that questions the nation-state's construction of modernity under the domination of global capitalism, such nativism inevitably wanes when global capitalism's deepening grip on the nation's experience and conception of modernity renders untenable a foreign-native oppositional conception of modernity. This is arguably what happened in China in the 1990s. As a full-throttle course of "reform" and integration into the global capitalist system brought relative material plenitude, consumerist enjoyment, and economic gains to many, especially those in the urban centers, the capitalist mode of modernity could hardly be distanced as foreign and alien, even if it could still be considered problematic in some quarters. The dissolution of a native-foreign oppositional conception of modernity, however, did not take away the issue of native place and the cultural politics associated with place under global capitalism that *xungen* nativism engaged by virtue of its emphasis on the notion of roots. Indeed, the significance of regional ethnic differences and rural marginalization highlighted in *xungen* nativism's focus on the marginalized hinterlands became even more salient as capitalist principles and relations took hold in China in the name of reform.

As widely observed, the 1990s saw an ascendance of cultural regionalism in China, with the provinces becoming a focal unit of regional culture and identity. That a political-administrative boundary should come to delimit cultural identity suggests intense cultural political maneuverings. Deliberately promoted by provincial leaders and local elites, such cultural regionalism is linked to a provincial discourse of development responding strategically to state economic policies that emphasized fiscal decentralization and local specialization to develop "comparative advantages" in a global market. As the central government's reform agenda called for self-reliance in the provinces, provincial leaders, especially those in the interior regions that had not been booming like the coastal areas under the open-door policies, faced a critical task of developing sources of revenue and attracting investment for local facilities in a larger economic environment of market competition. The promotion of a distinct provincial identity was a multipurpose attempt to achieve these ends by rallying local support, cultivating loyalty, and developing product specialization to claim particular market segments, with Shanxi, for instance, being transformed into a place of noodles and vinegar, or Guizhou into a liquor center.[5] Thus, unlike *xungen* nativism, the discourse of regionalism advanced is not critical of capitalist modernity at all. Rather, it is geared toward accommodating and aligning with the requirement and demand of transnational capital, so as to ensure the province's economic survival through plugging into the global capitalist circuit. In other words, it fits into global capitalism's transformation of place and place-based cultural differences into marketable features and selling points in investment decision and marketing strategies.

Notably, this discourse of cultural regionalism also differs from *xungen* nativism in its relation to the nation-state. If *xungen* nativism vaccinates between national identification and regional ethnic cultural identification, at times using the latter to question dominant ideological construction of the nation and the modernity it legitimates, the provincialism that developed in the 1990s glosses over any possible disjuncture and tension between the national and the regional. Itself an overdetermined, artificial composition from a diverse variety of local, place-based folk culture and customary practices within the province, the distinctive regional culture claimed is simultaneously touted as a preservation and continuation of an essentialized national tradition and Chineseness, making the region a cultural core of the nation. Thus, despite intimately felt local identities based on places within the province that are characterized by different dialects, customs, cuisines, music, and drama traditions, a Shanxi culture was diligently crafted by the provincial leadership to promote pan-local integration and highlight the province's cultural importance as the hearth of ancient Han culture.[6] Crucially, such regional culture is mobilized to support rather than challenge the national course of economic development through integration into global capitalism set by the central government. In promoting a regional culture that retains Chinese essence, the provincial leaders seek to not only recenter their cultural if not economic positions but also attract transnational capital from overseas Chinese capitalist elites who find neo-Confucianist culturalist claims persuasive and appealing. In other words, the construction of a congenial relation between regional and national culture is, at least partly, a strategic response to global capitalism's modus operandi in Asia, where transnational Chinese capital plays a central role in establishing concrete patterns of investment, offshore production, and trade that are heavily influenced by place-based factors such as common language and cultural backgrounds, ethnic ties, and spatial proximity. If inland provinces inevitably lose out to the coastal area in terms of spatial proximity, ease of access, and even specific diasporic ties to the place of origin, they have all the more reason to emphasize a special link between the regional culture and the Confucian Han-Chinese tradition that supposedly grounds the identity of a cultural Chinese, wherever he is geographically located. By virtue of such accommodation to the operational logic of global capitalism in Asia, the discourse of cultural regionalism in the 1990s enacts very different place-based politics vis-à-vis the national and the global than that of *xungen* nativism, though it similarly abstracts local practices into supralocal cultural traditions.

Against such cultural regionalism orchestrated from above, a different kind of place-based politics—one grounded in concrete everyday lives—is suggested in Han Shaogong's discussion of his return to Hunan. Rather than an abstraction of place-based practices, such as a local dance or opera, into provincial cultural traditions that are in turn translated into commodities for the global market, Han focuses on the physical and humanistic attributes of the place he chose to build a new home. While a pristine environment may also constitute an attractive selling point to tourists in the marketing of a province,[7] Han's account of the clean water and air of his place is emphatically tied to organic farming and not tourist attraction. That is, Han stresses the physical attributes of the place as an organic component of a way of life and not a marketable commodity.

Such an understanding of the importance of the physical environment in constituting place and the way of life it supports echoes the environmental consciousness and protests that are becoming increasingly important as China faces a deepening environmental crisis after decades of growth-oriented industrial development. Deforestation and water and air pollution have progressively worsened as the country stepped up its pace of development. Though these environmental issues eventually affect all, their immediate impacts are distinctly local. Deforestation leading to soil erosion means the loss of arable land for peasants in the region and water pollution directly affects the health and even reproduction of local villagers dependent on natural sources of water. Thus, environmental problems can easily accentuate the sense of belonging to a place and the need of collective struggle to keep the place a viable habitat for the local people. Unsurprisingly, then, environmental protests have become a prominent form of place-based politics in China, especially in the rural areas, since the promulgation of the country's first Environmental Protection Law in 1979. With the law promoting awareness about environmental problems and conferring legitimacy to the fight against polluters, local villagers immediately affected by particular development projects are empowered to seek remedies. Typically, the affected villagers will group together to stage direct protests in the form of petitions, lawsuits, and even sabotage. In these protests, place-based cultural institutions and practices such as kinship and lineage, popular religion, and customs in the everyday life of local villagers play an important role in identifying specific environmental issues, galvanizing collective action, and imagining solutions. For instance, in a case analyzed by Jun Jing, the strong lineage of a dominant local family in a Gansu village made a ready base for mobilizing protests against the contamination of a local stream by a fertilizer factory. Not only did the family ties help to congeal the protest group, but the polluter's threat to the fertility and reproduction of the clan constituted a palpable signifier of the environmental problem jeopardizing the life and welfare of the local villagers.[8] Hence, place in the sense of social relations situated in a specific bounded physical environment is doubly significant in grounding environmental protests against the excesses and abuses of industrial development.

If Han Shaogong's reference to clean air and water in his account of return to the native place implicitly evokes place-based environmental politics, his recentering agriculture as a valuable part of life brings up another place-related issue that is increasingly significant under the postsocialist state's program of market-driven development and modernization—namely, rural marginalization and exploitation. The rural village and its agricultural way of life is a telling site of social inequality and injustice in a national economy geared toward production for the market and articulation into the global capitalist system. While the emphasis on market competition and commercialization has created economic opportunities and consumerist choices for many in the urban cities, it has increasingly marginalized and impoverished the rural areas, subjecting the agricultural population to the plight of "comparative disadvantage" as market fluctuations and rising costs and falling prices for farm products leave them destitute with few options. Despite backbreaking hard work, farming can no longer sustain life for many in China's rural hinterland, especially those in agriculturally marginal regions in the west and southwest where poor soil quality can hardly produce enough to feed the peasant's own family. Even for farmers in better endowed areas, poverty is never far from the horizon. The burdens of expanding government grain quota, heavy taxes, rising production costs, and increasingly wide differentials between agricultural and industrial prices deplete them of savings to cushion against unforeseen emergencies and the vagaries of nature. In contrast, those in the countryside who had the opportunity to start up private industry and rural services in commerce, transport, repair, or construction, leaving agriculture behind or on the sidelines, have prospered. Consequently, a sharp widening in income inequality is evident within rural China, both between regions and within villages. This gap reflects the increasing plight of farmers in the hinterland who continue to eke out a living in agriculture while others have found greener pastures, so to speak, precisely off farming.

There is a further twist to this place-related inequality and injustice. Even as the agricultural way of life is in grave jeopardy, many in the rural population remain tied to the land without access to any possible exit. Labor migration, which has played and continues to play an important role in supplying cheap labor for rural and urban industries, is a costly and risky business for the rural villagers while highly profitable for the employers. As long as the central government continues to impose residence-permit restrictions on migrant workers from the countryside, the migrants will remain at the mercy of their employers, competing with one another for only the worst jobs and bearing the hefty cost of migrating in search of an elusive job in the first place. Even labor migration encodes a kind of place-based inequality. Only those from areas with established chain migration linkages and those who can afford the transportation cost and time to leave home to hunt for jobs may find labor migration a possible way out of the seemingly dead end of agriculture. It is an entirely different story for the otherwise placed. As Jonathan Unger observes, the obstacles are simply too high, the costs too great, and the potential rewards too precarious for villagers in the truly impoverished areas to try to engage in long-distance job migration.[9] The marginalization of the agricultural way of life is most poignant from the vantage point of these places.

The marginalization yet continued exploitation of farmers to support the industrialization process makes class an irreducible, albeit suppressed, dimension of place-based politics in China. Indeed, judging from the incidents of media reports on peasant protests and demonstrations against the excessive fees and taxes levied on them, the thorny problem of class inequality can no longer be swept under the carpet of economic development through opening the country's doors to global capitalism. If the excesses of class struggle under the Maoist period justified to some extent *xungen* nativism's emphasis on regional ethnic culture rather than peasant lives in its gloss on the marginalized hinterland, the aggravation of class inequality in a decade and more of postsocialist development calls for a re-vision once again of how the marginalized hinterland constitutes a critical site for interrogating the dominant conception of development and modernization. The promotion of cultural regionalism by provincial leaders has made clear the accommodating nature of regional cultural identification under the operational logic of global capitalism. The increasing plight of farmers who have to live off the land, on the other hand, suggests class to be a critical locus of intervention in the construction of modernity that takes seriously the importance of place in general and the native place in particular.

Interestingly, an opposite reversal has occurred in the politics of the native place in Taiwan. As in China, the notion of native place and place-based politics remained important but took on different forms in Taiwan after the wane of *xiangtu* nativism. The superimposition of a foreign-native and capitalist-labor opposition in *xiangtu* nativism collapsed with the transformation of Taiwan into a celebrated "little tiger" of global capitalist development. As Taiwan took advantage of the spatial proximity and cultural and ethnic linkage with China to become a key investor in the mainland coastal areas under the open-door policies, especially in the Fujian province, where some seventy percent of industrial outputs are generated by Taiwanese investment, the table was turned. While the common ethnic and cultural heritage of the Taiwan investors and Chinese laborers complicates a foreign-native oppositional understanding of this new relationship (Taiwanese investors have a legal status of "semiforeigner" in China), Taiwan's ascendance into the rank of "transnational capital" clearly makes implausible an identification of the native with manual labor. With the retraction of class issues from the imagination of the native place, the tricky native/national identification of Taiwan in the native place politics of *xiangtu* nativism takes the foreground.

The articulation of the native place as the basis on which to imagine a (new) national identity and future for Taiwan in *xiangtu* nativism reverberated politically after the cultural movement subsided. Taking clues from the *xiangtu* debates to respond to Taiwan's increasing isolation and diplomatic debacle, the Nationalist government under the leadership of Jiang Jingguo embarked on an indigenization process that sought to refocus national attention on pragmatic issues centering on Taiwan. Political reforms, including increasing the number of legislative seats elected from Taiwan and incorporating more Taiwanese into provincial government posts, were undertaken as part of a concerted effort to make Taiwan the locus of national identification. Significantly, if the ultimate connection of the native place to the Chinese nation was not openly questioned in *xiangtu* nativism, it became possible to do so with this indigenization movement. Though intended not to jettison the idea of Taiwan as ultimately a Chinese nation but to defuse ethnic polarization between the Taiwanese and Mainlanders, the indigenization policies did help to open up such a possibility. Underlying the indigenization strategy was a pragmatic depoliticization of Taiwan as the place where people of various Chinese origins dwell and live together in prosperity and economic progress. Thus, paralleling the indigenization efforts was a national development plan that focused on integration into the global capitalist system, stimulation of economic growth, commercialization, and raising standards of living. Included in the plan was also a call for cultural reconstruction that emphasized not only the dissemination of the Chinese tradition but also the promotion and protection of folk ethnic traditions, not to say the advancement of Western fine arts and other forms of high culture. As Allen Chun argues, this amounted to a commercialization of culture, Chinese and otherwise, as an object of desirable consumption in a free-market economy.[10] Taiwan, under this national development plan, is less a Chinese nation than a thriving marketplace and economic powerhouse under global capitalism.

If the Nationalist recentering of Taiwan highlights pragmatic economic development to deflect ethnic identification, the emphasis on Taiwan as a native place rather than Chinese nation took a different turn in the hands of the political opposition, who found an opening under the indigenization policies to advance their vision of a Taiwanese nation. With the gradual relaxation of political control and steps toward democratization, Taiwanese who had been excluded politically and culturally by the Nationalist-controlled state began to openly rally for a local-focused Taiwan consciousness that easily shifts into a Taiwanese consciousness with emphasis on Taiwan's distinct history and development under Japanese colonization, as noted in chapter two. Accentuating differences between the Mainlanders and Taiwanese, the controversial shift from Taiwan to Taiwanese consciousness in effect maps the native place onto Taiwanese ethnicity and even a Taiwanese nation. This is tantamount to a call for Taiwan independence that understandably leaves many in jitters, given China's ultrasensitivity to any suggestion of Taiwan separatism and the close economic ties that have been established between the two on top of cultural, historical, and ethnic linkages. Much of the political wrangles in contemporary Taiwan lies in such contentious mapping of the place called Taiwan.[11] Of potentially egregious economic and even military consequences for not only Taiwan but also the Asia-Pacific region and its relation to global capitalism, place-based politics is at its most acute here. This ongoing saga of indigenization also makes evident the global implications and complexity of efforts to identify the native/local in a given place. The accentuation of the idea of native place in *xiangtu* nativism turns out to be a Pandora's box with no closure in sight.

The dominance of Taiwanese identity politics in the indigenization of Taiwan, like the promotion of cultural regionalism in China, shows a conservatism that is often charged of place-based politics. Yet, it is important to note that there is nothing inherently conservative about place-based politics, though the tendency to inscribe place with established categories of identities and traditions is strong. It is precisely such reification that this book seeks to argue against through examining the class, ethnic, and gender mappings of the native in tension with the nation in the nativist contestation of post/modernity. Place-based politics in China and Taiwan after *xungen* and *xiangtu* nativism is no different in this respect. In China, the progressive challenge of environmental protests from below is no less significant a place-based politics than the accommodating conservatism of cultural regionalism from above. Similarly, however dominant Taiwanese identity politics is in structuring the reconstruction of Taiwan as a place, there are other forms of place-based politics with more critical and progressive potentials. The aboriginal movement is a case in point.

Seizing the political opening of the indigenization and democratization efforts, Taiwan's aboriginal groups formed an alliance to fight collectively for aboriginal welfare in 1984. If their initial efforts concentrated on addressing personal difficulties and social problems such as child labor, adolescent prostitution, and unemployment, their attention gradually shifted to the larger issues of resuming original family names and reclaiming ancestral land as the connection between personal problems and the societal placing of indigenous peoples as a whole became apparent. In other words, the aboriginal movement came to an understanding of the indigenous peoples' predicaments and problems in terms of marginality and displacement, and hence an appreciation of the significance of place-based politics in their struggle. Besides the demand for increased land rights, they fought for a change in the standard term of address for indigenous peoples from *shanbao* (mountain folks) to *yuanzhumin* (original inhabitants).[12] By asserting and demanding recognition of their prior claims to the land that now constitutes Taiwan, they insist on their right to partake in the (re)construction of the place and seek an equal place for themselves in the contemporary social order, including the right to study their native languages, history, and culture. Though ethnic identity is also a key dimension of this movement, the physical and social displacement of the aboriginals makes such claim to ethnic identification a strategic essentialism against marginality that is different from the conservatism in the Taiwanese majority's bid for a nation based on Taiwanese ethnicity.

This difference makes clear that place-based politics has different critical potentials in the struggle of differently placed social groups. Significantly, inasmuch as the place-based politics discussed above can be read as developing on the basis of issues opened up in the earlier nativist discourses, they also continue the gender bias of the earlier discourses. Women's concerns and perspectives tend to be marginalized from the place-based politics of cultural regionalism, environmental protests, and ethnic identification, even if women are often invoked as signs of the problems to be addressed. And yet, as Wendy Harcourt argues, women can and do engage in place-based politics that challenges global capitalism through networking on the basis of solidarity building around issues emanating from women's needs and experiences in everyday lives and livelihood.[13] Place, from the standpoint of women's lives and struggles, is differently constituted at several levels of intimacy and immediacy—first, the female body, which situates women and mediates their interactions in the dominant social order as mothers, sexual objects, natural being, and the other; second, the domestic place of the home, which circumscribes the primary social and cultural space of existence for many women; and, third, the "public" sphere outside the home, where women are largely silenced, marginalized, and at best tokenized. Women's place-based politics, then, potentially engages and articulates a whole range of issues spanning from the intimacy of sexual and body politics such as domestic violence and reproductive rights, to the workplace struggles of sexual discrimination and harassment, the social and political demand for gender equality and inclusiveness, and the national struggle for an "independent" development free from the domination of global capitalist powers and their transnational instruments such as the International Monetary Fund and the World Bank. These issues have different relevance and resonance in Taiwan and China as the two confront their respective national situations and pursue their development plans under global capitalism. With the emphasis on stimulating economic growth and the corresponding relaxation of political control, Taiwan, in particular, has seen a blossoming of women's groups and feminist activists and critics engaging in a variety of social and cultural struggle for rights, especially over sexual liberation and women's reclaiming their own bodies. China, on the other hand, has seen a retraction of official promotion of women's equality and participation, and a significant return of women to the domestic place of home as a result of factory closure and downsizing necessitated by the introduction of market forces under economic reforms. These involve complex place-based politics that cannot be adequately discussed within the scope of this study. Suffice it to note here that in light of the study's argument that gender bias and exclusion are crippling factors in the critical potential of nativist discourse, these place-based politics may precisely hold the key to the articulation of genuine alternatives under global capitalism. Including women's concerns and perspectives is vital to the formulation of place-based alternatives, under nativist conceptions and beyond.

Notes

Introduction: Interrogating (through) the Native

1. Rey Chow's essay "Where Have All the Natives Gone?" is exemplary of such a postcolonial articulation of the question of the native and its critical potentials. In Chow's terms, the native is a useful critical tool when its status as an image standing in for the unavailable moment of imperialism and its epistemic violence is taken seriously. If, on the other hand, the native is taken literally and given hermeneutic depth, the epistemic violence is reinforced and a conservative politics of nostalgia results. See Chow, "Where Have All the Natives Gone?" in *Writing Diaspora: Tactics of Intervention in Contemporary Cultural Studies* (Bloomington: Indiana University Press, 1993), pp. 27–54.

2. James Clifford, *Routes: Travel and Translation in the Late Twentieth Century* (Cambridge: Harvard University Press, 1997), p. 24.

3. On the local as a space of resistance under global capitalism, see, for example, Gillian Rose, "The Cultural Politics of Place: Local Representation and Oppositional Discourse in Two Films," *Transactions of the Institute of British Geographers* 19 (1994): 46–60; and Jon May, "Globalization and the Politics of Place: Place and Identity in an Inner London Neighborhood," *Transactions of the Institute of British Geographers* 21 (1996): 194–215. On the mutual implication of the global and the local, see Arif Dirlik, "The Global in the Local," in *Global/Local: Cultural Production and the Transnational Imaginary*, ed. Rob Wilson and Wimal Dissanayake (Durham: Duke University Press, 1996), pp. 21–45. On the complexity of cultural dynamics under global capitalism, see Lisa Lowe and David Lloyd, eds., *The Politics of Culture in the Shadow of Capital* (Durham: Duke University Press, 1997).

4. Prasenjit Duara, "Local Worlds: The Poetics and Politics of the Native Place in Modern China," *South Atlantic Quarterly* 99.1 (Winter 2000): 13–45.

5. *Xiangtu* literature is an important subgenre of modern Chinese literature that emphasizes the local color, traditions, and history of particular regions. Though it covers a range of styles, including the ambivalent ironic writings championed by Lu Xun and resistance literature against Japanese occupation of northeastern China, it is most often associated with the nostalgic pastoral work of Shen Congwen in the late 1920s and 1930s. Denounced by the Communist regime for being reactionary, Shen's work

enjoyed a revival in the 1980s with the demise of Maoist zeal, inspiring the (re)turn to regional cultures in *xungen* nativism. Of particular importance to the *xungen* advocates is Shen's legacy of strong regional identifications through embracing the "primitive" cultures of his native place in West Hunan. A comparison of *xiangtu* fiction in the 1920s and 1930s with *xungen* literature and Taiwan's *xiangtu* literature will be interesting, but beyond the scope of this study. For a literary reading of the relation between Shen's works and *xungen* literature, see Jeffrey C. Kinkley, "Shen Congwen's Legacy in Chinese Literature of the 1980s" in *From May Fourth to June Fourth: Fiction and Film in Twentieth-Century China*, ed., Ellen Widmer and David Der-wei Wang (Cambridge: Harvard University Press, 1993), pp. 71–106. The list of critical commentary on Shen's works is quite extensive. For example, see David Der-wei Wang, *Fictional Realism in Twentieth Century China: Mao Dun, Lao She, Shen Congwen* (New York: Columbia University Press, 1991); and Peng Hsiao-yen, *Antithesis Overcome: Shen Congwen's Avant-Gardism and Primitivism* (Taipei: Institute of Chinese Literature and Philosophy, Academia Sinica, 1994). A history of *xiangtu* literature from the perspective of contemporary scholars in the PRC can be found in Chen Zihui deng, *Zhongguo xiangtu xiaoshuo shi* [A History of Chinese Native Place Fiction] (Hefei: Anhui jiaoyu chuban she, 1999).

6. Gayatri Spivak makes an eloquent case for the importance of "rhetorically sensitive approaches" to cultural studies in "Thinking Cultural Questions in 'Pure' Literary Terms," in *Without Guarantees: In Honour of Stuart Hall*, ed., Paul Gilroy, Lawrence Grossberg, and Angela McRobbie (London: Verso, 2000), pp. 335–57. While Spivak focuses on the political effectiveness of reading literature literarily, her reminder that the rhetorical deployment of language matters in figuring out the political in the cultural applies in spirit here.

CHAPTER ONE. OF ALTER/NATIVES, MARGINS, AND POST/MODERNITY AT THE RIM

1. For classic discussions of China's response to the onslaught of Western modernity, see Benjamin Schwartz, *In Search of Wealth and Power: Yen Fu and the West* (Cambridge: Harvard University Press, 1964); and Joseph Levenson, *Confucian China and Its Modern Fate: A Trilogy* (Berkeley: University of California Press, 1968).

2. Mary Louise Pratt, "Modernity and Periphery: Toward a Global and Relational Analysis" in Elisabeth Mudimbe-Boyi, ed., *Beyond Dichotomies: Histories, Identities, Cultures, and the Challenge of Globalization* (Albany: SUNY Press, 2002), pp. 21–47.

3. Pratt, like many others, actually uses the term "periphery," following the core-periphery terminology adopted by Immanuel Wallerstein in his influential world-system theory. I decide to use "margins" instead to highlight the power structure of cultural differentiation on top of the political economic framework of the world-system theory, and to evoke current theoretical refiguration of marginality into a critical site for interrogating and interrupting the dominant universalizing discourse producing and consolidating the center.

4. Homi Bhabha, "Conclusion: 'Race', Time and the Revision of Modernity," in *The Location of Culture* (London: Routledge, 1994), pp. 236–56.

5. As Timothy Mitchell points out, recent efforts to decenter the dominant (Western) understanding of modernity through discussions of "alternative modernities" that emphasize the multifarious combination of forces shaping particular histories of development to produce different versions of modernity in different locations do not necessarily question an "underlying and fundamentally singular modernity" ["Introduction," in Timothy Mitchell, ed., *Questions of Modernity* (Minneapolis: University of Minnesota Press, 2000), xii]. Mitchell's own attempt at decentering, with a poststructuralist reading of modernity in terms of representation or a staging of history that is inherently incomplete, affirms the critical importance of treating modernity as primarily a discursive construct, which Pratt specifically foregrounds in calling it white Europe's "identity discourse." See Mitchell, "The Stage of Modernity," in Mitchell (2000), pp. 1–34.

6. Gayatri Spivak, *Outside in the Teaching Machine* (New York: Routledge, 1993), p. 63.

7. Lisa Rofel, *Other Modernities: Gendered Yearnings in China After Socialism* (Berkeley: University of California Press, 1999), pp. 16–17.

8. See Max Weber, *The Protestant Ethic and the Spirit of Capitalism* (New York: Charles Scribner's Sons, 1976); and *The Religion of China: Confucianism and Taoism* (New York: Macmillan, 1964).

9. See Theodore Huters, "Appropriations: Another Look at Yan Fu and Western Ideas," *Xueren* [Scholar], no. 9 (April 1996): 296–355; Gail Hershatter, *Dangerous Pleasures: Prostitutes and Modernity in Twentieth Century Shanghai* (Berkeley: University of California Press, 1997); and Shu-mei Shih, *The Lure of the Modern: Writing Modernism in Semi-Colonial China, 1917–1937* (Berkeley: University of California Press, 2001).

10. A helpful summary of the political economy of development in the Asia-Pacific can be found in Ravi Arvind Palat, "Introduction: The Making and Unmaking of Pacific-Asia," in Ravi Arvind Palat, ed., *Pacific-Asia and the Future of the World-System* (Westport, CT: Greenwood Press, 1993), pp. 3–20. On the subcontracting system specifically, see Gary Gereffi, "International Subcontracting and Global Capitalism: Reshaping the Pacific Rim," in Palat, pp. 67–83.

11. On Nihonjinron, see Kosaku Yoshino, *Cultural Nationalism in Contemporary Japan: A Sociological Enquiry* (London: Routledge, 1992). For an insightful collection on Japan's cultural relations to the West during this period, see *Postmodernism and Japan*, eds., Masao Miyoshi and H. D. Harootunian (Durham: Duke University Press, 1989).

12. Fredric Jameson, *Postmodernism, or, The Cultural Logic of Late Capitalism* (Durham: Duke University Press, 1991).

13. When, whether, and how postmodernism mattered in Taiwan and China are highly debatable issues both locally and cross-culturally. Fredric Jameson's identifica-

tion of a novel by Taiwan writer Wang Wenxing published in the 1980s as postmodernism was roundly criticized by Rey Chow for imposing a Western critical periodization on texts quite differently situated. [See Fredric Jameson, "Literary Innovation and Modes of Production: A Commentary," *Modern Chinese Literature* I.1 (1984): 3–18; and Rey Chow, "Reading Mandarin Ducks and Butterflies: A Response to the 'Postmodern' Condition," *Cultural Critique* 5 (1986): 69–93.] The identification and temporal location of postmodernism have been no less controversial among Chinese scholars ever since the concept was introduced into the Chinese cultural scene in the mid-1980s. Rehearsing the complex debates is beyond the scope of this discussion, especially since postmodernism is not the concern here, as I explained in the main text. Suffice it to say that despite charges of "inauthentic and blind borrowing" from the West, postmodernism has been creatively deployed by both cultural workers and critics in Taiwan and China to engage contemporary issues in their concrete social locations. For a good overview, see Arif Dirlik and Zhang Xuedong, eds., *Postmodernism and China* (Durham: Duke University Press, 2000).

14. David Harvey's justly influential book, *The Condition of Postmodernity*, gives a lucid summary of these developments and their cultural effects. For a Marxist historical treatment of the discursive emergence of postmodernity, see Perry Anderson, *The Origins of Postmodernity* (London: Verso, 1998).

15. Needless to say, this is not to deny the importance of other developments and factors within Euro-America in the rise of postmodern discourse, as discussed in countless studies on the subject. Particularly noteworthy is the coming to voice of ethnic minorities and other marginalized groups in the civil rights and feminist movements, which put tremendous pressure on the universalistic claims of the white male discourse of modernity. On the relation between the rise of postmodern discourses and the politics of marginality and difference, see, for example, Craig Owens, "The Discourse of Others: Feminists and Postmodernism," in Hal Foster, ed., *The Anti-Aesthetic: Essays on Postmodern Culture* (Port Townsend, WA: Bay Press, 1983), pp. 57–82; Andreas Huyssen, "Mapping the Postmodern," *New German Critique* 33 (Fall 1984): 5–52; Nelly Richard, "Postmodernism and Periphery," *Third Text* 2 (1987–8): 6–12; Anders Stephanson, "Interview with Cornell West," in Andrew Ross, ed., *Universal Abandon? The Politics of Postmodernism* (Minneapolis: University of Minnesota Press, 1988), pp. 269–86; bell hooks, "Postmodern Blackness," *Yearning: Race, Gender, and Cultural Politics* (Boston: South End Press, 1990), pp. 23–31; and Linda Nicholson, ed., *Feminism/Postmodernism* (New York: Routledge, 1990).

16. First published in 1979 by Harvard University Press, Ezra Vogel's *Japan as Number One: Lessons for America* was quickly adopted by a commercial press and became a best seller with notable impact well into the mid-1980s.

17. Since one of the hallmarks of postmodernity (and postmodernity discourse) is the putative disruption of the center-margins structure, maintaining the language of center and margins in our discussion is already to go beyond the signification system of postmodernity. The center-margins language draws attention to the fact that however decentered or, more exactly, multicentered the postmodern world of global capi-

talism, its power centers are still concentrated in cities that are predominantly Western, as Saskia Sassen has effectively shown, leaving the center-margins structure as relevant as ever, if somewhat displaced. See Saskia Sassen, *The Global City: New York, London, Tokyo* (Princeton: Princeton University Press, 1991).

18. See "Introduction: Postmodernism and China," in Dirlik and Zhang, *Postmodernism and China.*

19. See Arif Dirlik, "The Asia-Pacific Idea: Reality and Representation in the Invention of a Regional Structure"; Alexander Woodside, "The Asia-Pacific Idea as a Mobilization Myth"; and Bruce Cumings, "Rimspeak; or, The Discourse of the 'Pacific Rim'"; all collected in Arif Dirlik, ed., *What Is in a Rim? Critical Perspectives on the Pacific Region Idea*, 2nd edition (Lanham, MD: Rowland and Littlefield, 1998). See also Christopher Connery, "Pacific Rim Discourse: The U.S. Global Imaginary in the Late Cold War Years," *boundary 2*, 21:1 (1994): 30–56.

20. The miracle motif is evident in the titles of a wide range of publications on the East Asian economic development experiences, such as Chalmers Johnson, *MITI and the Japanese Miracle* (Berkeley: University of California Press, 1982); Thomas Gold, *The Taiwan Miracle* (Armonk, NY: M. E. Sharpe, 1986); Gary Gereffi, ed., *Manufacturing Miracles* (Princeton: Princeton University Press, 1991); and World Bank, *The East Asian Miracle: Economic Growth and Public Policy* (Washington, DC: Oxford University Press, 1993)

21. Martin Andersson and Christer Gunnarsson, eds., *Development and Structural Change in Asia-Pacific: Globalizing Miracles or End of a Model?* (London: RoutledgeCurzon, 2003), p. 3.

22. Bruce Cumings, "Rimspeak," p. 54.

23. Originally a geological term, the Pacific Rim refers to the rim of volcanic and tectonic activity around the Pacific Ocean.

24. The frontier connotation of the rim is well noted. Dirlik, Woodside, and Connery all draw attention to it without much elaboration.

25. Arif Dirlik, "Introduction: Pacific Contradictions," in *What Is in a Rim?*

26. Peter A. Gourevitch, "The Pacific Rim: Current Debates," *The Annals of the American Academy of Political and Social Science* 505 (1989): 8–23.

27. Herman Kahn, *World Economic Development: 1979 and Beyond* (New York: Morrow Quill Paperbacks, 1979), p.122.

28. See Roderick MacFarquhar, "The Post-Confucian Challenge," *The Economist*, February 9, 1980, pp. 67–70; Peter Berger, "An East Asian Development Model?" in Peter Berger and Hsin-huang Michael Hsiao, eds., *In Search of an East Asian Development Model* (New Brunswick, NJ: Transaction Books, 1988). Berger's ideas were first explored in an article published in a Taiwan magazine: "Yige dongya fazhan di moxing: zhanhou taiwan jingyan di wenhua yinsu" [An East Asian Development Model: Cultural Factors in the Experience of Post-war Taiwan], *Zhongguo luntan* [China Forum], no. 222 (December 25, 1984), pp. 19–23.

29. Hung-chao Tai, "The Oriental Alternative: An Hypothesis on Culture and Economy," in Hung-chao Tai, ed., *Confucianism and Economic Development: An Oriental Alternative?* (Washington, DC: The Washington Institute Press, 1989), p.7.

30. Besides social scientists, humanists of Chinese origins in US academies also actively participated in the so-called post-Confucian challenge. Most notable is Tu Wei-ming, a prominent scholar of Confucian philosophy at Harvard University, who not only took part in many forums and conferences on Confucianism and economic development in East Asia, but also played a central role in Singapore's promotion of Confucianism and design of a Confucian curriculum. His contribution can be gleaned from two edited volumes of speeches and interviews: Tu Wei-ming, ed., *Confucian Ethics Today: The Singapore Challenge* (Singapore: Curriculum Development Institute, 1984); and *Ruxue disan shiqi fazhande qianjingwenti* [On the question of the prospect of the third stage development of Confucianism] (Taipei: Lianjing chuban shiye gongsi, 1989).

31. The revival of (neo)Confucianism has been richly documented and discussed in various studies. For an informative analysis of the transnational activities and dynamics of the revival, see Arif Dirlik, "Confucius in the Borderlands: Global Capitalism and the Reinvention of Confucianism," *boundary 2*, 22:3 (1995): 229–73. Discussions of activities and receptions in the People's Republic of China can be found in Jing Wang, *High Culture Fever: Politics, Aesthetics, and Ideology in Deng's China* (Berkeley and Los Angeles: University of California Press, 1996), chapter 2; and Xudong Zhang, *Chinese Modernism in the Era of Reforms: Cultural Fever, Avant-Garde Fiction, and the New Chinese Cinema* (Durham: Duke University Press, 1997), chapters 1 and 2.

32. David Der-wei Wang, "Introduction," in Ellen Widmer and David Der-Wei Wang, ed., *From May Fourth to June Fourth: Fiction and Film in Twentieth-Century China* (Cambridge: Harvard University Press, 1993), pp. 2–3.

33. Rey Chow, "Between Colonizers: Hong Kong's Postcolonial Self-writing in the 1990s," Diaspora 2.2 (1992): 151–71.

34. Ibid., p. 156.

35. Rey Chow, *Primitive Passions: Visuality, Sexuality, Ethnography, and Contemporary Chinese Cinema* (New York: Columbia University Press, 1995), p. 49.

36. Chow, "Between Colonizers," p. 157.

37. David Harvey, *The Condition of Postmodernity: An Enquiry into the Origins of Cultural Change* (Cambridge: Basil Blackwell, 1989), p. 302.

38. Trinh T. Minh-ha, *Woman, Native, Other: Writing Postcoloniality and Feminism* (Bloomington: Indiana University Press, 1989).

39. Stuart Hall, "The Local and the Global: Globalization and Ethnicity," in Anthony D. King, ed., *Culture, Globalization and the World System: Contemporary Conditions for the Representation of Identity* (London: Macmillan, 1991), pp. 19–40.

40. Ben Xu, "'From Modernity to Chineseness': The Rise of Nativist Cultural Theory in Post-1989 China," *Positions* 6:1 (Spring 1998): 203–37; 214.

41. Kwame Anthony Appiah, *In My Father's House: Africa in the Philosophy of Culture* (New York: Oxford University Press, 1992), p. 60.

42. See Max Horkheimer and Theodor Adorno, *The Dialectic of Enlightenment* (New York: Continuum, 1990).

43. This means regarding nativism as a form of what Arif Dirlik calls "place-based imagination," aiming at "the creation and construction of new contexts for thinking about politics and the production of knowledge." See Arif Dirlik, "Place-based Imagination: Globalism and the Politics of Place," in Roxann Prazniak and Arif Dirlik, eds., *Places and Politics in an Age of Globalization* (Lanham, MD: Rowland and Littlefield, 2001), p.16.

44. Doreen Massey, *Space, Place, and Gender* (Minneapolis: University of Minnesota Press, 1994), pp. 120–21.

CHAPTER TWO. BENEATH THE CLAIMS OF NATIVE SOIL: CLASS, NATION, GENDER, AND *XIANGTU* NATIVISM

1. Martial law was imposed in 1952 and not lifted until 1987. For a discussion of martial law in Taiwan, see Richard C. Kagan, "Martial Law in Taiwan," *Bulletin of Concerned Asian Scholars* 14.3 (July–Sept., 1982): 48–54.

2. N. H. Jacoby, *U.S. Aid to Taiwan* (New York: Praeger, 1966), pp. 243–45; included in *The Taiwan Experience, 1950–1980*, ed. James Hsiung and others (New York: American Association for Chinese Studies, 1981), pp. 177–78.

3. As of 1970, U.S. and Japanese capital accounted for eighty-five percent of Taiwan's investment. See Thomas Gold, *State and Society in the Taiwan Miracle* (Armonk, NY: M. E. Sharpe, 1986), pp. 76–87, for a summary of the role of foreign capital in Taiwan's postwar economic development, and Hsiung, 1981, pp. 179–87, on the domination of the United States and Japan in foreign trade.

4. This situation, shared by many third world countries, provided the context for Latin American formulation of "dependency" theories [see, for example, Fernando Cardoso and Enzo Faletto, *Dependency and Development in Latin America* (Berkeley and Los Angeles: University of California Press, 1979)], which resonate with the analyses of Taiwan's postwar development by many of its leftist intellectuals. Hu Qiuyuan, Chen Yingzhen, and Wang Tuo were among those who articulated various versions of dependency in their works. The question whether Taiwan constituted a case of dependency development, given its exceptional ability among third world countries to generate economic growth, was one of the most contentious issues during the nativist literature debate. It also became an academic concern in the United States at the turn of the 1970s, with most scholars arguing that Taiwan's economic growth rendered it a "deviant" case of dependency. [See, for example, Alice Amsden, "Taiwan's Economic History: A Case of Etatisme and a Challenge to Dependency Theory," *Modern China* 5.3 (1979): 341–79; Richard Barrett, with Martin King Whyte, "Dependency Theory and Taiwan: A Deviant Case Analysis," *American Journal of Sociology* 87 (1982):

1064–89; and, for an alternative view that emphasizes the broader picture of Taiwan's structural position in the world capitalist system, see Hill Gates, "Dependency and the Part-Time Proletariat," *Modern China* 5.3 (1979): 381–407.] Focusing on the control of capital, technology, and market rather than economic growth, however, Taiwan's leftist intellectuals maintained that Taiwan's economy was a dependent one. Analyses of Taiwan's "development" by Chen Yingzhen and Wang Tuo can be found in their collected essays of social and cultural criticism; see, for example, Chen Yingzhen, *Zhongguo jie* [China Knots] (Taibei: Renjian chubanshe, 1988); Wang Tuo, *Jiexiang gusheng* [Drum Sounds in the Streets] (Taibei: Yuanxing chubanshe, 1977).

5. What constituted the nation in Taiwan was, of course, a thorny issue and continues to be so to this date. While the Nationalist government claimed representation of the Chinese nation against the Communist regime in mainland China, some local people came to see the Nationalists as "colonizers" of their Taiwan (Formosa) "nation," especially after the Nationalist army's bloody suppression of local protests against military brutality and persecution of the local people in 1947, and the subsequent imposition of a highly repressive regime as the Nationalists retreated to Taiwan in 1949. The issues of national identity and its relation to ethnicity in Taiwan were, unsurprisingly, a critical site of contention for nativist discourse, and will be taken up later in our discussion. For an account of nationalist feelings among the pre-Nationalist settlers (the local Taiwanese) and their descendants, see Douglas Mendel, *The Politics of Formosan Nationalism* (Berkeley and Los Angeles: University of California Press, 1970).

6. The magazine published thirty-one issues between July 1976 and January 1979. For a general introduction of the magazine and the role it played in radicalizing intellectual discourses in Taiwan, see Chen Guuying, "The Reform Movement among Intellectuals in Taiwan since 1970," *Bulletin of Concerned Asian Scholars* 14.3 (July–Sept. 1982): 32–47.

7. Diaoyutai, a string of tiny islands northeast of Taiwan, had remained under U.S. occupation after the end of World War II. Both the Japanese and the Chinese claimed sovereignty over the islands. In 1970, the United States accepted Japan's claim and agreed to turn them over as part of the reversion of Okinawa.

8. *Daxue zazhi* [The Intellectual], a magazine produced by a loose collective of intellectual and business elites as a forum for political discussion, was foremost in its protest against the transfer of Diaoyutai to Japan. Though not particularly influential among the general public, the magazine had a large following in university campuses. It played an important role in inspiring and reporting student movements to "protect Diaoyutai" and later to demand political participation and provide social services to the disadvantaged. While not directly critical of Taiwan's economic development, the magazine in its later issues showed increasing concern for social equity as part of modernity, probably reflecting a general sentiment among socially conscious intellectuals of the time. For a summary account of the magazine and its place in Taiwan's demand for political reform, see Li Xiaofeng, *Taiwan minzhu yundong sishinian* [Forty years of democratic movements in Taiwan] (Taibei: Zili wanbao, 1987), pp. 90–108. See also Mab Huang, *Intellectual Ferment for Political Reforms in Taiwan, 1971–73* (Ann Arbor: Center for Chinese Studies, University of Michigan, 1976).

9. The significance of Taiwan's international humiliation in the early 1970s to the rise of national and social consciousness, and their congealment into a nativist discourse in subsequent years is widely acknowledged in local writings. For discussions of the events' impact on the development of nativist literature, see Wang Tuo, "Nian shiji taiwan wenxue fazhan de dongxiang" [Taiwan literature's trend of development in the twentieth century], in *Jiexiang gusheng*, pp. 81–91; and Chen Yingzhen, "Wenxue lai zi shehui fanying shehui" [Literature arises from society and reflects society], in *Xiangtu wenxue taolun ji* [Collection on the Native Place Literature Debate], ed., Yu Tiancong (Taipei: Yuanliu Publishers, 1978), pp. 53–68. The collection will hereafter be referenced as *Xiangtu*. All translations from the collection are mine unless otherwise noted.

10. The term "internal colonialism" is taken from Michael Hechter's *Internal Colonialism: The Celtic Fringe in British National Development, 1536–1966* (Berkeley: University of California Press, 1975).

11. Because of its significant implications for Chinese nationalism and the mobilization of nationalist sentiments to contest modernity in Taiwan, the ethnic identity of the Taiwanese was an important issue not only between the advocates and opponents of nativist discourse but also among the former, as will be seen later.

12. Some cultural critics in Taiwan have indeed traced the development of a sociohistorical condition conducive to the cultural reception and espousal of postmodernism to the 1970s. According to Ping-hui Liao, for instance, it is Taiwan's "double marginalization" from the center of China and the world order in the wake of its forced departure from the United Nations in 1971 that opened up the postmodern condition in the politically and diplomatically isolated island-state. This double marginalization constitutes "a peculiar global/local cultural dialectics that stresses the urgency to negotiate from the periphery, to deconstruct Chinese-Western grand narratives of ideological mapping," fostering people's imaginative appropriation of global products and cultural trends, as well as their "desire to mobilize indigenous countertraditions in recognition of internal cultural dynamics." It thus prepared the ground for a flourish of postmodernist play in cultural production and identity politics once political repression was formally relaxed with the lifting of martial law in 1987. See Ping-hui Liao, "Postmodern Literary Discourse and Contemporary Public Culture in Taiwan," in Dirlik and Zhang, *Postmodernism and China*, pp. 68–88.

13. Besides the Mainlanders and the Taiwanese, there are of course the non-Chinese aborigines, whose drastic reduction in number owing to a long history of discrimination and oppression makes them a minority in the fullest sense of the word.

14. On February 28, 1947, the Nationalist army opened fire on a group of demonstrators who had taken to the streets to protest the Mainlander soldiers' brutality and rampant looting and pilferage since their arrival to reclaim Chinese sovereignty over the island after Japan's defeat in World War II. This began a pervasive persecution of the local people that claimed thousands of lives and effectively demoralized and eliminated the social elites. No public discussions of these events were allowed until the lifting of martial law in 1987. The significance of the "2–28 incident" in symbolizing Mainlander domination and congealing a Taiwanese identity can hardly be overestimated.

15. Before martial law was lifted in 1987, political identification based on provincial origins and ethnicity was officially repressed, though socially prevalent. Since then, the Mainlander-Taiwanese ethnic divide has become an important factor in political mobilization. For a discussion of the role of ethnic identification in Taiwan's contemporary politics, see You-ping Cheng, "The Interaction of Ethnicity and Party Politics in Taiwan," *Issues and Studies* 31.11 (Nov. 1995): 1–15.

16. As Hill Gates notes, "many people in Taiwan perceive their society as one in which Mainlanders are at once an ethnic group and a class that is superior to the ethnic group and class of Taiwanese" ["Ethnicity and Social Class" in *The Anthropology of Taiwanese Society*, ed., Emily Martin Ahern and Hill Gates (Stanford: Stanford University Press, 1981), p. 255]. Her later study of the working class based on fieldwork done in 1980 finds that her subjects still believed that ethnicity and social class largely coincided. See *Chinese Working-Class Lives: Getting By in Taiwan* (Ithaca: Cornell University Press, 1987), pp. 58–59.

17. See Wang Tuo, "Yongbao jiankang de dadi" [Embrace the healthy land], in *Xiangtu*, pp. 348–62.

18. Lin Yaofu, "Language as Politics: The Metamorphosis of Nativism in Recent Taiwan Literature," *Modern Chinese Literature* vol. 6 (1992): 7–22.

19. Ma Sen, "'Taiwan wenxue' de zhongguo jie yu taiwan jie—yi xiaoshuo wei li" [The emotional knots of Taiwaneseness and Chineseness in the notion 'Taiwanese Literature'—the example of narrative fiction], *Unitas* 89 (March 1992): 172–93; especially pp. 175–76.

20. In fact, writings from the colonial period were largely buried in history, and their rediscovery in the 1970s was an important aspect of the emergence and consolidation of nativist discourse.

21. The nature of "modernist" literature in Taiwan was (and continues to be) a deeply controversial issue. In the 1960s, Western modernist literature (including works by Franz Kafka, James Joyce, Virginia Woolf, William Faulkner, and D. H. Lawrence) was systematically introduced into Taiwan's literary scene by the literary magazine *Xiantai wenxue* [Modern Literature] founded by a group of students studying "foreign literatures" at the National Taiwan University. Literary works experimenting with modernist techniques, quasi-Freudian exploration of the human psyche, and existentialist themes soon abounded. It was against the heavy borrowing and "blind" imitation of Western literature in such works that some literary critics and writers began to (re)turn to the notion of nativist literature. On Taiwan's "modernist" literature, see Sung-sheng Yvonne Chang, *Modernism and the Nativist Resistance: Contemporary Chinese Fiction from Taiwan* (Durham: Duke University Press, 1993).

22. The full-scale public debate began with pointed criticisms of *xiangtu* literature delivered in the Symposium of Literary Workers, a conference initiated by the Nationalist government and held in August 1977. Voluminous articles in defense of the literature and rebuttals by state-sponsored writers and critics subsequently appeared in daily newspapers and various magazines. The debate intensified with the direct involvement of the Nationalist Party and the armed forces in organizing the

"National Forces Cultural Assembly" in January 1978. By late 1978, several prominent nativist literature advocates had decided to engage directly in political struggles and the debate subsided. For a convenient summary and discussion of the debate from a perspective of artistic autonomy, see Jing Wang, "Taiwan *Hsiang-t'u* Literature: Perspectives in the Evolution of a Literary Movement," in Jeannette L. Faurot, ed., *Chinese Fiction from Taiwan: Critical Perspectives* (Bloomington: Indiana University Press, 1980), pp. 43–70. A different interpretation of the controversy in terms of nationalist criticism and rejection of westernized modernist literature is offered in Chen Guuying, "The Reform Movement."

23. Yin Zhengxiong, "Fendi li nali lai di zhongsheng?" [From where in the graveyard does the bell-chime come?] in *Xiangtu*, p. 201; originally published in *Xianrenzhang*, no. 2 (April 1977).

24. Ibid., pp. 202–3.

25. Ibid., p. 200.

26. Peng Ge, "Butan renxing, heyou wenxue" [How can there be literature without recourse to humanity], in *Xiangtu*, 262, 249; originally published in *Lianhe bao* (United Daily News), August 17–19, 1977.

27. Peng Ge, "Dui pianxiang de jingjue" [Alert against erroneous tendency], in *Xiangtu*, pp. 235–37; originally published in *Lianhe bao*, July 27, 1977.

28. Peng Ge, "Baolei neibu" [Inside the fortress], in *Xiangtu*, 233; originally published in *Lianhe bao*, July 16, 1977.

29. Peng Ge, "Butan renxing," pp. 248–49.

30. Peng Ge, "Wenyou dunhou" [Gentle, kind, and sincere], in *Xiangtu*, p. 229; originally published in *Lianhe bao*, July 16, 1977.

31. Peng Ge, "Wenyou dunhou," p. 230; emphasis added.

32. The poem runs as follows:

In the eighth month, height of autumn, the wind angry howled,
Unrolled from off my roof three layers of reeds.
The reeds flew over the river, strewed the river's edges:
High, they hung in the tall tree tops;
Low, they whirled in the deep pools.
From Southern Village gangs of boys cheat me in my age and infirmity;
Heartlessly to my face they play the thief;
Openly with armfuls, go off into the bamboos.
Till my lips are burning, my mouth parched, I shout to no end.
So, I return, leaning on my stick and signing to myself.
In a while, the wind is still, the clouds ink colored;
The autumn sky silently approaches darkness.
My cotton quilt, after many years, is cold as iron;
My spoilt child, restless in sleep, trod the lining to shreds.
Over my bed the roof leaks; there is no dry place;
The streaming rain like hemp threads, never broken.

Since the rebellion seldom have I slept well:
The long night, soaked, how can I get through?
Where can I find a mansion of a million rooms?
To shelter every poor scholar, with a smiling face;
In wind and rain unmoved, secure as a mountain.
Oh when before my eyes there sprang such a house,
Though my hut alone were smashed and I froze to death, I should be content.

Translation taken from A. R. Davis, *Tu Fu* (New York: Twayne Publishers, 1971), pp. 79–80.

33. The movement was a major effort initiated personally by Taiwan's then president and longtime supreme leader, Chiang Jieshi (Chiang Kai-shek), to consolidate Taiwan's claim of representation of the Chinese nation against the People's Republic of China. The timing of the movement suggests that it was a deliberate response to the Cultural Revolution, which swept through the Chinese mainland in 1966. This is clearly stated in official and semiofficial documents on the movement. For an account of the movement and its ideological and historical foundation, see Warren Tozer, "Taiwan's 'Cultural Renaissance': A Preliminary View," *The China Quarterly* 43 (July–Sept. 1970): 81–99.

34. Zhang Gai, *Zhonghua wenhua fuxing yanjiu* [Study on Chinese Cultural Renaissance] (Taibei: Zhongyang dangbu, 1968), pp. 115, 116, 117. Translation mine.

35. For a summary account of these developments in the nativist debate and the different positions taken by various nativist advocates, see Lin Yaofu, "Language as Politics: The Metamorphosis of Nativism in Recent Taiwan Literature," *Modern Chinese Literature* 6 (1992): 7–22.

36. Ye Shitao, "Taiwan xiangtu wenxue shi daolun," in *Xiangtu*, p. 70; originally published in *Xiachao* 2.5 (1977): 68–75.

37. Ibid., pp. 70–71.

38. Peng Ruijin, "Taiwan wenxue ying yi bentuhua wei shouyao keti" [Taiwanese Literature should make nativization its primary task], *Wenxuejie* 2 (Summer 1982), p. 3.

39. Peng Ruijin, *Taiwan xinwenxue yundong sishi nian* [Forty years of new literature movement in Taiwan] (Taibei: Zili wanbaoshe wenhua chubanbu, 1991), p. 165.

40. Song Dongyang, "Xian jieduan taiwan wenxue bentuhua de wenti" [The question of nativization of Taiwanese Literature at the present stage], in *Taiwan wenxue de guoqu yu weilai* [Taiwanese Literature's past and future], ed. Chen Yongxing (Taibei: Taiwan wenyi zazhishe, 1985), p. 22.

41. Li Qiao, "Taiwan wenxue zhengjie" [The correct interpretation of Taiwanese Literature], *Taiwan wenyi* 83 (July 1983), p. 7.

42. See Xu Nancun [Chen Yingzhen], "'Xiangtu wenxue' de mangdian" [The blindspot of 'nativist literature'], in *Xiangtu* pp. 93–99; originally published in *Taiwan wenyi* 2 (June 1977).

43. Chen Yingzhen, "'Xiangtu wenxue' de mangdian," p. 95. For Chen's development of essentially the same argument in terms of third world literature later, see "Zhongguo wenxue he disan shijie wenxue zhi bijiao" [Comparing Chinese literature with third world literature], in *Guer de lishi, lishi de guer* [Orphan's history, history's orphan] (Taibei: Yuanjing chuban shiyegongsi, 1984), pp. 377–97. For his general discussion of Taiwan's nativist literature, see "Wenxue lai zi shehui fanying shehui" [Literature originates in society, reflects society], in *Xiangtu*, pp. 53–68.

44. Zhang Wenzhi, *Dangdai wenxue di taiwan yishi* [Taiwanese consciousness in contemporary literature] (Taibei: Zili wanbaoshe wenhua chubanbu, 1993).

45. Wang Tuo, "Shi 'xianshi zhuyi' wenxue, bushi 'xiangtu' wenxue" [It is 'realist literature,' not 'native place' literature], in *Xiangtu*, pp. 115–16; originally published in *Xianrenzhang* [Cactus] 2 (April 1977).

46. Wang Tuo, "Xiangtu wenxue yu xiangshi zhuyi" [Nativist literature and realism], in *Xiangtu*, p. 300; originally published in *Xiachao* [China Tide] 17 (August 1977).

47. Wang Tuo, "Shi 'xianshi zhuyi' wenxue," p. 116.

48. Social injustice was a particularly sensitive issue for the Nationalist government since it had consistently stressed its adherence to "the three principles of the people" (*sanmin zhuyi*), of which the last is people's livelihood and welfare, with equity and stability two of its pronounced goals in economic development. For an interpretation of Taiwan's economic development in terms of its successful implementation of the principle of people's welfare, see Chu-yuan Cheng, "The Doctrine of People's Welfare: The Taiwan Experiment and Its Implications for the Third World" in *Sun Yat-sen's Doctrine in the Modern World*, ed., Chu-yuan Cheng (Boulder: Westview Press, 1989), pp. 244–75.

49. Xu Nancun [Chen Yingzhen], "Shilun Chen Yingzhen" [An attempt to discuss Chen Yingzhen], in *Xiangtu*, pp. 164–175.

50. Wang Tuo, "Yongbao jiankang de dadi," in *Xiangtu*, p. 349; originally published in *Lianhe bao*, Sept. 10–12, 1977.

51. Chen Yingzhen, "Shilun Chen Yingzhen," p. 174; emphasis mine. "Xinsheng" literally means voice in the heart, that is, what is felt and thought at heart, but is not or cannot be voiced. To express the unvoiced thoughts and feelings of the people is an intellectual mission that is generally considered part of the Chinese cultural tradition.

52. Wang Tuo, "Yongbao jiankang de dadi," p. 350; emphasis mine.

53. Gayatri Chakravorty Spivak, "Can the Subaltern Speak?" in *Marxism and the Interpretation of Culture*, eds., Cary Nelson and Lawrence Grossberg (Urbana: University of Illinois Press, 1988), p. 275.

54. Spivak's provocative articulation of the issue in the statement "The subaltern cannot speak" has prompted much critical defense of the subaltern's ability to speak. See, for example, Benita Parry, "Problems in Current Theories of Colonial Discourse," *Oxford Literary Review* 9.1–2 (1987): 27–58. Henry Louis Gates, Jr. also criticizes Spi-

vak's formulation for closing off the possibility of cultural resistance in "Critical Fanonism," *Critical Inquiry* 17 (Spring 1991): 457–70. But for an argument in support of Spivak's position, see Rey Chow, "Where Have All the Natives Gone?" especially pp. 34–36. In response to the controversy, Spivak has reworked her argument to clarify her concern with the subaltern not being heard in the hegemonic mode of intellectual narrative production rather than her ability to speak. See *A Critique of Postcolonial Reason* (Cambridge: Harvard University Press, 1999), pp. 248–311.

55. Chang, *Modernism and the Nativist Resistance*, p. 159.

56. Chen Yingzhen, "Jianli minzu wenxue de fengge" [Establish the style of national literature], in *Xiangtu*, p. 337; originally published in *Zhonghua zazhi* [China magazine], 171 (1977). Similarly, another prominent nativist literature advocate Yu Tiancong writes: "in Taiwan, we see the great masses of people producing and constructing in the open, under the sun or in rain, everyday and thousands of soldiers being ready to sacrifice and struggle. It is in facing these people that we discover true national strength." ("Women de shehui he minzu jingshen jiaoyu" [Our education on social and national spirit], in *Xiangtu*, p. 27.)

57. An informative discussion of Taiwan's modernist literature can be found in Sung-sheng Yvonne Chang's *Modernism and the Nativist Resistance*. Chang argues that while Taiwan's modernist literature in its early stage of development tended to focus on form and language rather than content, as the nativist critics have charged, that was no longer the case for mature works. Embodying a humanist concern for individual experiences, she further contends, Taiwan's modernist literature appropriates rather than imitates Western modernist aesthetics and thematics to reexamine Chinese culture.

58. Wang Tuo, "Shi 'xianshi wenxue,'" p. 112.

59. Theodor Adorno explains negative aesthetics in this way: "Aesthetic identity is meant to assist the non-identical in its struggle against the repressive identification compulsion that rules the outside world. It is by virtue of its separation from empirical reality that the work of art can become a being of a higher order, fashioning the relation between the whole and its parts in accordance with its own needs." [*Aesthetic Theory*, trans. C. Lenhardt (London: Routledge & Kegan Paul, 1984), p. 6.]

60. Wang Zhenhe, "Xiaolin lai Taibei" [Xiaolin comes to Taipei], in *Jiazhuang yi niuche* (Taipei: Yuanjing chubanshe, 1977), pp. 219–49. The story is originally published in *Wenxue jikan* [Literature Quarterly] 2 (Oct. 1973). All translations are mine.

61. The story is, in fact, one of the three works explicitly named in Yin Zhengxiong's invective against native place literature. See *Xiangtu*, pp. 201–2.

62. Wang Zhenhe is known for his skillful play with languages, and his sophisticated command of linguistic and artistic styles suggests a modernist inclination that distinguishes his work from the generally more content-driven *xiangtu* fiction. His astute engagement with the politics of language use has prompted a critic to read his fictions as exemplifying a postcolonial construction of Taiwan's identity in cultural and linguistic hybridity. See Jiu Guifan, "'Faxian taiwan': jiangou taiwan houzhimin lunshu' ['Discovering Taiwan': Constructing postcolonial discourse in Taiwan], *Zhongwai wenxue* 21.2 (July 1992): 151–67.

63. "Xiaolin," p. 219.

64. The story tells of well-off women going to the United States to give birth and students taking flight and refusing to come home to Taiwan after studying in the West.

65. "Xiaolin," p. 220.

66. Ibid., pp. 230–31.

67. The cigar is obviously a loaded sign of Western culture here. In this graphic visualization of the manager's prostituting himself in sycophantic attention to the family of a wealthy businessman, a "boss," the link between Westernization and class oppression in Taiwan's modernity is again underscored.

68. "Xiaolin," pp. 229–30.

69. As Jiu Guifen has pointed out, the emasculated man is a central figure in nativist fiction of the 1970s. Integrating postcolonial and feminist theoretical arguments, Jiu situates this figure in the gendered power structure of colonial domination and reads it in terms of nativist fiction's resistance to (neo)colonialism. In so doing, however, her analysis inadvertently reproduces the androcentrism of the nativist works and overlooks the importance of gender power maintained in the actual relations between the emasculated men and the "native" women in their lives. See Jiu Guifen, "Xingbie/quanli/zhiminlunshu: xiangtu wenxue zhong de qushi nanren" [Gender/power/colonial discourse: castrated men in nativist literature], in *Dangdai taiwan nuxing wenxue lun* [Women and Contemporary Taiwanese Literature], ed., Cheng Minglee (Taipei: Shibao chuban gongsi, 1993), pp. 13–34.

70. "Xiaolin," pp. 232–35.

71. Ibid., p. 240; emphasis added.

72. Ibid., p. 224.

73. It is noteworthy that Mrs. Wang's last name signifies in Chinese a body of water; and, with phrases like *shuixing yanghua*, water when associated with woman carries the negative connotation of infidelity and promiscuity.

74. Elizabeth Wilson, *The Sphinx in the City: Urban Life, the Control of Disorder, and Women* (Berkeley: University of California Press, 1992).

75. "Xiaolin," p. 241.

76. Wang Tuo, "Jinshuishen," in *Jinshuishen* (Taibei: Xiangcaoshan chubanshe, 1979), pp. 189–256. Originally published in *Youshi wenyi* 260 (Aug. 1975). All translations are mine.

77. Ibid., p. 246.

78. Ibid., pp. 190–91.

79. That the characterization of Jinshuishen takes Wang Tuo's story beyond the analytics of class is also noted by Jing Wang. Reading Jinshuishen in terms of a "suffering Buddha incarnate," however, Wang sidesteps the importance of Mazu in anchoring the protagonist in the historically and socially specific "native place" of Tai-

wan. Furthermore, the argument that with such a characterization of Jinshuishen, "the story has manifested the success of the artist in transcending the stereotyped reaction of his class ethics[;] [i]ndividual experiences of the underprivileged class are raised to the dimension of suffering humanity" curiously ignores the story's ideological investment in a nativist/nationalist figuration of the suffering but enduring mother (Jing Wang, "Taiwan *Hsiang-t'u* Literature," p. 65).

80. See, for example, Zhou Shiyue, "Mazu xinyang ji qi zai taiwan de chuanbo" [The belief in Mazu and its propagation in Taiwan], in *Taiwan yanjiu shinian* [Ten Years of Taiwan Studies], ed., Chen Kongli (Taibei: Boyuan chubanshe, 1991), pp. 517–26.

81. See Wang Meiying, "Kaitai mazu" [Mazu, the Taiwan founder], in *Taiwan wenhua duanceng* [Cultural Faults in Taiwan] (Taibei: Daoxiang chubanshe, 1990), pp. 207–10. A further elaboration of the pivotal role of Mazu worship in establishing communal identification with Taiwan and the indigenization of Chinese society in the past and present can be found in her "Taiwan Mazu yu bentu rentong" [Taiwan's Mazu and identification with the indigenous], pp. 211–16, in the same collection of essays.

82. P. Steven Sangren, "Female Gender in Chinese Religious Symbols: Kuan Yin, Ma Tsu, and the 'Eternal Mother,'" *Signs* 9.1 (1983): 4–25; 16.

83. The notion of "national allegory" is obviously taken from Fredric Jameson's famous and well-critiqued essay "Third-World Literature in the Era of Multinational Capitalism," *Social Text* 15 (1986): 65–88. While I have problems with, among other things, Jameson's automatic identification of the collective entailed in "third world literature" as the nation, I find it useful to borrow his notion of national allegory to suggest that there is simultaneously a telling of the experience of the collectivity in the story of Jinshuishen's individual experience. Furthermore, on account of the symbolic meaning that the figure of Mazu has accrued, it is not implausible to associate the collectivity with a sense of "nation" in this case, although Wang Tuo has not openly espoused a Taiwanese nationalism.

84. See Harvey, *The Condition of Postmodernity*, especially pp. 10–38.

85. "Jinshuishen," pp. 255–56.

86. Xu Nancun [Chen Yingzhen], "Shiping 'Jinshuishen'" [A preliminary review of "Jinshuishen"], in *Jinshuishen*, pp. 11–12.

87. The legend of Mazu clearly reveals a strong grounding in and support of patriarchy. The veneration and official deificaton of Mazu were predicated on her filial piety reaching the sanctioned height of feminine self-sacrifice for the survival of present and future family patriarchs—her father and brothers.

88. "Jinshuishen," pp. 221–22.

89. Ibid., pp. 232–33.

90. Ibid., p. 241.

91. On the various ways in which women have been implicated in nationalism, see Nira Yuval-Davis and Floya Anthias, eds., *Women-Nation-State* (London: Macmillan, 1989), p. 7.

92. Huang Chunming, "Pinguo de ziwei," in *Luo* (Gong) (Taipei: Huangguan, 1985), pp. 137–72. Originally published in *Shibao fukan* (China Times Literary Supplement), Dec. 28–31, 1972. For a translation, see "The Taste of Apples," in *The Drowning of an Old Cat and Other Stories*, trans. Howard Goldblatt (Bloomington: Indiana University Press, 1980), pp. 158–84. Translations here are mine unless otherwise noted. Of all the Taiwan nativist writers in this period, Huang Chunming is arguably the most interesting, not least because his fictions show the development of a critical consciousness in response to social and historical changes. Widely praised for their "humanism," his early nativist stories are not short of sentimental valorization of the little people eking out a living in rural Taiwan. His representation of the self-sacrifice and redemption through motherhood of a prostitute in the celebrated story "Yuyehua" (Flowers in a rainy night) shows an uncritical affirmation of feminine, especially maternal, virtues under Chinese patriarchy that resonates with Wang Tuo's story discussed above. Against these earlier works, the critical interrogation of working class family dynamics in his later fiction, as discussed here, reflects a reflexive critique of his own ideological formation.

93. "Pinguo," p. 145.

94. Ibid., p. 152.

95. Ibid., pp. 149, 151.

96. Ibid., p. 162.

97. Ibid., p. 169.

98. On the national level, this is certainly an apt remark on the experiences of economic development in East Asia. It is, of course, the "exceptionality" of the East Asian countries in breaking out of the pattern of dependency that drew the attention of development scholars and administrators to the possibility of the so-called East Asian Development Model.

99. "Pinguo," p. 172.

100. Ibid., p. 140.

101. Ibid., pp. 170–71; emphasis added.

102. Ibid., p. 156.

103. Ibid., p. 142.

104. Ibid., p. 166.

105. For an elaboration of this point, see Ming-yan Lai, "The Intellectual's Deaf-Mute, or (How) Can We Speak beyond Postcoloniality?" *Cultural Critique* 39 (1998): 31–58.

CHAPTER THREE. BEYOND THE REACH OF ROOTS: MARGINALITY, MASCULINITY, AND *XUNGEN* NATIVISM

1. Postmodernism was introduced into China in the mid-1980s, especially with Fredric Jameson's lectures in Beijing in 1985. The lectures were promptly translated

and published in a volume, which helped to promote the concept not only in China but also in other Chinese-speaking areas, notably Taiwan. Arguably because of China's preoccupation with modernization to overcome its perceived backwardness, however, few in China found postmodernism a useful concept for discussing China in the 1980s. Xiaobing Tang, who translated the Jameson lectures, was exceptional in advancing the argument that China's cultural scene in the latter half of the 1980s could be productively discussed in terms of postmodernism. Citing the period's massive loss of faith in coherent metanarratives of telos and historical destiny after the traumatic changes and turbulent times under Maoist socialism, Tang finds postmodernism the most apt characterization of a contemporary Chinese culture that lacks legitimate normativity and affords neither stability of meaning nor utopian beliefs. See Xiaobing Tang, "The Function of New Theory: What Does it Mean to Talk about Postmodernism in China?" in Liu Kang and Xiaobing Tang, eds., *Politics, Ideology and Literary Discourse in Modern China: Theoretical Interventions and Cultural Critique* (Durham: Duke University Press, 1993). Such a characterization is of course highly controversial and has been vigorously challenged by Jing Wang, among others. Indeed, the relation between China and postmodernism has been a hotly debated topic among scholars both inside and outside China. Even among those who identify postmodernism in China, it is generally attributed to the 1990s, when mass consumerism took hold of the country under the government's active promotion of market economy to disarm and neutralize the silenced discontent of the populace over the 1989 Tiananmen suppression. In their landmark collection on the topic, however, Arif Dirlik and Xudong Zhang follow Tang to locate postmodern resonance in China as early as the 1980s, though they employ a significantly different line of reasoning with a focus on the broad reference of the postmodern rather than postmodernism. In short, Dirlik and Zhang contend that "spatial fracturing and temporal desynchronization" under a simultaneous juxtaposition of incompatible modes of production, which disrupts the spatial and temporal teleologies of modernity in the form of the nation-state and the development of a national market and culture, makes postmodernity a useful rubric for analyzing changes in China since the country's pragmatic departure from socialism. See Dirlik and Zhang, "Introduction: Postmodernism and China," in *Postmodernism and China*.

2. A classic discussion of this Chinese struggle with the legacy of Confucianism, leading to the traditional culture's relegation to and retention in emotional attachments, can be found in Levenson, *Confucian China and Its Modern Fate*.

3. Maurice Meisner, *The Deng Xiaoping Era: An Inquiry into the Fate of Chinese Socialism, 1978–1994* (New York: Hill and Wang, 1996), p. 286.

4. Liu Binyan, *China's Crisis, China's Hope* (Cambridge: Harvard University Press, 1990), p. 354.

5. Shenzhen and three other southern coastal areas were designated special economic zones in 1979. With the goal of attracting foreign capital and technology, the SEZs offered exceptionally favorable conditions in labor supply as well as tax and fiscal arrangements for foreign investment in export-oriented industries. In essence, they were China's version of the export processing zones that facilitated the offshore production of multinational companies and the advent of global capitalism.

6. Among these efforts to bring modern Western knowledge and thoughts to the Chinese cultural arena, two series were considered particularly influential: the "Zouxiang weilai" (Marching toward the future) series masterminded by Jin Guantao, which focuses on theoretical and methodological developments in the natural sciences in order to introduce scientific rationality into the study of Chinese history and society; and the "Wenhua: zhongguo yu xijie" (Culture: China and the World) series overseen by Gan Yang, which seeks to introduce Western theoretical developments in the humanities to illuminate the project of modernity for China. A summary introduction of these two series can be found in Chen Lai, "Fulu: Sixiang chulu de sandongxiang" [Appendix: Three orientations in the outlet of thoughts], in *Zhongguo dangdai wenhua yishi* [China's Contemporary Cultural Consciousness], ed. Gan Yang (Hong Kong: Joint Publishing Co., 1989), pp. 581–87. See also Edward X. Gu's informative discussion of these two series in terms of the formation of a cultural public space in "Cultural Intellectuals and the Politics of the Cultural Public Space in Communist China (1979–1989): A Case Study of Three Intellectual Groups," *The Journal of Asian Studies* 58, no. 2 (May 1999): 389–431.

7. Wang, *High Culture Fever*, pp. 56–64, 86–93.

8. Gan Yang, "Bashi niandai wenhua taolun de ji ge wenti" [Problems in cultural discussions of the eighties], in *Zhongguo dangdai wenhua yishi*, p. 32.

9. For an informative account of the important events leading to and during the Culture Fever, as well as a critical discussion of the main currents of the debates, see Wang, *High Culture Fever*, pp. 48–117. A totalizing analysis of the Culture Fever from a professedly Hegelian perspective can be found in Xudong Zhang, *Chinese Modernism in the Era of Reforms: Cultural Fever, Avant-garde Fiction, and the New Chinese Cinema* (Durham: Duke University Press, 1997). Both studies include the projects of Jin Guantao and Gan Yang in their discussions. For the purpose of this study, I limit my attention to the advocates of renewed focus on traditional Chinese culture.

10. Li Zehou, *Zhongguo xiandai sixiangshi lun* [Essays on modern Chinese intellectual history] (Beijing: Dongfang chubanshe, 1987), p. 312.

11. For an example of the refutation of Tu Wei-ming's New Confucianism by Chinese intellectuals keen on adopting Western knowledge for China's modernization, see Bao Zunxin, "Rujia lunli yu 'yazhou silong'—'ruxue fuxing shuo' boyi" [Confucian ethics and the 'Four Dragons of Asia'—a rebuttal of the thesis of 'Confucian renaissance'], *Xinhua wenzhai* [Xinhua Digest] 4(1988): 157–62.

12. Wang, *High Culture Fever*, p. 234.

13. See "Editors' Postscript" in *Lun Zhongguo chuantong wenhua* [Essays on Chinese traditional culture], edited by Li Zhonghua and Zhang Wenting for the Academy of Chinese Culture Lectures Editorial Board (Beijing: Sanlian, 1988); emphasis added.

14. Tang Yijie, "Introduction," *Lun Zhongguo chuantong wenhua*, pp. 9–10.

15. See, for instance, Liu Wei, "Dangtai Zhongguo wenhua yanjiu zhuangkuang de hongguan sikao" [Thinking about the condition of contemporary study of Chinese

culture on a macro scale], *Xuexi yu tansuo* 2(1986), reprinted in *Xinhua wenzhai* 6(1986):185–87; and Wang He, "Chuantong wenhua yu xiandaihua" [Traditional culture and modernization], *Zhongguo shehui kexue* 3(1986), reprinted in *Xinhua wenzhai* 7(1986):188–94.

16. Germane here is Geremie Barme's critique of Chinese artists' failure in the post-Mao years to break out of a "velvet prison" where the desire for individualistic and autonomous expressions is (self-)repressed after years of "living as salaried company men and . . . sharing in political power." See Geremie Barme, "The Chinese Velvet Prison: Culture in the 'New Age,' 1976–89," *Issues and Studies* 25.8 (August 1989): 54–79.

17. Li Zehou, "Shitan Zhongguo de zhihui" [On Chinese wisdom], in *Lun Zhongguo chuantong wenhua*, p. 36. Li made clear his conscious effort to stay within the ideological parameters of the official rhetoric on modernization in his repeated assertion that his notion of Western substance with Chinese function is equivalent to what is meant by "the Sinification of Marxism" and "Socialist road with Chinese characteristics." On this and further clarification of his ideas, see, in addition to the quoted article, "Manshuo 'xiti zhongyong'" [Notes on 'Western substance, Chinese function'] in *Zhongguo xiandai sixiangshi lun*, pp. 311–45; and "Zhongguo sixiangshi zatan" [On Chinese intellectual history], *Fudan xuebao* 5(1985), reprinted in *Xinhua wenzhai* 12(1985):176–80. The proximity of Li's ideas to the ideological underpinnings of the Deng regime has been noted by Li Min, who goes further to suggest that "Li's ideas have become the philosophical premises underlying Deng's modernization programme . . . [and] aided the formulation of several cornerstones of the political ideology that legitimizes Deng's reforms." (Li Min, "The Search for Modernity: Chinese Intellectual Discourse and Society, 1978–88—the Case of Li Zehou," *China Quarterly* 132 (December 1992), p. 971).

18. "Zhonggong zhongyang guanyu shehuizhuyi jingshenwenming jianshe zhidao fangzhen de jueyi," *Xinhua wenzhai* 11(1986), p. 2. The translation is from the official English document, "Resolution of the Central Committee of the Communist Party of China on the Guiding Principles for Building a Society with an Advanced Culture and Ideology," printed in *Beijing Review*, vol. 29, no. 40 (October 6, 1986). That the directive on spiritual civilization is in essence an injunction for the "modernization of the people" is argued explicitly in an article published in the official newspaper, *Renmin ribao*. See Xue Dezhen and Yuan Zhiming, "Jingshenwenming jianshe shi yizhong zhutixing de jianshe" [The construction of spiritual civilization is a construction of the subject], *Renmin ribao*, November 14, 1986. On a direct discussion of what the modernization of the people means for contemporary China, see Xu sumin, "Ren de xiandaihua" [The modernization of the people], *Qingnan luntan* 1 (1984); *Xinhua wenzhai* 2(1985): 108–10.

19. See Meisner, *The Deng Xiaoping Era*, especially chapter 11.

20. See, for example, Wang Bosen, "Shilun jingji gaige yu daode jinbu de guanxi" [On the relationship between economic reform and moral advancement], *Wenhui bao* (Shanghai), July 13, 1984; and Yuan Zhiming and Xue Dezhen, "Lun 'fu'—dang de fumin zhengce duanxiang" [On 'wealth': thoughts on the Party's policy for getting people rich], *Remin ribao*, August 3, 1984.

21. Xudong Zhang, for example, aligns *xungen* literature with misty poetry (*Chinese Modernism*, pp. 137–42) and Jing Wang situates it in a modernist search for subjectivity in *High Culture Fever*.

22. See, for example, Michael Duke, "Reinventing China: Cultural Exploration in Contemporary Chinese Fiction," *Issues and Studies* 25 (1989): 29–53.

23. See Han Shaogong, "Wenxue de 'gen,'" *Zuojia* 4(1985): 2–5. It was later reported that many of the ideas covered by Han's article were raised and discussed in a literary meeting held at the end of 1984 and attended by many of the writers who were later associated with *xungen* literature. See Li Qingxi, "Xungen: huidao shiwu benshen" [The search for roots: return to the thing itself], *Wenxue pinglun* 4(1988): 14–23.

24. In a rather typical discussion, Li Shulei makes a distinction between two kinds of *xungen* literature, "primitive root-seeking" (*yuanshi xungen*) and "cultural root-seeking" (*wenhua xungen*). Works of the first kind, he argues, depict primitive and semiprimitive lives outside of normative Han culture in order to affirm a new ideal of humanity that incorporates the vitality and creativity of nature and primitive life, leaving behind the weak personality permeated with traditional Confucian-Daoist culture. As such, they are in sync with the "progressive" march of life and reflective of modern cultural consciousness. In contrast, works of "cultural root-seeking" celebrate traditional Han culture, thus joining force with the conservative countercurrent. See Li Shulei, "Cong 'xunmeng' dao 'xungen': guanyu jinnian wenxue biandong de zhaji zhiyi" [From the search of dreams to the search of roots: reading notes on literary changes in recent years], *Dangdai wenyi sichao* 3 (1986): 42–49.

25. See A Cheng, "Wenhua zhiyuezhe renlei" [Culture conditions humanity], *Wenyibao* July 6, 1985. On the relation of A Cheng's work to Daoist aesthetics, see, for example, Su Ding and Zhong Chengxiang, "'Qiwang' yu daojia meixue" ['The Chess King' and Daoist aesthetics], *Dangdai zuojia pinglun* [Review of Contemporary Authors], 9 (no. 3, 1985): 20–26. See also Jing Wang's different argument in *High Culture Fever* (p. 185) that while the Dao is important to A Cheng's work, especially "Qiwang" (Chess king), he does not glorify the Daoist tradition or makes it the renewed foundation of life in the present. A similar argument can be found in Xin Xiaozheng, "Du A Cheng xiaoshao sanji" [Random notes on reading A Cheng's fiction], *Dangdai zuojia pinglun*, 11 (no. 5, 1985): 26–31.

26. In an interview, Han Shaogong makes a distinction between two "levels" of recovering culture in literature that reflect a similar difference in emphasis: a "low" level of making culture the object of description, as in works that depict the social manners and customs of people in particular regions; and a "subjective" level of incorporating culture into literary production, in the sense that culture informs the aesthetics and modes of thinking and feeling underlying the literary production, whatever the topic or object being treated. It is noteworthy that whereas the former "level" is marked clearly as "regional culture," the latter is characterized by a contrast between "Oriental culture" and "Occidental culture." As his explicit ranking of the two levels indicates, Han sees himself as more in tune with the "subjective" recovery of culture, though, he admits, he also writes about the rural native scene and strives to give Hunan and Chu

"flavors" to his works. See Lin Weiping, "Wenxue yu renge—fang zuojia Han Shaogong" [Literature and moral character: an interview with Han Shaogong], *Shanghai wenxue* 11(1986): 68–76.

27. The critic Li Tuo offers an interesting reconciliation of these two trends of evaluation in suggesting that *xungen* is a reconstruction of Chinese culture which combines the contradictory moves of a critical reflection of Chinese traditional culture on a systemic scale and a "reasonable" assimilation of Chinese literary, artistic, and aesthetic traditions. See Lin Weiping, "Xinshiqi wenxue yixitan—fang zuojia Li Tuo" [A conversation on literature in the New Era: an interview with Li Tuo], *Shanghai wenxue* 10(1986): 90–96.

28. Lei Da, "Minzu linghun de faxian yu zhongzhu—xinshiqi wenxue zhuchao lungang" [The discovery and recasting of the national soul: a synoptic discussion of the main waves of literature in the New Era], *Wenxue pinglun* 1(1987), p. 27.

29. Zhou Zhengbao, "Xiaoshuo chuangzao de xin qushi—minzu wenhua yishi de jianghua" [A new trend in fiction writing: the strengthening of national cultural consciousness], *Wenyibao* August 10, 1985.

30. Han Hang, "Wenxue xun 'gen' zhi wojian" [My views on the search for 'roots' in literature], *Xinhua wenzhai* 5(1986), p. 159.

31. Wang Dongming, "Wenhua yishi de jianghua yu dangdai yishi de ruohua" [The strengthening of culural consciousness and weakening of contemporary consciousness], *Wenyibao* September 21, 1985.

32. Chen Sihe, "Dangdai wenxuezhong de wenhua xungen yishi" [The cultural search for roots in contemporary literature], *Wenxue pinglun* 6(1986), p. 24.

33. Qian Niansun, "Wenxue zhi 'gen' de duoxiang shenzhan he xun 'gen' yanguang de kuoda" [The multi-directional extension of the 'roots' of literature and the expansion of the vision of search for 'roots'], *Wenyibao* November 9, 1985.

34. In his interpretation of the rise of interest in Chu culture and growing identification with the values of southern China, glossed primarily as "dynamism," "openness, mobility, and decentralization," in the 1980s, Edward Friedman emphasizes "the rise of a southern-oriented national identity" to replace the ideologically bankrupt northern-centered "anti-imperialist nationalism" of the Mao era (Edward Friedman, "Reconstructing China's National Identity: A Southern Alternative to Mao-Era Anti-Imperialist Nationalism," *The Journal of Asian Studies* 53.1 (1994), p. 85). My reading suggests that Han-nationalism based on cultural traditions originating from the north still dominated the PRC in the 1980s, and attention to the "southern" cultures of Chu and Wu-Yue, as in the case of *xungen* nativism may well be a subtle challenge to nationalist discourse rather than an alternative nationalism in the making.

35. The number of recognized "minority nationalities" varies greatly in the history of modern China, testifying to the extremely contentious and political nature of the definition of nationality. From the early identification of only four minority nationalities by Sun Yatsen—Mongols, Manchus, Tibetans, and Muslim Turks (referring mainly to the Uygurs in Xinjiang), the number of recognized minority nationali-

ties has swelled to fifty-five by the 1982 census, and accounting for about eight percent of the Chinese population according to the 1990 census.

36. This suggests a possible implication of race in the Chinese notion of *minzu*. Emphasizing the importance of patrilineal descent and lineage institution in the conception of *minzu*, Frank Dikotter argues in *The Discourse of Race in Modern China* (Stanford: Stanford University Press, 1992) that there is a conflation of "race," descent, and nation in the term's usage throughout the twentieth century.

37. See Dru C. Gladney, *Muslim Chinese: Ethnic Nationalism in the People's Republic* (Cambridge: Council on East Asian Studies, Harvard University, 1991), pp. 81–87.

38. As many scholars of minority nationalities in China have pointed out, Sun Yatsen played an important role in developing the notion of *minzu* and shaping the idea of a Han nationality. On Sun's tendency to dismiss the importance of the minority nationalities in the constitution of the Chinese nation, see Colin Mackerras, *China's Minorities: Integration and Modernization in the Twentieth Century* (Oxford: Oxford University Press, 1994), pp. 55–56. On the importance of race in Sun's theory of *minzu*, and in modern Chinese conceptions of the nation in general, see Dikotter, *The Discourse of Race in Modern China*.

39. Etienne Balibar, "The Nation Form," in Etienne Balibar and Immanuel Wallerstein, *Race, Nation, Class* (London: Verso, 1991), p. 96.

40. See Leo J. Moser, *The Chinese Mosaic: The Peoples and Provinces of China* (Boulder: Westview Press, 1985). The extent of silence on this subject can also be gauged from a collection titled *Unity and Diversity: Local Cultures and Identities in China*, edited by Tao Tao Liu and David Faure (Hong Kong: Hong Kong University Press, 1996), in which contributors discuss the historical constitution of local/regional cultural identities and their relation to a "common Chinese culture" without addressing the question of ethnicity explicitly. Yet matter-of-fact references to ethnic differences among Han Chinese are by no means lacking in academic discussions, as, for example, in the following observation: "The regionally defined groups . . . Cantonese, Shanghaiese, and Taiwanese . . . have obvious ethnic differences in speech, dress, customs, religious beliefs, and so on" [David Yen-Ho Wu, "The Construction of Chinese and Non-Chinese Identities," *Daedalus* 120.2 (1991), p. 167]. There are also exceptional anthropological studies that focus on the formation of different ethnicities among the Han Chinese. Particularly notable is Emily Honig's *Creating Chinese Ethnicity: Subei People in Shanghai, 1850 1980* (New Haven: Yale University Press, 1992), which documents the creation of a Subei ethnicity, partly through job segregation and discrimination of migrant labor, in Shanghai.

41. Chen Pingyuan, Qian Liqun, and Huang Ziping, "'Ershi shiji zhongguo wenxue' sanren tan: wenhua jiaodu" (A conversation on 'twentieth century Chinese literature': cultural perspectives), *Dushu* 1 (1986), p. 85. In the conversation, Qian Liqun's appreciation of *xungen* nativism is, interestingly, not shared by Chen Pingyuan and Huang Ziping, who question the distinctiveness of regional cultures and the continued importance of "historical" cultures different from Confucianism-centered Han culture in modern China.

42. The idea of ethnic identification employed here is informed by both the "primordialist" and "boundary" approaches to ethnicity. Works that have helped me think through the idea include: Clifford Geertz, "The Integrative Revolution," in Clifford Geertz, ed., *Old Societies and New States* (New York: Free Press, 1963); Fredrik Barth, *Ethnic Groups and Boundaries* (London: Allen & Unwin, 1969); John Hutchinson and Anthony D. Smith, ed., *Ethnicity* (New York: Oxford University Press, 1996).

43. Prasenjit Duara, *Rescuing History from the Nation: Questioning Narratives of Modern China* (Chicago: University of Chicago Press, 1995), pp. 177–204.

44. Interestingly, it is Deng Xiaoping's policy of letting certain regions—mainly the geographically better endowed coastal areas—get wealthy first under his program of "modernization" through importation of Western capital and technology that intensified the significance of place and heightened general awareness of spatial differences and inequalities. Such awareness arguably contributed to the development of regional consciousness in *xungen* nativism.

45. The phrase "the global imaginary of identity" is taken from Xiaobing Tang's *Global Space and the Nationalist Discourse of Modernity: The Historical Thinking of Liang Qichao* (Stanford: Stanford University Press, 1996), which gives a succinct argument on the spatiotemporal logic of hegemonic Western modernity. Leo Ou-fan Lee offers a suggestive reading of *xungen* fiction in terms of margins and periphery in "On the Margins of the Chinese Discourse: Some Personal Thoughts on the Cultural Meaning of the Periphery," in Tu Wei-ming, ed., *The Living Tree: The Changing Meaning of Being Chinese Today* (Stanford: Stanford University Press, 1994), pp. 221–38.

46. Shi Shuqing, "Mengjing zhong de gaomi dongbeixiang—yu dalu zuojia Mo Yan duitan" [The northeastern village of Gaomi in dreams: a conversation with mainland writer Mo Yan], in Shi Shuqing, *Wentan fansi yu qianzhan—Shi Shuqing yu dalu zuojia duihua* [Reflections and anticipations in the literary world: Shi Shuqing's conversations with mainland writers] (Hong Kong: Mingbao chubanshe, 1989), p. 113. "Zhiqing" refers to a generation of educated youths who were relocated to rural areas to work with and learn from the peasants in the Cultural Revolution period (late 1960s to mid-1970s).

47. Having come of age before the onslaught of the Cultural Revolution, Zheng Wanlong is a notable exception to this pattern. While he has also been assigned to work in rural areas, his experience was not that of a *zhiqing*'s disillusioned dislocation and subsequent struggle to reclaim some collective meaning for that displacement. This difference is arguably reflected in his much more individualistic conception of the search for roots and its meaning, focusing on male subject constitution rather than regional ethnic culture, as will be discussed later.

48. In the words of Cai Xiang, *xungen* literature presents all kinds of "man" (*hanzi*) who exude the "masculinity we have long yearned for, namely vigor, valor, frankness, faithfulness to one's words and promises, an adventurous spirit, and steadfastness in feelings . . . the manly man who seems to have become so rare in our lives today" (Cai Xiang, "Yeman yu wenming: pipan yu zhangyang" [Barbarism and civilization: criticism and publicization], *Dangdai wenyi sichao* 3 (1986), p. 32).

49. See Kam Louie, "The Macho Eunuch: The Politics of Masculinity in Jia Pingwa's 'Human Extremities,'" *Modern China* 17.2 (1991): 163–87. The quoted phrase is from p. 167.

50. In an overview of *zhiqing* literature, Guo Xiaodong traces the preoccupation with subjectivity and self-affirmation in *zhiqing* writings of the early 1980s to the writers' historical struggle with the "religious" mentality developed in the Cultural Revolution years, which still made it difficult for them to identify with the material culture blossoming in society after they emerged from the shadow of self-abnegation under authority (Guo Xiaodong, "Lun zhiqing zuojia de qunti yishi" [On the collective consciousness of *zhiqing* writers], *Wenxue pinglun* 5 (1985): 37–44). Though *xungen* literature is not mentioned particularly in Guo's discussion, its focus on masculine subjectivity can certainly be understood in a similar light. Guo's discussion, however, pays no attention at all to the gender specificity of the subjectivity evoked in *zhiqing* writings.

51. A discussion of the politics of signification in this particular coding of gender power can be found in Xueping Zhong, *Masculinity Besieged? Issues of Modernity and Male Subjectivity in Chinese Literature of the Late Twentieth Century* (Durham: Duke University Press, 2000).

52. Wang, *High Culture Fever*, p. 218.

53. Since the mid-1980s, complaints from Chinese writers and critics about the lack of popular interest in "serious" literature and the massive popularity of "vulgar" fictions by Hong Kong and Taiwan writers such as Jin Yong, Yi Shu, and Qiong Yao have become rather common. The anxiety this paucity of readership created in the "serious writers," among whom the *xungen* writers are ranked, is reflected in Zheng Wanlong's lament over the prevalent tendency to commodify literature and the loneliness and poverty of those "few" writers who continue to take the production of literature seriously in a literary meeting organized by *Wenxue pinglun* and *Wenxue ziyoutan* in late 1987. See "Miandui dangjin wentan de lengjun chensi" (Grim reflections on the contemporary literary scene), *Wenxue pinglun* 3(1988): 4–10, especially pp. 5–6.

54. Jia Pingwa's "Shangzhou" series of writing are generally taken to be important *xungen* literature. The writer himself, however, did not position his works as such. In the preface to a four-volumes collection of his Shangzhou stories, Jia notes that his works have been classified as "*xiangtu wenxue* (native soil literature), *xungen wenxue*, and even something called *diyu wenhua* (regional culture)," but to him, "they are stories about peasants, though they are not written for peasants only" [Jia Pingwa, "Preface," in *Shangzhou: shuobujin de gushi* (Shangzhou: endless stories), Vols. 1–4 (Beijing: Huaxia chubanshe, 1995), p. 4]. Jia's almost dismissive reference to the notion of "regional culture" contrasts sharply with the affirmation of regional ethnic cultures by such *xungen* advocates as Han Shaogong and Li Hangyu. His refusal to be associated with regional culture came at least in part from his belief that Shangzhou, as the place of origin of the system of rule that enabled Qin Shihuang to unify China, is central to the Chinese nation and culture. This is also reflected in his stories of the mid-1980s, which incorporate ethnographic details of the Shangzhou area only to show how Chinese peasants react to the agricultural "reforms" of the Deng regime and how their cul-

tural "backwardness" hampers the progress of modernization. For a good example, see "Gubao" (Old fortress, 1986).

55. Han Shaogong, "Wenxue de 'gen,'" *Zuojia*, no. 4 (1985): 2–5. All translations are mine.

56. Ibid., p. 3.

57. Ibid., p. 5.

58. A similar argument is made by the Chinese critic Li Jiefei in "Ping zhongguo wenxue de minzu yishi" [On national consciousness in Chinese literature], *Shanghai wenxue* 1(1989): 74–80.

59. Chow, *Primitive Passions*, p. 23.

60. See Han's later essay "Xunzhao dongfang wenhua de siwei he shenmei youshi" [Search for the advantages in the thoughts and aesthetics of Oriental Culture] (1986) in Han Shaogong, *Yexingzhe mengyu—Han Shaogong suibi* [Dream words of the nocturnal traveller: informal notes of Han Shaogong], (Shanghai: zhishi chubanshe, 1994), pp. 22–25.

61. As the most prominent of four southern coastal areas designated as special economic zones in 1979, Shenzhen dramatized the power differences between China and the capitalist West, and symbolized to some Chinese observers the corrupting influence of Western capitalist excesses on the Chinese people. Han's pointed comparison of the SEZ to Hong Kong is clearly meant to call up these issues.

62. "Wenxue de 'gen,'" p. 4.

63. Such a resort to folk culture for indigenous alternative is reminiscent of the folk literature and folksong collecting movements initiated by intellectuals in the 1920s to recover and preserve subaltern cultural traditions as a source of cultural vitality to counter Confucian orthodoxy and Western encroachment. For a discussion of these movements, see Chang-tai Hung, *Going to the People: Chinese Intellectuals and Folk Literature, 1919–1937* (Cambridge: Harvard University Press, 1985).

64. Shi Shuqing, "Niao de chuanren—yu Hunan zuojia Han Shaogong duitan" (The descendent of bird: a conversation with Hunan author Han Shaogong), in Shi Shuqing, *Wentan fansi yu jianzhan: Shi Shuqing yu dalu zuojia duihua*, pp. 124–40. Han Shaogong's views on the cultures of the minority nationalities expressed here parallel the exoticization and eroticization of minority cultures in contemporary Chinese paintings that Dru Gladney critiques in his article "Representing Nationality in China: Refiguring Majority/Minority Identities," *The Journal of Asian Studies* 53.1 (1994): 92–123. However, there is no such representation of minority cultures in his fictional writings, which do not focus on the minority nationalities at all.

65. This discursive strategy is akin to anthropology's denial of coevalness to the "others" it studies that Johannes Fabian has powerfully critiqued in his *Time and the Other: How Anthropology Makes Its Object* (New York: Columbia University Press, 1983).

66. Han Shaogong, "Bababa," in *Xiepi* (Addiction to shoes) (Wuhan: Changjiang wenyi chubanshe, 1993), pp. 63–102.

67. Ibid., p. 68.

68. Such a reading was advanced soon after the story's publication by Yan Wenjing in "Wo shibushi shangle nianji de bingzai?" (Am I an aged Bingzai?), *Zuopin yu zhengming* 2 (1986): 66. Along similar lines, Liu Zaifu identified Bingzai's "sick mentality" as a general state of "primitive ignorance" (*yuanshi yumei*) among the Chinese people that resulted from the nation's traditional culture in "Lun Bingzai" (On Bingzai), *Guangming ribao*, November 4, 1988. See also Fang Keqiang, "A Q he bingzai: yuanshi xintai de chongzu" (Ah Q and Bingzai: the reconstruction of primitive mentality), *Wenyi lilun yanjiu* 5 (1986): 10–11; Meng Fanhua, "Qimeng jiaose zaidingwei: chong du 'xungen wenxue'" (Repositioning the Role of Enlightenment: Rereading 'xungen wenxue'), *Tianjin shehui kexue* 1 (1996): 59. Similar readings can also be found in English language critical essays, for instance, Michael Duke, "Reinventing China: Cultural Exploration in Contemporary Chinese Fiction," *Issues and Studies* 25 (1989): 29–53; and Joseph S. M. Lau, "Visitation of the Past in Han Shaogong's Post-1985 Fiction," in *From May Fourth to June Fourth: Fiction and Film in Twentieth-Century China*, ed. Ellen Widmer and David Der-Wei Wang (Cambridge: Harvard University Press, 1993), pp. 19–42.

69. "Bababa," p. 101.

70. Ibid., p. 68.

71. C. T. Hsia, "Obsession with China: The Moral Burden of Modern Chinese Literature," in *A History of Modern Chinese Fiction*, 2nd ed. (New Haven: Yale University Press, 1971), pp. 533–54.

72. Li Hangyu, "Liyili women de 'gen'" [Attending to our 'roots'], *Zuojia* 9 (1985): 75–79.

73. Li Hangyu, "'Wenhua' de ganga" [The embarrassment of 'culture'], *Wenxue pinglun* 2 (1986): 50–54.

74. The critic Zeng Zhennan has identified in Li Hangyu's works what he calls a "Southern life-force" and "Southern solitude"—clearly alluding to the popular *One Hundred Years of Solitude* by Gabriel Garcia Marquez, whose Nobel Prize in 1982 has greatly inspired Chinese writers and critics to envision the possibility of a Chinese version of magical realism propelling Chinese literature into the ranks of modern world literature. Instead of reading them in terms of a "Southern" challenge to the orthodox culture rooted in the North, however, Zeng treats them as "reflecting on [the Chinese] national soul" and illumining "the psychological dilemma and intention of the modern Chinese." See Zeng Zhennan, "Nanfang de shengli yu nanfang de gudu—Li Hangyu xiaoshuo pianlun" [Southern life-force and Southern solitude: a discussion of Li Hangyu's fictions], *Wenxue pinglun* 2(1986): 64–72.

75. Li explains in an interview that though he was inspired by the real-life conditions of his native region, he deliberately chose a fictional name for the area in his stories to give room to his imagination. See Liang Lifang, "Li Hangyu: 'Gechuanjiang'shangde xunjinzhe" [Li Hangyu: seeker on the 'Gechuanjiang'] in *Cong hongweibing dao zuojia: jiaoxing yidaide shengyin* [From Red Guards to writer: voice of the awakened generation] (Taipei: Wanxiang tushu gongsi, 1993), p. 164. William

Faulkner's fictionalization of his native region into the famous "Yoknapatawpha" County is clearly a role model here.

76. Li Hangyu, "Gechuanjiang shang renjia" [Families on the Gechuanjiang], in *Zuihou yige yulao'er* (Taipei: Hongfan shudian, 1988), pp. 1–30. All translations are mine unless otherwise stated.

77. Ibid., p. 8.

78. Ibid., pp. 10, 29.

79. Ibid., p. 24.

80. Laosi's attitude toward his lack of a male heir suggests that the Gechuanjiang culture is inherently patriarchal, just like the Confucian tradition to which it is implicitly opposed. With its focus on the negative effects of Laosi's patriarchal thinking and behavior on Sishen and Qiuzi, who demonstrate their "manly" capability as navigators, Li's story is certainly critical of the patriarchal nature of the Gechuanjiang culture on the descriptive level. Yet, this critical attitude toward traditional gender ideology and practices remains superficial and is not translated into the meaning structure of the story itself, which, as I argued above, problematically associates women with pragmatic calculation to further its advancement of the Gechuanjiang culture as an alternative value system.

81. In another story, "Shazao yifeng" [Shazao's inherited custom, 1983], Li again uses the motif of the last practitioner of a traditional occupation—in this case, the specialized painting of decorative features on external house walls—to dramatize both the passing of a traditional way of life and the dignity of someone who struggles against all odds to hang on to the life that defines his being. See "Shazao yifeng" in *Zuihou yige yulao'er*, pp. 55–89.

82. Li Qingxi, "Xu" (Preface), in *Zuihou yige yulao'er*, pp. 1–10.

83. See Rita Felski, *The Gender of Modernity* (Cambridge: Harvard University Press, 1995), pp. 35–60.

84. In a review of the sociological conception of nostalgia in the Western context, Bryan Turner includes the idea of a loss of personal authenticity and emotional spontaneity as part of the nostalgia paradigm. See "A Note on Nostalgia," *Theory, Culture, and Society*, vol. 4 (1987): 147–56. This aspect is certainly prominent in Li's nativism but it is embedded in a discursive environment significantly different from nostalgia.

85. Li Hangyu, "Shanhusha de nongchaoer," in *Zuihou yige yulao'er*, pp. 115–52. All translations are mine.

86. In "'Wenhua' de ganga," Li mentions that he recognizes the inevitability of new styles of life and new cultural modes brought about by modern material civilization, but he wishes only that "their costs could be lower" (p. 52).

87. "Shanhusha," p. 119.

88. Li Hangyu's admiration for Ernest Hemingway's literary construction of the masculine hero is clearly evident here.

89. "Shanhusha," p. 119.

90. Li Hangyu refers to this marginalization and repression in his article "Liyili women de 'gen.'"

91. As the critic Zeng Zhennan points out, Li's characterization of Wu-Yue cultures deliberately deviates from the received image of southern culture as feminine, leisurely, gentle, and graceful (Zeng Zhennan, "Nanfang de shengli yu nanfang de gudu," pp. 66–67). The culture associated with Xian in Li's story, however, fits in with the stereotypical portrayal of northern culture. On the common juxtaposition of northern and southern cultures, see Lung-ChangYoung, "Regional Stereotypes in China," *Chinese Studies in History* 21.4 (1988): 32–57.

92. "Shanhusha," p. 123.

93. Ibid., p. 135.

94. Maurice Meisner, *Mao's China and After* (New York: Free Press, 1986), p. 442.

95. Class in China under the rule of the Communist Party is an issue highly charged and deeply imbued with contradictions. Richard Curt Krauss's perceptive study shows that there were different theories of class circulating in the PRC during the Maoist years, each attaining different importance and attention at different times and for different purposes. By the eve of the Cultural Revolution (1966–1969), "class" was signified by three different systems: (1) class origins established prior to socialist transformation; (2) location in the new state-party bureaucratic structure; and (3) political consciousness and behavior [Richard Curt Krauss, *Class Conflict in Chinese Socialism* (New York: Columbia University Press, 1981), p. 88]. With the economic "reforms" of the Deng years and the ideological repudiation of the Maoist emphasis on class struggle, the scenario is different but no less controversial. Now, it is arguably the bureaucratic structure, together with the differential opportunity it affords for taking advantage of the newly instituted market mechanisms, that plays a decisive role in the emerging class system, which the regime takes pains to rationalize with reference to the objective needs of modernization, and against which the general public indirectly protests by objecting to systemic corruption. A thorough analysis of the rise of a class of "bureaucratic bourgeoisie" under the Deng regime and the effects of economic reforms on peasants and workers are given in Meisner, *The Deng Xiaoping Era*.

96. "Shanhusha," p. 131.

97. Li Hangyu, "Zuihou yige yulao'er" in *Zuihou yige yulao'er*, pp. 31–54. All translations are mine. A translation of the story can be found in "The Last Angler," *Best Chinese Stories (1949–1989)*, Beijing: Panda Books, 1989.

98. Ibid., p. 52.

99. Ibid., pp. 47, 48.

100. This series of stories is collected in Zheng Wanlong, *Shengming de tuteng* [Totems of Life] (Beijing: Zhongguo wenlian chuban gongsi, 1986). Quotations from the stories given here are all taken from this collection. All translations are mine unless otherwise stated. For a translation of the first ten stories in the series, see Zheng Wan-

long, *Strange Tales from Strange Lands: Stories*, edited and translated by Kam Louie (Ithaca: East Asia Program, Cornell University, 1993).

101. Interestingly, in his "theoretical" discussion of *xungen* as a general trend in Chinese literature, Zheng Wanlong readily evokes national cultural psychological structure in elucidating the meaning of roots. This arguably reflects the *xungen* advocates' theoretical tentativeness and the common discrepancy between "theoretical" discussion and actual practice that plague them, which many Chinese critics have pointed out. It also suggests the hegemonic effects of a culturalist conception of the Chinese nation. Apparently, Zheng believes that an individual naturally embodies his nation's culture, as he notes in an interview: "I have in my body everything that this nation has, whether good, bad, stupid, or backward." (Liang Lifeng, "Zheng Wanlong: fajueliao chuangzuode jinkuang" [Zheng Wanlong: A goldmine of creation excavated], in *Cong hongweibing dao zuojia*, p. 420). On this assumption, a focus on an individual's root-seeking will automatically be an engagement with national culture as well. On Zheng's general discussion of the key ideas underlying *xungen* literature, see Zheng Wanlong, "Zhongguo xiaoshuo yao zouxiang shijie—cong zhigen yu 'wenhua yanceng' tanci" [Chinese literature must move towards the world: speaking of planting roots in the 'rock stratum of culture'], *Zuojia* 1(1986): 70–74; and "Xiandai xiaoshuo de lishi yishi" [Historical consciousness in modern fiction], *Xiaoshuochao* 7(1985): 79–80.

102. Zheng Wanlong, "Wo de gen," in *Shengming de tuteng*, pp. 310–14. To the extent that Zheng acknowledges in this personal manifesto a larger cultural context to which his individual cultural roots belong, he characterizes it as "Oriental" rather than national (p. 314).

103. Ibid., p. 310.

104. It is worth noting that this Han-Sinocentrism also pervades critical reception of Zhang's *Yixiang yiwen* series. The majority of critical essays takes for granted the primitive wildness and "barbarism" of the place, and leaves unquestioned the imperialistic implications of Zhang's literary appropriation of the Oroqen homeland to stage the "human" drama of masculine self-construction in battling wilderness. For examples, see Li Shulei, "Cong xun 'meng' dao xun 'gen'" [From seeking "dreams" to seeking "roots"], *Dangdai wenyi sichao* 3(1986): 42–49; Cai Xiang, "Yeman yu wenming—pipan yu zhangyang' [Barbarism and civilization: criticism and praise], *Dangdai wenyi sichao* 3(1986): 29–35; and "*Yixiang yiwen* yu wenxue de xun 'gen'—Zheng Wanlong zuopin taolunhui" ["Strange tales from other lands" and the search for "roots" in literature: a symposium on the works of Zheng Wanlong], *Beijing wenxue* 3(1986): 64–79.

105. Zheng only spent his early childhood in Heilongjiang, where his father worked as a gold-digger. He left for school in Beijing when he was eight and is identified as a Beijing rather than Heilongjiang writer.

106. "Wo de gen," p. 313.

107. This is affirmed by Zheng's statement in an interview that "root-seeking is primarily about self-understanding." See Liang Lifang, "Zhang Wanlong," p. 420.

108. On Western modernism's primitivization of other cultures, see Marianna Torgovnick, *Gone Primitive: Savage Intellects, Modern Lives* (Chicago: University of

Chicago Press, 1990); *Modernist Anthropology: From Fieldwork to Text*, ed. with an introduction by Marc Manganaro (Princeton: Princeton University Press, 1990); *Prehistories of the Future: The Primitivist Project and the Culture of Modernism*, eds., Elazar Barkan and Ronald Rush (Palo Alto: Stanford University Press, 1995); Richard Price and Sally Price, *Primitive Art in Civilized Places*, 2nd ed. (Chicago: University of Chicago Press, 2001); *Primitivism and Twentieth-Century Art: A Documentary History*, eds., Jack Flam and Miriam Deutch (Berkeley: University of California Press, 2003); and Carole Sweeney, *From Fetish to Subject: Race, Modernism, and Primitivism* (Westport, CT: Praeger, 2004).

109. For a discussion of post-Mao Chinese eroticisation of non-Han cultures through a combination of the strategies of minority-as-woman and commodity-as-woman, see Louisa Schein, "Gender and Internal Orientalism in China," *Modern China*, 23.1 (January 1997): 69–98.

110. *Shengming de tuteng*, pp. 16–7.

111. See Kam Louie, "Masculinities and Minorities: Alienation in 'Strange Tales from Strange Lands,'" *China Quarterly* 132 (1992): 1119–35. Whatever the potential merits of reading Zheng's male protagonists along the line of machismo, Louie's rather mechanical application of the "script for macho personality" given by two sexologists ends up reducing Zheng's stories to the "predictable" elements of "fight," "danger," and "callous sex."

112. *Shengming de tuteng*, p. 20.

113. Ibid., p. 21.

114. Zheng Wanlong directly criticized the "money is supreme" mentality fostered by the state's economism in a forum on "literature and morality." China's economic reforms, he said, have led to an increasingly "materialistic, utilitarian, and pragmatic" outlook among the Chinese people, making it necessary to "rebuild a new morality (rather than amorality) on the basis of traditional morality" [See Tang Yin, Meng Weizai, and Zheng Wanlong, "Wenxue yu daode—zuojia sanrentan" (Literature and morality: a conversation among three writers), *Guangming ribao* Dec. 18, 1986].

115. Other stories in the *Yixiang yiwen* series, such as "Goutoujin" (Dog-head gold) and "Taoguan" (The earthen urn), suggest the same principle negatively by demonstrating the futility of materialistic pursuit and greed.

116. The stereotypical representation is probably related to the fact that most of the Oroqen stories are Zheng's rewriting of widely circulated stories he has heard. The stories of "Huangyan" (Yellow smoke), "Zhong" (The clock), and "Yang pingzi di'er" (The blue glass bottle bottom) belong to this category, as the prologues to the stories indicate.

117. *Shengming de tuteng*, pp. 28–30.

118. Ibid., p. 35.

119. Ibid., pp. 39–40.

120. Chen Mo, "Qiantan 'Yixiang yiwen' de bu zu" [A brief discussion of the shortcomings of "Strange tales from other homelands"], *Beijing wenxue* 3(1986): 72–74.

121. *Shengming de tuteng*, p. 71.

122. Ibid., p. 77.

123. Ibid., p. 72.

124. Ibid., p. 76.

125. Ibid., p. 78.

126. Ibid., p. 77.

CHAPTER FOUR. GENDERING NATIVES, ENGENDERING ALTERNATIVES

1. Women's relation to nationalism has seen increased attention in recent years. Kumari Jayawardena's *Feminism and Nationalism in the Third World* (London: Zed, 1986) provides a classic overview on the subject. Another groundbreaking volume is the collection of essays *Nationalisms and Sexualities* edited by Andrew Parker, Mary Russo, Doris Sommer, and Patricia Yaeger (New York: Routledge, 1992), which includes discussions of various intersections in the discourses of gender, sexuality, and nationality from different disciplinary approaches. For considerations of the issue with reference to transnational developments, see Caren Kaplan, Norma Alarcon, and Minoo Moallem, eds., *Between Woman and Nation: Nationalisms, Transnational Feminisms, and the State* (Durham: Duke University Press, 1999). On the relation of women to nationalism in modern China, see Wendy Larson, "Women, Writing, and the Discourse in Nationalism," in *Women and Writing in Modern China* (Stanford: Stanford University Press, 1998), pp. 7–43; Sally Taylor Lieberman, "The Mother from Hell and the Emasculated Nation-Builder" in *The Mother and Narrative Politics in Modern China* (Charlottesville: University Press of Virginia, 1998), pp. 76–103; and Susan L. Glosser, "'The Truth I Have Learned': Nationalism, Family Reform, and Male Identity in China's New Culture Movement, 1915–1923," in *Chinese Femininities, Chinese Masculinities: A Reader*, eds., Susan Brownell and Jeffrey N. Wasserstrom (Berkeley: University of California Press, 2002), pp. 120–44.

2. Felski, *The Gender of Modernity*.

3. Deniz Kandiyoti, "Identity and its Discontents: Women and the Nation," in Patrick Williams and Laura Chrisman, eds., *Colonial Discourse and Post-Colonial Theory: A Reader* (New York: Columbia University Press, 1994), pp. 376–91.

4. Besides Felski, see Elizabeth Wilson, *Adorned in Dreams: Fashion and Modernity* (Berkeley: University of California Press, 1987), and *The Sphinx in the City: Urban Life, the Control of Disorder, and Women* (London: Virago, 1991); Rachel Bowlby, *Just Looking: Consumer Culture in Dreiser, Gissing, and Zola* (New York: Methuen, 1985); Janet Wolff, "The Invisible Flaneuse: Women and the Literature of Modernity," *Theory, Culture, and Society*, 2.3 (1985): 37–46; Andreas Huyssen, "Mass Culture as Woman: Modernism's Other" in *After the Great Divide: Modernism, Mass Culture, and Postmodernism* (Bloomington: Indiana University Press, 1986); Christine Buci-Glucksmann, "Catastrophic Utopia: The Feminine as Allegory of the Modern," *Rep-*

resentations, 14 (1986): 221–29; and Griselda Pollock, "Modernity and the Spaces of Femininity," in *Vision and Difference: Femininity, Feminism and the Histories of Art* (New York: Routledge, 1988).

5. Such a mapping can be seen in both traditional Left and feminist critiques, and has been criticized for an ascetic emphasis on production and a nostalgia for authenticity and natural "needs" that overlooks the possibility of agency and active negotiation of meaning in consumption. See, for example, Mica Nava, "Consumerism and Its Contradictions" and "Consumerism Reconsidered: Buying and Power," in *Changing Cultures: Feminism, Youth, and Consumerism* (London: Sage, 1992).

6. Carolyn Steedman, *Landscape for a Good Woman* (London: Virago, 1986), quoted in Sue Thornham, *Feminist Theory and Cultural Studies* (New York: Oxford University Press, 2000), p. 128.

7. Douglas Kellner, *Critical Theory, Marxism, and Modernity* (Baltimore: The Johns Hopkins University Press, 1989), p. 91; quoted in Felski, *Gender of Modernity*, p. 7.

POSTSCRIPT: PLACE-BASED POLITICS IN CHINA AND TAIWAN TODAY

1. Ma Ke, "Yu Han Shaogong tanxin" [Talking with Han Shaogong], *Shenzhen shangbao*, March 28, 2003, quoted in He Yanhong and Yang Xia, *Jianchi yu dikang: Han Shaogong* [Perseverance and Resistance: Han Shaogong] (Shanghai: Shanghai renmin chubanshe, 2005), p. 236.

2. "Han Shaogong de nongjia dayuan" [The rural compound of Han Shaogong], *Wenyibao*, April 12, 2001, quoted in He and Yang, *Jianchi*, p. 242.

3. Jia Mengwei, "Wennuan de sixiang" [Warm thoughts], *Wenyi zhengming*, 1 (2003), quoted in He and Yang, *Jianchi*, p. 244.

4. Shu Puyu, "Xiwang zhishifenzi geng youxiu yixie—fang zuojia Han Shaogong" [Wishing for a better intelligentsia—interview with Han Shaogong], *Zhonghua dushubao*, September 25, 2002, quoted in He and Yang, *Jianchi*, p. 242.

5. See David S. G. Goodman, "Structuring Local Identity: Nation, Province and County in Shanxi during the 1990s," *The China Quarterly* (2002): 838–62; and Tim Oakes, "China's Provincial Identities: Reviving Regionalism and Reinventing 'Chineseness,'" *The Journal of Asian Studies* 59.3 (2000): 667–92.

6. See David S. G. Goodman, "King Coal and Secretary Hu: Shanxi's Third Modernization," in *The Political Economy of China's Provinces*, eds., Hans Hendrischke and Feng Chongyi (New York: Routledge, 1999).

7. See, for example, this promotion of Guizhou: "Nature is still pristine here, and people still preserve their traditional cultures. . . . Guizhou's environment gives people a sense of returning to nature. This is something the people of the developed countries long for," in Deng Zongyue, "Shanguo tiantang de shuguang: guanyu Guizhou fazhan luyouye yu kaifa ziyuan zhi yantao" [Dawn of a mountain kingdom

paradise: a discussion of Guizhou's development of tourist industry and extraction of resources], paper presented at the Mainland-Taiwan Tourism Conference, Taipei, 1993, quoted in Oakes, "China's Provincial Identities," p. 682.

8. See Jun Jing, "Environmental Protests in Rural China," in *Chinese Society: Change, Conflict and Resistance*, eds., Elizabeth J. Perry and Mark Selden (London: Routledge, 2000), pp. 143–60.

9. Jonathan Unger, *The Transformation of Rural China* (Armonk, NY: M. E. Sharpe, 2002), p. 129.

10. Allen Chun, "Democracy as Hegemony, Globalization as Indigenization, or the 'Culture' in Taiwanese National Politics," *Journal of Asian and African Studies*, 35.1 (2000): 7–27.

11. On the domination of the issue of indigenization, or *bentuhua*, in Taiwan, see John Makeham and A-chin Hsiau, eds., *Cultural, Ethnic, and Political Nationalism in Contemporary Taiwan: Bentuhua* (New York: Palgrave Macmillan, 2005).

12. For an interesting discussion of the "*Yuanzhumin* subjectivity," see Michael Rudolph, "The Quest of Difference versus the Wish to Assimilate: Taiwan's Aborigines and their Struggles for Cultural Survival in Times of Multiculturalism," in *Religion and the Formation of Taiwanese Identities*, eds., Paul R. Katz and Murray A. Rubinstein (New York: Palgrave Macmillan, 2003), pp. 123–56. Rudolph's article effectively argues how the development of self-consciousness and self-confidence among the Aborigine activists was, in part, a response to the state promotion of Taiwan as a "multicultural society" in the 1990s, and the new attention given to the Aborigines and their cultures by various interested parties, including the political opposition, Taiwanization-oriented circles within the government, ethnologists, human rights organizations, and environmental protection groups.

13. Wendy Harcourt, "Rethinking Difference and Equality: Women and the Politics of Place," in *Places and Politics in an Age of Globalization*, pp. 299–322.

Index

SUNY SERIES, EXPLORATIONS IN POSTCOLONIAL STUDIES

Emmanuel C. Eze and Arif Dirlik, editors

Laura Rice, *Of Irony and Empire: Islam, the West, and the Transcultural Invention of Africa*

Anjali Prabhu, *Hybridity: Limits, Transformations, Prospects*

M.T. Kato, *From Kung Fu to Hip Hop: Globalization, Revolution, and Popular Culture*

Natascha Gentz and Stefan Kramer (eds.), *Globalization, Cultural Identities, and Media Representations*

Sandra Ponzanesi, *Paradoxes of Postcolonial Culture: Contemporary Women Writers of the Indian and Afro-Italian Diaspora*

Sam Durrant, *Postcolonial Narrative and the Work of Mourning: J.M. Coetzee, Wilson Harris, and Toni Morrison*

Patrick Colm Hogan, *Empire and Poetic Voice: Cognitive and Cultural Studies of Literary Tradition and Colonialism*

Olakunle George, *Relocating Agency: Modernity and African Letters*

Elisabeth Mudimbe-Boyi (ed.), *Beyond Dichotomies: Histories, Identities, Cultures, and the Challenge of Globalization*

John C. Hawley (ed.), *Postcolonial, Queer: Theoretical Intersections*

Alfred J. Lopez, *Posts and Pasts: A Theory of Postcolonialism*

S. Shankar, *Textual Traffic: Colonialism, Modernity, and the Economy of the Text*

Patrick Colm Hogan, *Colonialism and Cultural Identity: Crises of Tradition in the Anglophone Literatures of India, Africa, and the Caribbean*